Soul Murder

A novel
based on true events
in the life of
Charles "Butch" Allee

Brett Valette

Doug Preston, best selling thriller writer:

"I read Soul Murder with great interest. I think it's a very good book, a gripping read, with well-portrayed characters and a compelling narrative that drives right along. I can see a lot of excellent research went into it, which makes all the difference between an average thriller and one that stands out. *Soul Murder stands out.*"

James Redford, director and screenwriter:

"In "Soul Murder" Brett Valette doesn't shy away from the most compelling and primal of human emotions. Desire, fear, revenge - they are all major players in his well-crafted and action-packed story of a deep and unrelenting injustice."

Butch Allee   Photo by the author

Soul Murder

A novel by Brett Valette
Published in the United States of America
V&V publishing

Copyright: Brett Valette January 1, 2014. All rights reserved

www.brettvalette.com

First edition: 2014

ISBN: 978-0-9849848-1-7

Full releases to write and publish this story were obtained from
Butch Allee, Cindy Allee, Charles Allee, Margaret Allee and
Lea Allee.

Gitanjali
By Rabindranath Tagore (May 7, 1861 - August 7, 1941,
Calcutta India)
Gitanjali is a collection of poems by the Indian poet
Rabindranath Tagore. The original Bengali collection of 157
poems was published on August 14, 1910.

Author's note

This story is based on actually events.

I interviewed Butch, his family, local folks involved and various people who were impacted by the killing that occurred.
 A man lost his life and another lost his soul. No one, in this tragedy won or walked away unscathed. Life, at times, has been cruel to everyone involved.

I still keep in touch with Butch. He, his family, and his story had an influential impact on my own life. Even now when Butch and I get together, there is a sadness, an emptiness that lives in his eyes. The events of that day still haunt him, it changed his, and his family's life forever. It forever changed the lives of the other family involved, too.
I also changed.

Butch and I are from two very different worlds but we've grown to accept each other, like each other, and respect each other. So much so that when we meet he 'chops' the air and calls me, 'Brother.'
I also, call him, 'Brother.'

Brett Valette

Acknowledgements

I want the reader to know that the letters that Butch Allee wrote to his family, which are included in this book by his permission, are his actual writings.

There were many people I interviewed that gave me their time and their view on the events. Most did not want to be mentioned and I will not. But thank you for your interest and your story.

The reading group of Lita, Lisa and Julie. Thank you for the feed back and suggestions. All three of you consistently help improve my writing and story telling.

Jennifer Atkins at Atkins Editorial. My editor, who takes my words and rearranges them so they make sense. She also cuts most of my ramblings.

John Marlow. As a story consultant John gave invaluable suggestions in weaving the details and events into Soul Murder. His insights and creativity have taught me to be a better story teller.
www.selfeditingblog.com and www.makeyourbookamovie.com

Carol Ruzicka who creates impressive book covers. Thank you so much. www.carolruzicka.com

I want to thank my readers. This was more than a story to me; I hope it's more than just a story to you also.

Justice
Even when it works, steals your soul.

One

A holding cell at the Kersey County Justice Center

Butch Allee's tattooed fingers felt no hesitancy as he knotted the corner of the bed sheet around the bars of his cell door. He grabbed the sheet's other end, twisted a loop in the center, and reaching upward, tied the remaining end securely to another bar.

He gave it a firm tug.

He only had a few more minutes alone as his public defender, Mark Moore, had just informed him that the verdict was in. He had already spent six months in jail, most of it in solitary confinement, some of it in psychotic delirium. A guilty verdict would send him to a worse place. And it didn't matter if it was real or in his own mind, it would be forever. Butch knew he wouldn't make it. Reciting a short prayer he asked for forgiveness from his family.

He had always taught his kids to be strong. Stand up for what's right.

He just didn't have any strength left for himself.

His vision watered. His fingers tattooed with L-O-V-E quickly wiped them away.

On tiptoe he slipped his head inside the loop of the secured bed sheet and settled his back against the cell bars. Then just a whisper of words; "God. Please, help me."

Butch let his knees relax and immediately felt the tightness around his neck. Urgency now rushed into his fingers so he clasped them tightly together behind his back. Butch sucked in a final breath, and pulled his feet off the ground.

Faint footsteps echoed down the concrete hallway, but he couldn't be sure as the loop of bed sheet quickly cut off the flow of blood to his brain.

His eyes fluttered.

Around him the stainless steel toilet, sink, and cement bunk whirled. Spun. And went black.

Mark Moore, Butch's public defender, sounded upbeat as he walked the hall toward the holding cell.

"Jury's ready Butch. We got a good chance here, let's face the music."

Mike abruptly halted as the triangles of white cloth poked into view from Butch's cell. "Oh, shit!" Mike ran to the cell door, "Guard! Guard!" He frantically pulled at the knots on the bed sheet, "Come on, come on." He yelled out again, "Get this fucking cell door open!"

Two

Kersey County Courtroom

The verdict was delayed for one hour as an EMT attended to Butch Allee's suicide attempt. Fortunately, the guard in the holding cell arena reached between the bars, and using his folding knife sliced through the bed sheet. Butch collapsed onto the floor; alive, and breathing.

Mark Moore waived a psychological evaluation at this point, everything was already done and decided. And no one in the courtroom was aware of what had happened and the verdict proceedings were resumed.

Butch Allee sat at the little wooden table in the tiny little courtroom, waiting. Struggling to hold himself together. Mark Moore sat next to him.

This was Mark Moore's first murder trial. He had been a public defender for two years and nothing in that two years had prepared him for this trial. Especially defending someone like Butch Allee -- defending the man who had killed the Wyoming State wrestling champion in his own front yard in the tiny farming town of Kersey.

Kersey was a spit of a town on the plains of Wyoming; silent to ever being spotlighted in the news. The fact that an upstanding young wrestling champion, father of two, was brutally killed created sensational headlines. The fact that he was killed by a biker, a loner, and by some reports an ex-Hells Angel created national headlines. And the fact that Butch Allee had a wavy fire tattoo emblazoned across his forehead provided great photos to accompany those headlines; his face sold the story.

The murder of the State wrestling champion flew from the pages of the local news to the state news and onto the national news. Even Brian Williams mentioned it at 6 O'clock.

With trembling fingers Butch grabbed at the paper cup at the center of the defendants table and gulped the warm water.

The jury room door flung open and Butch jumped.

The first juror stepped out.

It all seemed unreal.

The jurors, looking like worn out hound dogs after a long, hot afternoon rabbit hunt, milled about, taking forever as they settled into their seats. Some were sweating, some were coughing and making uncomfortable noises. For most of them their postures were heavy, faces worn, eyes agitated.

Torturous minutes passed, he wiped his forehead. Butch's quivering tattooed fingers pulled and twisted his foreign-feeling white dress shirt. He had yanked the shirt tail out of his black pants and unknowingly was knotting and unknotting the scratchy, starched cloth soaked and sticking to his body under his "three-times-in-my-life" black suit.

As the jury fell silent Judge DeBeque -- his mini floor fan tucked beneath his desk blowing dry farm air up his robe -- looked tired and worn too. He usually fished the North Platte on Fridays but today he asked the question everybody already knew the answer to: "Has the jury reached a verdict?"

Butch grabbed a breath through his open mouth.

As she struggled to her feet the female foreman responded, "Yes we have your Honor."

"Will the defendant please rise."

Butch sat there, hoping by a miracle if he sat there long enough the verdict would float away on the wind. The dusty dry air raked his sinuses and chafed his nerves. It was his time but he didn't want to move. He couldn't move.

"Butch it's time to get up," whispered Mark Moore looking down at him. He didn't let on but he was scared too. Mark Moore had grown to like this man. Trusted him. He had trusted him so much that he had taken a bold legal risk: He called only one witness to testify. One single witness to impact the jury for an acquittal. That one witness was Butch Allee. Now he would know if that move had paid off.

Butch shuddered, ground his teeth and nervously blinked as he forced himself to stand. His shirttail, wrinkled from fear, hung out of his pants. With the twenty pound weight loss in solitary his legs were trembling. To steady himself he laid his large callused hands on the table. Faded blue letters, creased by age, were crudely etched onto the fingers of his left hand spelling out

L-O-V-E.

F-U-C-K adored the other.

"What say you?" asked the Judge, spreading his legs so his mini floor fan blew farm air up his robe.

"In the matter of Charles Butch Allee – " Butch sucked air "— charged with second degree murder in the death of Len Lamont..."

Suddenly every authority figure he had ever hated now seemed to be screaming in his brain: Loser. Fuck-up. Freak. They were right. They were all right. Now he was going to hear the same thing from the jury and spend his life in a prison cell.

"...we find the defendant... "

A primitive child-like moan escaped his lips.

"...not guilty."

The courtroom exploded. Tension from the spectators burst free, a mixture of boos and hisses mixed with whistles and hoots and cheers filtered throughout the room.

Mark threw his arms up in celebration. *Not guilty!* Butch felt weak, dizzy. He collapsed into the wooden chair.

His mouth dropped open and soft words escaped, "They believed me? Oh God, oh God thank you." He looked up at Mark Moore who was grinning like a kid on Christmas morning. Butch's face was wet, but not with sweat. Mark grabbed Butch about the shoulders and shook him with glee.

Sheriff John McCallum sitting at the prosecution table, went ashen as the verdict was read. Roy Parker, the district attorney, obese and sweating, sweat more. With those two words his career imploded and he suddenly craved a snickers bar and a pint of *Ben and Jerry's*.

At the same instant a scream jolted everyone in the tiny courtroom. "No! No! It ain't fair. This is wrong!"

Alisha Lamont, Len's wife, stood, trembling, stabbing the air with her finger at Butch. "He's a murderer, he ain't innocent." She now stabbed at the jury, "You're lettin' him go?! Oh God I can't believe this. This is all wrong." She felt weak and grabbed comfort from anyone close. "He murdered my husband, my babies Daddy and you're lettin' him go?"

Judge DeBeque slammed his palm repeatedly on the wooden console, "Everyone sit down, *now*. Everyone, be quiet. Quiet! Now!" The electrified courtroom fizzled with the admonition. "I want order in here now."

Judge DeBeque looked down at the defendant's table, "You're free to go Mr. Allee. Court adjourned."

Cindy Allee, who was sitting right behind Butch, ran around the bench and grabbed him, her face pressed against his chest as her tears disappeared into his already wet shirt. She pulled away and grabbed his face between her hands, "I'm so happy, Butch. I'm so relieved."

"Cindy, they believed me." Butch quickly turned to watch the jury file out. He felt the urge to wave at them or give them a thumbs-up. He didn't know if that was the right thing to do so he stood there, watching in disbelief.

Cindy whispered in his ear, "They believed you because it was the truth."

He smiled awkwardly, looked nervously at the crowd gathering about him and hugged her again. "I gotta get out of these clothes."

"Congratulations Butch. We did it. We won." Mark Moore said as he squeezed Butch's free hand.

"It's strange, I don't feel like I won." He glanced through the courtroom doors: A mob of reporters and cameras were waiting for him. "You're the only one who believed in me, Mark." Butch looked him in the eyes.

"*They* believed you," Mark nodded to the jury box. "I told you we'd win. We might as well get out you of here Butch. You're a free man." Mark unclenched his jaw and for the first time during the trial, allowed a smile to creep along his lips.

The words sounded strange to Butch, heavy with responsibility. A *free* man. Butch glanced back at Alisha Lamont who was being comforted by family. He watched as she wept in their arms. He had killed a man. A father. The town hero. He felt Cindy take his arm and pull him from the courtroom into the suffocating crowd.

Cameras flashed as reporters spat out their questions: "Your son's trial for accessory is next week are you confident of another not guilty verdict?"

Butch was quickly forced back into the moment, "My son ain't guilty. He was just defending himself, just like I did."

"Did Sheriff McCallum set you up, Butch?" A reporter stepped in front of him blocking his way.

"I know the Sheriff don't like me, but I don't know if he set me up or not. All's I know is that Sheriffs shouldn't be actin' the way he did."

"Where's the bat Butch? The DA said you hid the murder weapon."

"Parker's a buffoon," growled Mark Moore as he walked along side Butch deflecting the question.

"You know a lot of folks are going to say you murdered the town hero and walked free—" Butch stopped, his eye's flashed fire and surrounded by the flaming tattoo they blazed. He crowded the reporter, "I didn't murder anyone," -- the reporter stumbled backward into the crowd -- "and the jury said so."

Cindy reached out and pulled him toward the truck; they climbed into their '89 Dodge pickup, rolled the windows down for air and drove off.

As Cindy and he drove home Butch began to feel at ease. The cool breeze from the open window washed over his face - a feeling he hadn't had in months. He breathed in the sweet smell of cow and farm mixed with a whiff of diesel. The smell of freedom. The smell of home. Butch shut his eyes. There was an easiness in allowing his eyes to close without anxiety or fear.

At that moment Butch had no idea that the worst part of his life was not over.

The next day the *Kersey Sentinel* headline screamed: *Murderer Walks.*

Three

Six Months Later

Dr. Alexander Dalton pushed through the doors of Aspen Grove Psychiatric Hospital. It was 2:30 in the afternoon and he was beat after testifying at a morning trial. He liked court, it was familiar to him. But after his wife was murdered at the hands of his own client, he vowed never to go back to defending criminals. It was then he left his law practice and became a psychologist.

He liked the safety of being a psychologist. But safety brought loneliness. Boredom.

He flopped into his high backed leather chair and briefly took in the comfort of his office isolation. He really just wanted to go home, but work numbed his emotions. Home seemed to create them. He closed his eyes.

Be calm.

Calm.

Quiet.

Let it go. Relax.

He repeated the mantra.

But the forced meditation wasn't cutting it, and he knew his blood pressure was up. Or was it anxiety? Maybe fear?

Probably all three, but it was more than just the trial that was causing his uneasiness.

He glanced up at his *Three Stooges* calendar that was thumb tacked to the wall.

The Anniversary.

The weeks leading up to the Anniversary were always the most difficult for him. The count-down was emotionally excruciating: It was weeks, then days..., then the hours. He desperately wanted to be home, but he needed to be here, the staff and patients needed him here.

He took in a long slow breath. Another feeble attempt at relaxation.

And exhaled.

It wasn't helping.

He could still see that tattooed monster...his hands around his wife's neck. It sickened Alex that he had defended him.

Alex forced his eyes open and swiveled his chair toward his desk. He was greeted by a pile of patient charts that had to be reviewed and signed today. Sitting atop the charts was a paperback book. He scooped it up reading the note taped on the cover: *Thought you might like this. Sandra.*

He didn't want to, but the note made him smile. Then grief, old but fresh bubbled up. It still overtook him, even after all these years. And after all these years it still caught him by surprise; how easily and quickly it was there.

He blinked to dry his eyes, then thumbed through the obviously worn pages of the used paperback book. He stopped at no particular spot, then read:

> *"Thou hast made me known to friends*
> *whom I knew not.*
> *Thou hast given me seats in homes not my own.*
> *Thou hast brought the distant near and made*
> *a brother of the stranger."*

He couldn't read anymore and tossed the paperback behind the unread stack of charts. The tears, sadness, the hollowness, were now too thrown away, buried beneath the clinical façade of detachment.

With his elbow on the desk and his forehead resting in his palm he stared at the overwhelming pile before him. "Shit." He grabbed the first chart within reach and opened it.

He was startled by a voice from behind him: "You aren't going to sweep all those into the trash can are you?"

Alex spun around.

Nurse Sandra Kelly was standing at the open door of his office. His look to her conveyed 'maybe.'

"You've got a psych eval to do before you do any house cleaning."

"Now? Before my afternoon espresso?" His eyes pleaded with her like a little boy begging for chocolate before breakfast.

"Before *anything*, Dr. Caffeine."

He threw the chart back on the desk and glanced at his empty coffee mug. Rubbing his face he unsuccessfully tried to wipe away the days heaviness. "I had the murder trial today."

"The guy who cut off his girlfriends head?" Sandra asked as if they were discussing yesterdays lunch.

"Yes. And it was murder on me too."

She looked at him, concerned. She wanted to walk over and put an arm around his shoulders, but she knew she couldn't cross that boundary with her boss. "Did they bring up..."

"Yes." He spun around and began searching through his papers. "Thanks for the poetry book."

"Have you heard of him?" she said, her eyes sparkling.

"I didn't look, I read one paragraph...ah excuse me, *verse*, then you walked in."

"It's a book about *life* Alex." She waited for a visual cue from Alex.

None came.

"It's by Rabindranath Tagore. He's Indian."

Alex eyebrows raised. "American Indian?"

"East Indian."

"Eastern American Indian? Massachusetts?" He spun around and looked at her.

"Will you stop." She made a face at him. "I hope you don't mind, but I thought it might help."

"Thanks Sandra, but I don't *need* any help. Remember? I'm the psychologist." He broke his gaze with her. "Okay, back to work. Who's the eval on?"

She crossed her arms trying to warm herself from his sudden coldness. "He came in a couple hours ago. Self admit."

He saw her demeanor change but he didn't interpret it correctly. "What's going on? Is it someone I know?"

"I hope not."

"What's up?"

"Alex, talk to me. We've known each other--"

He cut her off with a raised palm, "— Not now Sandra, okay? It's just...not a good time."

"It's never a good time, that's why talking is good." She rolled her eyes, "Here I go, counseling the doctor." She knew he wasn't going to let her in. "Okay, Alex. Fine. Your next patient. He's in the waiting room. You'll like him."

"He's not a family member?"

She looked at him funny, "No. Command hallucinations and suicidal ideation."

"Wonderful." An added heaviness developed in his face. "First patient --"

"---And before your espresso. Tsk, tsk, you poor baby." She was still irritated but she smiled at him anyway.

"Is he on a hold?"

"No, he walked in. His intake sheet's on your desk, if you can find it."

He grabbed the chart, flipped to the intake sheet and focused on the preliminary diagnosis written by the intake staff. "If he's hallucinating why hasn't Sizemoore seen him?"

"Are *you* serious? Dr. Sizemoore won't see these guys until you've checked 'em out first. He isn't going to get abused or spit on. You know the rule: The psychologist gets 'em first, wears 'em out, then Sizemoore gives 'em their meds."

Dr. Alexander Dalton leaned back into his chair, "If the poor guy is out of it, he should have a med consult first. Sizemoore is such a pussy. Alex feigned an apologetic smile, "Sorry. Now, would you *please* get me some coffee while I go check on this guy."

She cocked her head, "I'm not your waitress, Alex." She turned on her low heels and walked out the door.

"I tip twenty percent," he yelled to her.

Alex reluctantly stood up from his chair, stretched, grabbed the intake sheet and walked down the yellowed linoleum-floored hall toward the waiting room.

Alex just didn't want to be here.

He pushed open the waiting room door, glanced at the name on the intake sheet, "Butch Allee," Alex called out.

Only then did Alex take an interest and look for his first patient.

Butch Allee stood up and at that moment Alex didn't need his coffee any more and he reflexively took one step backward. Instantly this patient triggered memories. Bad ones. A split second of panic engulfed him, he tried to swallow but there was no spit.

Without turning his back Alex took another step backward as Charles "Butch" Allee walked toward him.

The man who had walked into *his* hospital was wild, unkept and had a garishly colored flame tattoo on his forehead. The beard, earrings and chains all added to the scary image.

It's not him. It's not him. Alex was reciting without even being aware of it. Judgmental assessments popped in Alex's mind like defiant psychological popcorn. This guy looked like Charles Manson. And they both looked like *him*. Albert Soccoro.

His throat seemed to close as he spoke, "I'm Dr. Dalton. We're going down the hall to my office, Mister Allee, right down there on your left." Alex stiffly pointed. He watched Butch obediently shuffle toward his open office door, his head down, slightly hunched over.

At forty-nine years of age Dr. Dalton had seen it all: Teenage girls, their thighs and arms adorned with cigarette burns and self inflicted cuts. The Crooked Neck Man, who, with his daughters jump rope, failed at hanging himself from the backyard apple tree. The Acid Man, who brewed up home-made acid in his bathtub, then would slowly lower himself into the skin-eating solution, bathing in it, slowly burning himself to death. Alex had seen it, dealt with it, and moved on. But Butch Allee...for the first time in years, took his breath away. The others were pitiful, depressed and intentionally hurt *themselves*. But this patient could hurt *him*. And he had been there before. And he didn't like going back there.

Terror was grabbing hold of Alex and he didn't quite know what to do.

Butch stopped at the office door.

Dr. Dalton quickly walked in and sat beside his desk. A hot cup of coffee with three spoonfuls of sugar was waiting for him. A sense of familiar comfort enveloped him. But just for a second.

Alex quickly covered his fear with aloofness: "Have a seat, Mr. Allee. I want to review your chart. Then I'll have some questions." Alex assessed the man sitting across from him: No eye contact. Disheveled. Head down. Long matted graying hair. Scraggly beard. Cut-off shirtsleeves, a leather vest. *White Power* was tattooed on his left arm. Beneath it, the typical naked woman with fantasy breasts. An eagle with wings outstretched flew across his right. Blue spider webs stretched across the web and back of his hands and as

Butch's fingers gripped his knees Alex read, upside down, *Love* across the knuckles of one hand and *Fuck* on the other. Both arms were a mosaic of professional and amateur designs, pictures and words. Human graffiti.

Alex hated all graffiti, human or otherwise.

Butch slid his hair behind his ears revealing the untamed flames etched across his forehead.

Alex was struggling with the likeness between his new patient and the client that strangled his wife to death.

I hate these guys, he thought, if I met him on the street...

Stop! Alex scolded himself. Just stop. He blinked fast, grabbed for his coffee and took a sip. Enough. He came to you for help. Alex pushed away the rebellious emotions. You're a psychologist, help this man. Alex forced himself to regrouped for the session. "Mr. Alley, would you like something to drink?"

Butch fidgeted. "No."

Butch had pulled the front of his shirt from his pants and was tugging and knotting the end of it. Alex watched, analyzing, assessing, judging. Butch looked like a beaten up Rottweiler.

Alex started the session: "Why are you checking yourself into Aspen Grove Psych-Care?"

Butch looked up at Alex, his eyes were bloodshot, weary. "I killed a man."

Alex bolted upright jerking his cup of coffee, the black goo splashing against the rim. Holy fucking shit! He set the mug on his desk not taking his eyes off the man before him. I knew it, fuck. Today, of all days. "When!? When did you do this Mr. Allee?"

Therapy was over even before it had begun. Alex's professional responsibility now required him to assess danger. *Danger to self or others.* And right now Alex was feeling the 'danger to self or others' may include him. "*Where* did you do this *Mr*. Allee? I need to know *now*."

Butch shrunk, cowering at Alex's intimidating intensity. He chewed his lower lip, looked at the floor and leaned away from Alex like a little boy anticipating a quick swat from his Pa. He licked his dried lips then squinted up at Alex. "In my front yard."

Goddamn it! I should have gone home, I *wanted* to go home. Listen to your intuition next time! Fuck! This is exactly why he had left his criminal defense practice. And damn it, it was following him right to the psych-ward. How fucking ironic, I'm in a psych-ward!

"When did you do this? Today? Yesterday? I need to know Mr. Allee or I'm bound by law to call the police."

Butch was now breathing hard and fast. He wanted to run. "A year ago. The cops know. That's why I was in jail."

A year ago! The locked-unit security alarms in Alex's head went silent and he immediately relaxed. Good. Good! A year ago. Alex was a wreck. He needed to settle down and deal with the situation before him. He grabbed his coffee mug and sipped the calming sweet brew. He breathed easier, then laughed at himself for freaking out. Alex's words slowed now, "This happened a year ago? And you said you were in jail?"

Butch settled along with Alex and he nodded, "Maybe you heard 'bout me. I killed Len Lamont."

Alex shook his head, "No, I've never heard of him." And he wouldn't have forgotten Butch. "This was a year ago? And you're not in prison now, what happened?"

"I spent six months in jail, but the jury found me not guilty."

I'm sure you did something else those six months made up for, thought Alex remembering his lawyer days and knowing that criminals do far more crimes than they ever get nabbed on. "Okay, Mr. Allee, let's start over. Tell me what happened, and why are you here now?"

Butch's fingers moved faster, twisting and tugging at his shirt. He lowered his face and tears fell, spotting his dirty jeans.

Alex squinted and cocked his head, this was not what he expected from this wild man.

"Doc, I need some help. Can you give me something for these voices?" Butch stared at the doctor and slowly started rocking back and forth twisting his shirt tighter.

Alex immediately softened. He could now see it. The agitation, the fear. This was a man in pain certainly suffering a severe major depression. For being found not guilty he was an emotional mess. Alex set his coffee mug on the desk.

"What are the voices saying to you Mr. Allee?"

More kneading and then a grimace of pain washed over his worn face. Butch gripped his knees and rocked more, looked up at Alex, then away.

"Tell me what they're saying to you Mr. Allee. I can't help you unless you talk with me." Alex watched him: The grizzled un-kept beard on his chin trembled, his mouth moved with no words and he continued to rub his thighs with his palms, back and forth, back and forth. Then his face wrinkled in pain and his breath trembled through clenched teeth. With a quick gasp, he blurted out: "They scream at me. Alisha Lamont's scream...they say I'm a murderer."

Butch's eyes went wide and they rolled about as he rocked. There was a burst of panic on his face, his muscles tightened, his chest heaved and sweat rolled down into his beard.

Alex was sure that Mr. Allee was reliving the killing right there in the office and he didn't want him to decompensate any more than he already had. Alex needed to pull him out of it quickly. "Mr. Allee. Mr. Allee, look at me."

Alex knew the signs of psychological decompensation and it was happening right now in front of him. Butch's eyes rolled, stopped, then jumped about the room. He was listening to the voices. Alex knew he needed to influence Mr.

Allee, to overpower the voices with therapeutic sanity. He could call Dr. Sizemore to administer a sedative but Alex liked the power of words. The power of emotion. If he was to save Mr. Allee, he needed to do it right now. "Mr. Allee, listen to me. I need you to look at me." Alex leaned forward and Butch caught his movement. His eye's went wild like a caged animal.

"Mr. Allee, you're safe here. You are safe here. Be with me. It's safe. Stop and look at me. I want you to breath deeply and slowly."

Alex could see Butch straining to make eye contact. Struggling to trust him. Probably digging down deep into his past to allow this authority figure to guide him to safety.

Alex slowly reached out and touched Butch's knee. "The voices you hear are false. What they are saying to you is not true. Listen to my voice Mr. Allee. My voice. Hear only my voice."

Butch settled his eyes onto Alex. "Stay looking at me, Mr. Allee. That's right. Yes. Breath deep and slow Mr. Allee." Alex demonstrated so Butch could mimic the rhythm of Alex's chest. "Just calm and breath. That's good. No one is going to hurt you here Mr. Allee, I'm here to help you."

Alex continued to breath slowly and watched as his patient's muscles relaxed, his eye's focused and the agitation began to melt away. "Alright. That's better. Lets just sit here a few minutes together, both of us, we'll just continue to breath and relax.

Four minutes pasted as Alex and Butch breathed together.

"Okay, now, how are you feeling?"

Butch's fingers tugged at his beard, "Them voices Doc. They tell me to kill myself." He hesitated, it was an option he had thought about many times. "Can you make 'em stop Doc?" He again looked at Alex, his expression was desperate, his eye's brimmed with tears, "I need it to stop...I'm going crazy."

Alex placed his right palm on his chin, his fingers caressing his cheek. He unconsciously did this when he felt empathy for a patient, or a friend, or a tough biker guy crying in his office. "Is the screaming *inside* your head? Or do you hear the screaming *outside* your head? Is the woman screaming *at* you?"

Butch resumed the rocking, it seemed to calm him like a child sucking it's thumb, rocking itself to sleep. His fingers gripped his knees. "She's screaming at me. I hear it all the time."

"Have you ever intentionally hurt yourself, Mr. Allee?"

He shook his head, his hair falling from behind his ears, "No. Call me Butch."

"When did the voices start?"

"A few months ago, I guess. Maybe a little longer. I was hearing stuff in jail too."

"And you hear them every day?"

"Most days. They got worse after my son Charles was arrested for drugs." He looked at Alex with fearful eyes. "He never did drugs before, Doc. I tried to teach him right. And we was best friends, but this killing and the time I spent in jail...I couldn't be there for him, like a father should be. It's my fault and Cindy is going to leave me if I don't get better."

Alex exhaled.

"Here's what we'll do...Butch. I'll get you set up with Dr. Sizemoore, our staff psychiatrist. You need a medication evaluation and I'll make sure that he sees you today. I don't believe in long term use of medications, but for now, let's get the voices under control and then we'll spend some time together. Just you and me. I think you should stay here for a while, a couple of weeks, maybe a month. This will help."

The agitated rubbing on his thighs ceased and Butch's biceps relaxed. "Do you think you can help me Doc?"

"I do. You have to trust me, Butch."

Those words.

It's what Mark Moore had told him almost a year ago.

Four

Aspen Grove Psychiatric Hospital

One week later

Butch was already waiting in Alex's office when he arrived. This time Alex comfortably greeted him. "Hey Butch, how's that Wellbutrin working for you?"

"It's helping Doc. Man, I'll tell you I feel a lot different." Butch's hair was combed and his beard was thick and clean from a morning bath. He sat upright with life in his eyes.

"You certainly look better too," kidded Alex.

"Them voices are gone." He shook his head, "I didn't like them voices. I couldn't sleep or be around anyone cause they kept telling me I was no good."

Alex sat and listened.

"I was afraid I was going to hurt myself. Cindy hid my gun."

"Cindy's your wife? Does she still have your gun?"

"Yeah, she hid it somewhere's. She's coming down here today with Lea and Margaret."

"Your daughters. And your son Charles, he's still in jail?"

"Yeah. I'm sick about that."

Alex thought he saw Butch's eyes moisten.

"He's my best friend and *they* caused this."

"Your son is your best friend?" Alex asked.

Butch looked suspicious at Alex, "He's the only one I trust."

Alex nodded. "You said 'they caused this.' Who's *they*?"

Butch's eyes narrowed. "Sheriff McCallum and Roy Parker, that District Attorney. They knew it was self defense, what I did. But they were friends with the Lamont's and I killed Len Lamont and they were going to get me."

Alex scribbled notes, occasionally looking up at Butch. "Why do you think that a Sheriff and a District Attorney would be out to get you?"

"They was all friends and I killed their friend. It didn't matter to them if it was fair or not. They was mad and they were going to get me to pay. Hasn't anyone come after you for something you done?"

Alex felt like cement was just dumped into his stomach. He squirmed. "Let's stay focused on your issue Mr. Allee." Alex swallowed, then quickly reviewed his notes. "Now that the voices are gone and you seem more comfortable, lets start from the beginning. Do you want something to drink?"

"Okay, maybe a *Coke*."

"I only drink *Dr. Pepper*. Have to be loyal to the profession."   Butch smiled for the first time. And for the first time actually looked friendly. There was something soft in Butch, but Alex still couldn't get past those flames blazoned across Butch's forehead; it was disarming. Alex got up and opened the mini-fridge in his office. "I want to ask you something." He handed the *Coke* to Butch. "Why do you have that tattoo on your forehead?"

Grinning and sheepish, Butch ran his fingers over the red and blue flames. "It was my fortieth birthday present. I always wore bandanas whenever I rode my Harley, so I just decided I'd get a tattoo instead."

"Do people look at you?"

"I don't know. I don't pay no attention."

Alex leaned back. "Really? You don't pay attention?"

"No. Why should I?"

"Well...I mean...it looks scary. You're hair, the beard, the tattoo on your forehead. The other tattoos. I think most people would be scared of you."

Butch stiffened. "Why would they be scared of me? Unless they're judging me." Butch sat the *Coke* on the side table like he was disgusted and wasn't going to drink this Doctors offering. "People have no right to be judging me. That whole trial was about judging people. The town thinks I murdered someone cause they said I looked like a murderer. And that ain't right." The expression on Butch's face changed, his eyes mirrored decades of anger. "When my car broke down and I rode my bicycle to work people looked at me funny. I know they was thinking 'Oh, he can't afford a car.' Or if I had a hole in my jacket, 'Oh, he's poor he can't afford a better jacket.' People are always judging. They look at you and think you're a loser." Butch crossed his arms. "I raised my kids not to be like that."

Alex fidgeted, it felt like Butch peered into his psychological closet and named all the articles of judgment hanging inside. He stopped writing and set the note pad on the side table.

"So from what you just said to me, you *do* care how people judge you? Or at least what they think about you?"

"I don't. Not anymore."

"But the jury...they judged you. Positively in fact." Alex arched his eyebrows. "They found you not guilty."

Alex could see Butch struggling with the seemingly contradictory words...judging positively. This being their first actual session he gently confronted Butch's belief system: "So not *everyone* judges you negatively."

Butch just sat there.

"Okay let's leave it at that for now. Why don't you take me back to the beginning. How did all this start?" Alex took a swig of *Dr. Pepper*.

Butch tugged on his beard and squinted sideways at Alex. He would do many times in future sessions. "I never talked about this to anyone before. Except Cindy."

"I'll let you be the guide Butch. Share with me only what you want to."

Butch leaned forward his strong forearms resting on his knees, "It all started when Sheriff McCallum came to town."

Five

Kersey, Wyoming

Like reading Braille, Sheriff John McCallum traced his thick index finger over the sharp angled letters carved into the backboard of the Kersey park bench.

"Lea Allee," he said softly as his finger tips read the name. A sharp sting followed and Sheriff John McCallum jerked his hand away, gave it a quick shake, then examined his finger tip.

A splinter.

With his thumb he pushed up the splinter of dark wood and pulled it out with his teeth. One small drop of red appeared as he squeezed his fingertip between his forefinger and thumb. "First blood. In Kersey of all places." All those years policing in Vegas and he never shed a drop. McCallum chuckled then straightened from his squat.

John McCallum stood six feet four inches and was wide as a door, he peered through the sparsely equipped Kersey Park. With his thumb he tilted the brim on his Stetson upward then sucked the blood from his finger and rubbed it dry.

Kersey Elementary let out at 2:30 and little groups of little kids would then be walking home. There was no bus service as most the kids lived within a rocks throw of the school.

John McCallum was sitting on the park bench as four young girls made their way through the park. "Hello girls."

He gave them a nod of respect. "I'm the new sheriff in town. Any of you know Lea Allee?"

The girls stopped giggling and kinda shuffled about forming a straight line, shoulders touching.

"Hi Mr. New Sheriff. I'm Lea."

The girls giggled again.

John stood up and pointed to the names carved in the bench. "Did you girls carve this?"

Lea's eyes darted between the bench and the Sheriff, then to her friends. Back and forth. "Yes," she managed to squeak out. Her chest was not letting her breath.

"That's public property. Did you know young lady that defacing public property can get you thrown in jail?"

Lea almost peed her pants as her little heart beat way out of control. "I'm sorry." She had never been in trouble with the law before. "I'm sorry, Sheriff. I didn't mean to do anything wrong."

John shifted his eyes to the other girls. "You also carve your names here?"

The girls looked terrified and remained stoic and silent.

"I don't want to make a big deal outta this, but we all need to respect this park. I know none of you want to go to jail, but jail is where disobedient girls go."

Lea couldn't hold it in and tears spilled from her eyes. "I don't want to go to jail, Sheriff. I'm sorry Sheriff, I won't do it again. I promise. I don't want to go to jail."

"Well then, lets get some sandpaper..." before he could finish Lea Allee bolted.

Six

Butch grabbed the torn rag hanging from the handlebars of his Harley and wiped his face as his sweat dripped into the pan of dirty engine oil creating fat round rainbows. He jerked upright when the screaming pierced his ears.

Squatting, he turned on bare heel and spied Lea running down the street toward him. Butch sprung up kicking over the pan of oil, coating his bare foot in greasy black. "Damn." He gave his foot a shake, then bolted toward the end of the driveway past Cindy's little rock garden as Lea jumped into his open arms.

Lea was sobbing and blubbering, "I'm sorry Daddy, I'm sorry Daddy, don't let 'em put me in jail, please don't let 'em put me in jail."

Butch wrapped his strong arms around her little body, held her close and stroked her red hair with his stained fingers. A large blue winged eagle tattoo became her pillow as she sobbed into his hairless, muscular chest.

"Lea, baby, what happened?" His heart ached. "Tell me what happened, no one is goin' to put you in jail. Don't worry baby, no one will put you in jail."

Her trembling eased as her Daddy held her tight, her sobbing softening into whimpering. Then between breaths: "The sheriff, the sheriff, he said...." She couldn't get it out. "The new sheriff...the sheriff said, he said, I was going to jail. He was going to put me in jail."

Instant rage erupted in his gut squashing the ache, "The sheriff! For what Lea? Why did he say you was going to jail?"

"Because I...I'm sorry Daddy, I didn't know it was wrong."

"What was wrong Lea, just tell me, I won't be mad at you."

"I carved my name on the park bench...and the sheriff said I was going to jail for it."

"You carved your name on the bench? In Kersey park?" She nodded with fear.

"That new Sheriff? He stopped you and told you that?" She kept nodding.

"Lea that's not bad, everyone in town's done it. You go on inside baby. Mom's at the store, but I'll be right back." He kissed her on the top of her head. "You didn't do nothin' wrong Lea, you're not going to jail."

"I'm not? You won't let 'em put me in jail Daddy?"

He kept the rage hidden, now smiling at her. "Lea, I won't let anyone put you in jail. I'm here to protect you, Charles and Margaret too. Now go on inside and wait for Mom." He stroked the top of her head then said, "Go on now. It's okay." It killed him inside to see her so scared, goddamn cops. She hugged him again.

"I'll be right back," he whispered in her ear.

Lea let go of her Daddy and reluctantly walked the gravel driveway to the porch. He nodded at her and she smiled as she stepped onto the weathered steps.

Rage and sour churned his gut. Cops! Always pushing around their authority. This is gonna end right now, he thought. Sweat broke out on Butch's flame tattoo and it wasn't because of the weather.

Barefoot and shirtless he swung his leg over the leather seat of his '66 Harley. With the force of stomping in a cops skull he kick-started the hog, gave a quick glance back at the porch and blew Lea a kiss. "When your Mom gets home, tell her I went to welcome the new sheriff to town." He gave her a wink and a nod.

Holding tight onto the sweeping handle bars he gunned the fine-tuned engine, careened out the driveway and barreled down the street, his back-length hair waving behind him.

Seven

In the living room of the one story converted house which served as the Sheriff's quarters, the three Kersey Councilmen waited. Back in the kitchen, Deputy Logan Pike busied himself pouring iced tea into tall green tumblers. A silly crooked grin expressed Logan's anxiety that came with serving important people. Though he grew up in Kersey and knew everyone by first name, he was still in awe of political authority.

Sheriff McCallum strutted into the living room: the nerve center of justice in Kersey. It was hot and there was no air conditioning, just the opened windows allowing the prairie breeze to flutter the thin, print curtains that hung from iron fence posts converted into curtain rods. The occasionally summer squall, fast moving and furious, would soak the curtains and drench everything within four feet of the open window. The gusts of dry wind would follow and blow the wet papers all over the floors and fill the place with a heavy smell of cow.

John McCallum had set up the meeting and as he approached, Councilmen Ted Rodgers stuck out a calloused hand, "Glad to finally meet you Sheriff McCallum I've heard a lot about you." He pumped his hand like he was yanking on a cows udder. "Welcome to Kersey. This is Coby Dyer and this is my brother Fred Rodgers."

John shook all their hands -- rough and cracked from farming. "So..., Ted and Fred? And you're both on the city council."

Fred, who tended to miss the subtleties of conversation, and life in general, added with a big grin, "Yeah, Ted and Fred, our Mamma and Daddy had a good sense of humor."

"They musta been drunk every time they named one of us," added Ted. "We got two more brothers too, Jed and Ned." He snorted a laugh, then took a glass of tea, "Thanks Loogy. How's Rhonna doing?" he asked.

Logan smiled wide, "Oh she's great."

"Any little deputies on the way?" Ted asked, winking at Logan and giving him a fatherly grin.

Logan blushed that Councilman Ted openly implied that he and Rhonna had sex. He looked at the floor, "No. And I don't know if they would be deputy's or not."

Everyone in town called him Loogy. Logan Pike grew up in Kersey, barely graduated high school, and married Rhonna VanMeetter, the neighbor girl with one eye.

Rhonna's right eye was poked out – yanked out really -- in a freak corn harvesting accident when she was fourteen and she wore a red checkered patch over it. Her Momma sewed the patch from her Daddy's torn work shirt, the very one he wore when that piece of corn stalk flew from the stripper and pierced her right eye. When it happened, Rhonna let out a short scream and tugged the spike of corn stalk right out, along with her full eyeball dangling off the end of it. Her parents never took her to a doctor, 'too dang expensive', her Dad said, besides 'nothin' we can do 'bout it now.'

Twice a day her Momma rinsed the hole with hydrogen peroxide and it healed up just fine.

Rhonna kept here eye in a relish jar, but grew bored changing the milky water every few days. Her Mamma threatened to throw it out 'cause she was worried it would start stinking up the entire house. Over the course of a few weeks it didn't even look like an eye anymore and Rhonna flushed it down the toilet.

Rhonna never warmed up to the hole there. It just kinda nagged at her every time she looked in the mirror, so she stuck one of her brothers cleary-marbles in it. It seemed to work just fine. She's the only girl in town with a red checkered patch covering a cleary-marble. She felt special.

The three councilmen, all weathered and thin with that, *no one works harder than me attitude*, walked out onto the porch with John McCallum. They all took seats on wicker chairs and a log bench. The stuffiness of the living room was replaced by the dustiness of Kersey. Logan followed with the pitcher of iced tea and set it on a TV tray.

Ted started, the tone serious. "Sheriff, we brought you to Kersey to keep tabs on the folks 'round here. Our last Sheriff was forced to resign...let's just say he was too friendly with everyone."

"Caught smoking weed back of the church one night with Bob and Sue Parker," added Logan grinning from one long ear lobe to the other.

Ted shot him a "shut-up" look, Logan stopped smiling and dropped his head staring at the rotting creaky floorboards of the porch. Ted continued, "Like any small town in the God fearing good Ole USA we have a few problems. Domestic violence, some weed smokers, a lot of speeding but we don't concern ourselves with that much. If I was to name one big issue around here it would be the unchristian-like behavior of some folks. Fights at the Oasis Bar, stiffing their tab...adultery!" The three nodded at that one. "Stuff like that."

John looked at the four of them and wondered what kind of lunacy he had gotten himself into.

"So anyways, we appreciate you coming from Las Vegas. It's a big change I'm sure."

John eyed him. "No change but the weather, Ted. Crime is crime whether it's busting girls on the Vegas Strip or busting pot smokers behind the barn. Makes no difference to me." John tilted back his cowboy hat. "Except Vegas is probably busier." They all chuckled. "There's bad people everywhere and they're all the same. But I want to be clear here. I'm not the Moral Police. What people do in their own house doesn't concern me, unless it's illegal."

Fred, Ted and Coby raised their tumblers in a sun-tea salute just as the roar of a Harley broke their moment of bonding. Logan's eyes went wide, "Jesus Christ, it's Butch Allee." There was an edge to his voice, "I know that hog anywhere."

The three councilmen scrambled to their feet and stared at the thunder rumbling up Main street.

"Butch Allee? Lea Allee's father?" asked John who remained seated. He rubbed his finger.

"He's that Son's of Silence biker I told you 'bout. With all them tattoos on his body."

Coby added, "*He's* why we brought you here, Sheriff. He's more than immoral, he's full of *illegal*. Folks in town say he's killed a couple people too."

"No ones proved that," said Fred.

"Cause he's a sneaky bastard," whispered Logan shaking his head while he kept hidden behind Ted.

"He's one of our bad ones, Sheriff. Criminal history as long as a stallions dick. Even beat his wife a few times too" said Ted.

"Everyone is just plain scared of him," Fred chimed in.

Logan peeking from behind Ted's shoulder and with obvious anxiety in his voice. "FBI got pictures of him at one of those KKK rallies. Took his son with him too. They's a whole bunch of nigger haters."

Like a giant owl John's head rotated round and stared at the four of them. *These people run this town?*

The gunning of the engine choked the quiet and all four watched, scared, like the Devil just rode in. John turned his attention back to the man on the bike and remained seated. "I take it none of you like him."

The Harley spit dirt and stones as Butch skidded the bike to the bottom stair of the porch. A black, oil stained bare foot slid the kick stand down and Butch defiantly sat on the Harley and looked up at the group on the porch who were staring down at him.

No one moved.

With a slow steady sweep of his leg, Butch swung it up and over the leather seat, stood tall and then strode up the wooden steps, his sinewy legs accented by sweat and dirt, one foot still covered in black oil.

Logan took one step backward.

Butch commanded the top step of the porch and with fire in his eyes said, "You the new sheriff?"

John McCallum hadn't moved. His eyes followed Butch up the stairs then peered upward as Butch stood over him. John pursed his lips like he was going to spit, then, slowly, steadily raised himself off the chair, straightened his knees and finally standing, all six foot four inches of him. At two hundred forty pounds he out stood and out weighed Butch by a full human being. John McCallum stared down on Butch, eyed his long hair, his un-kept beard, his skin or what he could see of it. His eyes cased Butch's torso: White power. A naked lady, a flying eagle, spider webs, a heart, a dagger with blood dripping off the point. The red and blue flames decorating Butch's forehead was a new one for John. The others, John knew immediately as prison tattoos. In the joint these guys tattooed themselves and each other. Ink and a straight pin. The result: Bleeding blue lines and crude designs. John could count how many times a guy had been locked up by the number of prison tattoos on his body. And Butch Allee was covered with them.

Butch took a step toward John McCallum. "Did you tell my daughter you were going to put her in jail for carving her name on the park bench?"

Logan went pale, remembering he'd carved his own name there.

"Aren't you cold, Mr. Allee?" John said dead-pan. The councilmen giggled and Fred nudged Ted with a brotherly fist.

Butch abruptly realized he was only wearing cut-off shorts. "Just answer my question Sheriff ." His words hid the sudden feeling of vulnerability he had with the authority figure towering over him.

John stared right into Butch's eyes, "Mr. Allee, I don't want any trouble from you. Defacing public property is a crime and I'm here to enforce the law. I didn't mean to --"

"Enforce the law my ass, you're picking on a little girl who done what every other kid in this town has done." He shot a look at Logan, who took another step back. "You have no right to tell her you're going to lock her up in jail. She came home crying. Is that what you want? *Little girls* scared of you?" Butch's eye's flashed and his lids narrowed, "You stay away from my family."

John hadn't moved, "Mr. Allee if you and your family obey the law, I'll have nothing to say to you except 'Hi,' and ..." John smiled, "I do suggest you get a shirt on."

"You going to arrest me for that? Is there a law says I can't go without a shirt?"

"No. No law like that Mr. Allee, I'm just concerned about your health."

"Fuck you!"

John's face tightened, caustic words were restrained from years of practiced patience, he instead seethed out, "Disrespect to a law enforcement officer can get you ticketed, *Mr.* Allee." But he was talking to Butch's thick back covered by long hair that hadn't felt scissors in fifteen years.

Butch sauntered down the steps and slid onto his Harley, kick started the hog and drove off sputtering stones and rocks and dirt at all of them. Like his ghost, dust lingered about the porch.

John never took his eyes off Butch, "I want tabs on Allee. You got that Logan?"

"Yes sir. We already got a file on him full of stuff, I'll get it." Logan spun around and ran into the house like a kid after free candy.

With a thick movement of his body John turned back toward the councilmen. "I can see why this town needs some honest and direct policing."

"Some honest and direct ass kicking if you ask me," said Ted, "and Butch is the first asshole that should get it." He looked at John, "Folks are scared of him. He deals with conflict through intimidation, just like he tried to do now, just look at him. Little kids are even scared of him, all those wicked tattoos and that hair and beard. Heaven knows there's nothing good about him. And I'll tell you, if anything happens to his kid Charles," he shook his head, "Butch is on their ass."

"He even goes to church on Sundays," said Coby with a snort of indignation. "No way he's a Christian. God forgive his devilish soul." Coby gazed upward and took a a few moments of Right-Wing silence.

Ted's anger withered a bit, "I still can't figure out why little Cindy Graff married him. She could have had any boy in this town." He gazed down the street at the one and a half story little cookie-cutter homes with little porches and little un-kept yards. "She had her pick. Any boy she wanted from this town."

"*You* wanted her."

"Shut up Fred." His reverie interrupted.

"Whose Cindy Graff?" John asked.

Ted looked at John sideways with a look of lost opportunity. "Graff Farms. Her Daddy owns a good bunch of the turf farms 'round here, supplies all the turf at the stadiums, even Mile High." His lips tightened. "Got some serious money he does."

"A lot of serious money," said Fred. "Could have been ours Ted, but you lost her to the Tattoo Man."

"Will you shut up Fred," Ted's lean body tightened and sweat broke out on his balding head, "Now just shut up."

The sparkle of dreams in Fred's eyes vanished at the scolding. "I was just--"

Ted shot him another look and turned back toward John. "Cindy grew up here in Kersey. Her Daddy was real successful and everyone thought she'd marry one of the town boys."

"I dated her once," interrupted Fred.

"I never dated her," added Coby. "You never dated her did you Loogy? You were too young."

"I like old women," Logan quickly added.

"She ain't old," said Coby in defense. "She was hot. Still is. Got to first base with her too."

Logan was wide eyed with respect for Coby's sexual experiences.

Ted ignored them both. "Anyways all of a sudden she left town and got married to *him*. They moved back to Kersey, Butch had lost his job or something, and everyone in town was shocked when they moved here...Little Cindy Graff married to this freak. Of all the boys here none seemed good enough for her, so she went out of town and got *him*." Ted looked at John, "You know it kinda felt like your own sister kicking dirt on your family, like they wasn't good enough. He's an outsider. A loner. Doesn't socialize with anyone. No friends here. You drive by any day and his Harley is parked in the driveway. He doesn't work. Cindy works full time just to pay the bills while he sits home and watch's TV." Ted gazed down Main street as the dust cloud settled onto the dirt covered road. "Kersey never been the same since."

John wasn't sure if he was ever going to be the same either.

Eight

Butch's Home

The screen door banged as it hit the wooden door frame as Cindy came in with an armful of shopping bags. She spied the collection of wild flowers arranged in a chipped opaque vase in the middle of the Formica kitchen table. "Oh how nice."

"I picked 'em for you," Butch said, leaning against the flaked kitchen door frame.

"You old softy."

He grinned, "I ain't that old." With three steps in the tiny kitchen he was next to her. Cindy wrapped her arms about his waist and laid her head on his chest, then a sigh, "You ready for work?"

"Yeah." He stroked her short blonde hair. "I hate it that you just get home and I have to leave." He squeezed her, feeling exactly the same as she did when they were dating. Even after three kids she was still tiny and firm. And she smelled so comforting.

"I hate it too, but one of us has to be home with kids. And the clinic needs me in the day—"

"—And the bindery needs me at night."

She looked up into his eyes, "I guess it's good we both are needed, huh?"

"Pays the mortgage."

She let him go, "I need to get these groceries put away."

"I want to show you something first." He took hold of her arm and walked her out the back door. "Look what I did for you."

The back yard was home to one very large, very old oak tree that shaded the entire tiny back yard.

"Permanent. For everyone to see."

Extending from one side of the trunk to the other was a large, red, spray painted heart with a jagged spray painted arrow piercing the center. The initials B and C above it and TLA below it.

"It'll always remind me that I truly love you."

Cindy stood on her tip toes and wrapped her arms around his neck. "I truly love you too." "Our lives are pretty perfect aren't they?"

"They are," she said, her smile genuine and full of love. She let her arms slide from his neck. "You're the most thoughtful man I've ever known. We're lucky we found each other."

"God brought us together," he added.

"And we're staying together forever." She gave him a squeeze.

"Where are the kids?" she asked as they walked back into the kitchen.

Butch took hold of a grocery bag and emptied it onto the counter, "Charles went to a wrestling try-out at school. Margaret is playing next door and Lea is recovering in her room."

Cindy stopped and turned around, a concerned look splashed on her face, and a can of Sloppy Joe mix in her hand. "Recovering from what?"

Butch spoke as he put groceries away. "She got stopped by that new Sheriff. On her way home from school. He told her he was going to throw her in jail for carving her name on the Kersey Park bench."

"Are you serious?" She put down the can. "He said that? Put her in jail?"

"Yeah. She came home crying and I went over to see him. I told him that she didn't do nothing wrong and to back off."

"What did he say to that?"

"Not much, he was there with Loogy and those council members."

She felt her chest heaving. "Everyone in town has their name on those benches. Why did he pick on her?"

"He's a big city cop with a big city attitude." Then he chuckled. "I drove the Harley over there with only my shorts on." He let out a laugh. "You should have seen their faces."

"This isn't funny, I don't like this one bit Butch. How's Lea?"

"She's fine. I told her no one was going to put her in jail. Don't worry, she's okay now."

"I want to talk to her." Cindy moved toward the living room but Butch caught her by the arm.

"Cindy, she's okay, lets not make a big deal of this with her. I dealt with it and she knows I talked to Sheriff McCallum."

"That's his name...McCallum?"

"Yeah John McCallum. Big guy in a big cowboy hat. Don't worry he ain't going to be pushing us around."

"But why Lea? Did he say?"

"I'm sure Loogy or those councilmen put him up to it. You know how they are, always giving me shit."

Cindy *did* know how they were. The petty intrusions into their lives, the stares when she was out with Butch and the kids. Since moving back to Kersey, it's never let up. It's like the Town resented her for bringing Butch here. She walked past the flowers and slowly put the cans of pork and beans into the cabinet.

"Don't worry Cindy, it's okay. I put that Sheriff in line." He kissed her on the top of the head. "I gotta go, see ya' in the morning." He strutted out the back door to his Harley, got on and drove out the driveway.

Cindy never liked hearing the Harley's roar soften in the distance as Butch rode away and now she liked it even less.

Nine

Aspen Grove

Alex sipped his coffee and made a face. Cold. From years of experience he knew that some patients told all kinds of wild stories and most had to be interpreted through a sieve of clinical skepticism. He felt Butch just might be one of them.

"They really hassled you about not wearing a shirt?"

"Yeah, they hassled me about all kinds of stuff. The cops were always watching me."

"Why would they be watching you?"

"I don't know. I never did nothing wrong there. I just don't like cops." Butch's face crinkled with defiance. "Never have never will."

Butch fidgeted in the chair and looked about Alex's office. It was uncomfortable for him being in this office that was a lot nicer than his house.

"Why don't you like cops?"

Defiance on Butch's face melted into confusion. "Who does? I don't trust any of 'em. They was always stopping me for no reason to check my drivers license. Routine, they'd say. But they was just trying to catch me with an expired one. Or we'd be driving in the station wagon and they stop us to see if we were all safe and wearing our seat belts. There were times they'd drive by the house real slow, just looking about. Ten minutes later, they'd drive by again."

"Do you have a record?"

Butch coiled back in his chair and looked at Alex as if he was a cop asking for his license. "Why? Does it matter here?"

"No actually. I was wondering about your past."

"I've done a few things. But they *are* in the past."

Alex nodded. "Like what?"

"I'm good now. I don't like going back there."

Alex nodded again, I bet you don't. He made a mental note that Butch evaded the question and again found Butch staring at him. Intensely staring, like criminals do when they want you to back off.

"If the police watched you all the time, you wouldn't trust them either," Butch added, then looked away.

"That's probably true. Do you trust *me*? This place? You must have trusted this hospital since you checked yourself in."

Butch's chest noticeably heaved. "Cindy was going to leave me if I didn't."

Alex decided not to push the trust issue anymore, he still needed Butch on his side if he wanted to get anywhere in the therapy. "So the sheriff, he was really concerned about Lea carving her name in that park bench? Sounds extreme to me."

Butch sat upright, alert, "Hey, that's what Cindy said. Some friends of ours said the same thing. Everyone in Kersey had their names carved there and all of a sudden it's against the law for my daughter to do it. It don't make any sense. He was trying to act big and tough with little girls."

"You're probably right."

Alex watched Butch's posture soften with the affirmation.

"What kind of work does Cindy do?"

"She's a nurse assistant at the local medical clinic. She worked days and I worked night shift binding scrap paper into bales."

Alex unconsciously leaned forward and looked Butch in the eyes. Binding scrap paper? "That's how you earned a living? Eight hours a night?"

"Twelve. Twelve hours, five nights a week. Sometimes six. We needed the money. I did some motorcycle fixing for a while, but it didn't pay enough. I was stupid and quit school, wanted to work, you know, get some money, date girls, work on my bike." He grinned then looked at the floor again, "I didn't have much guidance at home so I kinda did what I wanted. I only got an eighth grade education."

Eighth grade and working? Alex knew that was the fate of poor kids, of the luckless, the kids on the other side of the tracks. Now here was one of those kids. One of those whose luck never seemed to change.

"I tried to teach my kids to stay in school and get a good job, then they won't end up like me," Butch said.

He has some insight, Alex thought. "Did they follow your guidance?"

Butch's eyes lit up, "Yeah, they did, and their grades are good. I have good kids, Dr. Dalton." Then his eyes dimmed, "But after they put me in jail, and I couldn't be home and we had no money, Charles kinda went astray. I wasn't there to guide him, to be a good father to him. And Charles being charged with accessory to assault...and thrown in jail...." Butch stopped and wiped his eyes with his big calloused fingers, "That does bad things to a seventeen year old." He was silent for a few long minutes and avoided looking at Alex.

Alex sat silent with him.

As a *recovering* criminal defense attorney - as Alex referred to himself - he knew from experience that criminals were the master deceivers; the chameleons of the human race. When he practiced law he really didn't care who they were as long as they got a fair trial, and that he was paid in some form of tangible goods. Money was good. Gifts were sometimes welcomed along with all expenses paid exotic trips. At times even Alex was impressed with what some of his clients were willing to "trade" for his valuable services: Unlimited use of a clients beach house in Cancun, A Jaguar rental for a year or two, corporate jet to anywhere in the world. Of course he was also offered cocaine, escorts, part ownership of a pot farm in Columbia. He refused these payment methods. He never did anything illegal, but at times bartering was fun. Life was good. Very good. All that changed when Lisa was murdered. And now, as a psychologist, Alex *needed* to know who they were. He *wanted* to know. Being paid wasn't an issue.

Alex felt he needed to change direction a bit with Butch and said, "What was your childhood like?"

Butch leaned back into the chair. "Oh pretty normal I guess. Grew up in Commerce City doing kids stuff. Smoking cigarettes, ditching school, hopping the train outta town."

Alex eyebrows jumped. "That's normal kid stuff? Hopping trains?"

"Everyone did it. Ride the train outta town for the weekend, hang out in Denver."

"You'd hang out in Denver? Did you live on the streets?"

"Yeah. It was kinda scary, but kinda fun." Butch laughed as he heard himself say it now.

"How old were you?"

"About sixteen."

"And that was normal for you at sixteen?"

"Normal for us kids who lived in my neighborhood."

The making of a delinquent. "Where was your family?"

Butch looked confused. "They was home."

"Butch, kids just don't hop trains and ditch school. That's not *normal* kid stuff. What did your parents say?"

There was more confusion on his face and Butch thought a moment. "Nothing I guess. By then I was pretty much on my own. That's how I started getting into trouble."

Well, I guess. "So why did you start doing this?"

Butch thought a moment again. "Well we was Mormon."

Now Alex was confused. "Mormon? What does being Mormon have to do with you getting into trouble? I thought Mormons *stayed out* of trouble."

"We was brought up Mormon but I left the church when I was about fourteen. That's when I started getting into trouble. I ran away to California, stole a car. Then ended up in jail in Wyoming. I had a few probation violations, little stuff like that."

Alex was trying to fit all these misshapen pieces into a logical, clinically significant puzzle, but it wasn't working. "Okay let me get this straight you left the church and lost your way and got into trouble."

Butch's look was cold. "I didn't lose my way. The Church made me get into trouble."

Alex confronted him. "I don't understand. How did the church *get* you into trouble?"

Butch looked agitated and began rubbing his hands again. "When I was twelve or fourteen the Elders of the church had a talk with me and asked me what sins I did for the week that I wanted to be forgiven for. I told them I didn't do any sins. They said everyone sins. That kinda made me angry so I asked them what sins did *they* do. They got all mad and said they were Bishops they didn't sin. Right then I knew they was lying to me and I told 'em so, right to their faces. They told me to get out of their church, so I did and never went back to church again until I got outta jail when I was about twenty three."

Alex thought the whole thing was unbelievable. But he had heard worse things about church and the so called Christian forgiveness. "So you felt like the church elders lied to you and the church let you down."

Butch's eyes lit up again, "Yeah. That's right. I never thought of it that way but the Church did let me down. I never trusted authority figures after that. I was taught by my parents that church people were children of God. I thought they was perfect. But then I found out they were liars."

Alex couldn't argue with that last bit of disillusionment. "Did you teach your kids about authority figures?"

Butch's body visibly tightened. "Yeah. Don't trust any of 'em. Cops, church, none of them."

Alex filed that away. He changed the subject again. "So what's your relationship like with your son?"

Butch smiled, "We're like brothers, Charles and me. Best friends. We always were. We did everything together. He and I would talk about our problems or dream about building our own car and painting it." Butch tugged on his beard. "We had some good times."

"You said Charles got into wrestling?"

Butch suddenly looked sick, his gaze went out the window. "I wish he never had."

Ten

Kersey High School

The shrill whistle echoed through the gymnasium, the voice following was harsh and commanding, "Hustle, hustle, hustle. I want two *girls* out here now. Allee and Bouchard! You two."

Len Lamont dripped sweat as he motioned for the two wrestling candidates to move into the center of the mat. "Referee position," he barked. "Allee on top."

Frankie Bouchard knelt on all fours and Charles readied himself next to him. "Hold on," said Charles. He jogged to the bleachers and gently placed his wire rimmed glasses on the wooden bench then ran back to the center of the mat where Frankie was waiting and Len was impatient.

"Ready now four eyes?"

Charles nodded meekly and knelt down wrapping one arm around Frankie's mushy belly that hung down from eating too many burgers and fries at the Kersey McDonalds. The other hand gripped Frankie's left elbow.

Len squatted his gaze intense. "Okay sissies, I want it fast and furious. No pussy pulling, the first down walks and the winner goes on." Len winked, then smiled. His tobacco stained teeth seemed out of place in his twenty seven year old mouth.

"Wrestle!"

Charles dug his toes into the mat and pushed forward, but Frankie had the weight and spun around, crushing Charles beneath him. But Charles was wiry and strong and

54

kept his shoulder off the mat and bucked Frankie off his chest rolling him like a thick piece of dough, Charles sprung on top, leveraged his body with his legs and kept Frankie on his back.

Len was down on his stomach watching, he slapped the mat three times, "Match!" Within seconds it was over. "Bouchard get outta here. Allee you stay."

Charles stood and nodded at Frankie, still friends. Breathing hard, Charles slowly walked toward the bleachers but was stopped dead in his tracks by a large hand grabbing his shoulder from behind, then a whisper into his ear, "I knew you could amount to something." Then louder, "Good job Allee." Len playfully kicked Charles in the butt and chuckled as he strutted back onto the matt.

Charles swallowed, said nothing, and sat on the bench. He took his glasses, slipped them on and watched Len dominate the next wrestling team.

The water was cold, each drop seemed to create it's own goose bump on his hot, sweaty skin. Charles turned the shower handle further to the left as warmer water soaked his short, brown hair. He felt the warmth penetrate his sore muscles.

"Charles!" The familiar voice of Tommy Turner reverberated in the naked antechamber of shower heads.

"Hey Tommy," said Charles as he grabbed a bar of slimy soap.

"Awesome, we both made the team," said Tommy as he turned on the water and soaped up. "Man, you really pounced on Frankie."

Charles was still feeling bad about it. "Yeah."

"I'd have beat your ass, Allee." Tommy lathered up his hands and threw soap suds at Charles freshly rinsed hair.

"Hey ass-wipe!" Charles impulsively flung the slimy bar of soap at Tommy. It sailed passed missing him, hitting the shower wall where it stuck fast. They gawked as the bar clung to the soap-scum-stained tile and watched as it slid down that tile like a soft-shelled white snail leaving a sticky foamy trail.

"Whoa! You put that shit in your hair Allee? Someone spunked on it! Ha! And you washed your hair with it!" He snorted a laugh.

Charles wasn't into the tease, "Shut up Tommy." He grabbed a fresh bar of soap and rewashed his hair.

"I think we're going to win this years wrestling tournament," said Tommy as he bent over and washed his feet. "We got a great team this year and with Len coaching... we can't lose."

Charles looked at him, "You think so?"

"Hell yeah. Len's the best. State wrestling champion and everything." Tommy let the warm water run over his head.

"If he's so good why's he teaching at Kersey High?"

Tommy thought a moment, then slicked his hair back with his hands, "Cause he married Alisha. He can't go nowhere's else."

"I don't *want* to go *nowhere's* else."

Charles and Tommy spun around.

Standing naked, six foot two and two hundred and twenty five solid pounds, Len was listening and watching. "For your information *girls*, I can teach and coach anywhere I want. New York, L.A., Wichita. But I like it right here, besides, I get free dinners at *Grandma's*."

Len moved under the shower head between Tommy and Charles.

Ever since Len won the Wyoming State wrestling championship, the folks in Kersey treated him like royalty. While the rest of Wyoming went on it's way, the Kersey City Council kept the title *and* the prestige alive, making October 21, the day he won, as Len Lamont Day. It's not a legal holiday, so no one takes off work and school still goes on, but the town has a parade and everyone ends up drinking beer at the Oasis Bar. Len Lamont put Kersey on the map and the town intended to keep it that way.

"Allee...you got anymore tattoos?" Len motioned with his head toward Charles' left shoulder where an *A* was etched into his skin. His eyes slowly cased Charles sinewy, teenage body.

"No," Charles replied dully.

Len's lips pursed with disgust. "I can't believe a proper Christian man would give his own kid a tattoo."

Charles felt the pressure. "My Dad did it when I was four. It's an A for Allee."

"Duh! A, Allee. I got that four eyes. But why?"

Charles glanced at Tommy, then back at Mr. Lamont. "My Dad said if anyone kidnapped me he'd be able to identify me."

"Whoa, no kiddin'? Why would anyone kidnap you Allee?" Len squatted and washed his legs and feet. "Can't remember when a kid was ever kidnapped from Kersey." He stood. "I think it was....*never*!" Len looked disgusted by it all. "Did he do it to you himself?"

Len wasn't washing now, just standing letting the water flow over his naked body.

"My Dad told me he used some ink and a needle."

"Man that must have hurt, you just being four."

"I don't remember it."

"At four huh? That's really weird, Allee." Len grabbed some shampoo. "But what can you expect from *your* old man."

A few more boys walked into the showers and Len purposely spoke louder, "You did good out there Charles all one hundred and thirty five pounds of you." He threw a glance again at Charles body. "You work at it, put some decent effort into it and you could be *very* good. A bit skinny, but your wiry and quick." He grinned. "It's how I like my women, wiry and quick."

The open showers were now full of naked teenage boys and Len turned the water colder. He had stopped washing and kept his eyes focused on the green tiled wall. "You're Daddy causin' any trouble lately?"

Charles turned off the shower acting like he hadn't heard Mr. Lamont. He walked out over to his locker, dried off and got dressed.

Eleven

The Oasis Bar

8:35 pm

The narrowing stick of shiny wood felt comfortable and familiar in Len's right hand. It belonged there. His left hand relaxed, hung down by his side gripping a bottle of *Coors*. Len Lamont was always the tallest and the largest guy in the bar. He brought the bottle up to his lips, gulped deeply, finished it off then tossed it over the pool table, "Think quick!"

Bobby Rogers instinctively interrupted the path of the glass projectile sailing at his face and snatched the bottle in the air with a free hand, his pool cue remained tight in his other. "Fuck you Lamont."

The catch impressed Len. "I was hopin' to knock you out. Save you embarrassment from losing this game."

"Shoot ass-hole," Bobby said, setting the beer bottle on the floor.

Len leaned forward, holding his bulk above the table, "Eight in the center pocket." He gripped his custom pool cue the same way he had over the last ten years: Rough and clumsy, but with the precision of a sniper. The blue tipped cue jabbed the white cue ball with no follow through. The tired old ball smacked the *eight* shooting it across the worn green felt; it banked the pocket nearly jumping off the table and clumsily dropped into the center hole. "You owe me

Rogers. Pay up." Smug, Len straightened up and kissed his cue.

With his jaw flexing, Bobby Rogers reluctantly fished into his jean pocket, pulled out a ten and threw it on the table. Before the note had a chance to un-wrinkle, Evan Thomas snatched it up.

"This is for your tab Len. And you owe me more." Evan turned and walked back toward the bar.

Len eyed the back of Evan's head. A grin crept across his lips, he held up his right hand like a toy gun, index finger straight out, thumb up. He picked a spot right at the center of the rubber band that held Evan's thinning gray ponytail and clicked his tongue as he fired his thumb, then blew away the imaginary smoke.

Bobby watched and shook his head. "Want to lose some more money to Evan, Lamont?" he asked.

Len cocked his head, "I'll wrestle ya. In the parking lot. Twenty bucks." His eyes had that blurry glaze.

Bobby stared. The *Coors* that Len had thrown at him was Len's sixth, maybe seventh for the night, it was just enough to make Len irritable and nasty, just enough to push a challenge, even with a long time friend like Bobby. "Shut up." He was used to Len's drunken challenges.

"Pussy," Len said under his breath as he leaned his pool cue against the table, "Hey Evan! Hows about some beer over here."

Evan glared at him from behind the bar. "Shit no, Len! Not another beer till you pay down your tab. I'll call Alisha if I have to." Evan was busy mixing a drink for a trucker sitting at the bar. "If all my customers were like you, I'd be outta business." Evan served the trucker his drink then turned his attention to the old RCA TV precariously fixed to a rickety bracket in the corner.

The hard clicking of cowboy boots on the worn floor was drowned out by the hockey game on TV, but Evan jumped when the slam of Len's wide palm hit the oak bar.

"*Evan*! Give-me-a-fuckin' *Coors* or I'm goin to rip this fuckin' place apart..." his eye's glared, the blurriness gone for the moment, "...or maybe just *you*."

Evan's stomach churned and sweat slipped onto his upper lip. Evan was an ex-biker, and in his day one tough son of a bitch. But those days were long over and he was now a bar owner, replacing his biker-braun with a bit of business savvy, far from the bar destroyer he used to be. He didn't want to give in, but he knew that his fighting skills were very un-polished. Without taking his eyes off Len, Evan slowly slid the cooler lid open, pulled out a beer and slid it across the counter. "One on the house Len."

Len grabbed it. "Don't have the courtesy to even open it for me." He laid the bottle top on the edge of the bar and with his palm slammed it open sending the bottle cap clicking onto the floor. A nick was all that Len left on the edge of the polished wooden bar and without a word he walked back to the pool table.

Evan went for the phone.

Twelve

Sheriff McCallum pushed through the grimy swinging doors and stepped into the Oasis bar. With his Stetson, cowboy boots and gun at his side, he felt like a true Wyoming cowboy, except the place he stepped into was a metal modular building with a tin roof and red neon sign glaring in the window.

McCallum quickly cased the place which was now packed with obnoxious human noises and good country music being strangled by worn juke box speakers. He walked toward the bar where Evan greeted him.

"Thanks for getting over here Sheriff. Len's over there," he nodded over to the booth where Len, Bobby and a few others were sitting. "He ain't caused no trouble yet, but he just might. He did threaten me, that's why I called. He owes me a large tab too. Is there a law against that Sheriff?"

"I'll take care of it," John said, and walked toward the booth.

"Mr. Lamont?" Sheriff McCallum towered over the table as he looked down at Len.

Len no longer being the tallest or largest in the bar, gave John a quick once over.

"Hey Sheriff. You're the new guy in town. Welcome to Kersey." Len scooted out of the booth and stood nearly eye to eye with Sheriff McCallum. "I'm Len Lamont." He shook the Sheriff's hand. "This here's Bobby Rodgers, the *Councilmen's son,* and Frankie and Sue Woodman, they're married."

Len was acting way too friendly and John knew that overly friendly behavior meant something was up. "Mr.

62

Lamont I was called here because it seems you've had too much to drink and you were getting rather...lets just say a little nasty with Mr. Thomas."

"Too much to drink?" Len went wide-eyed with animated surprise. "Nasty? With Evan?" He glanced toward the bar, happily waved at Evan. "No way. We go way back." He tried to look the Sheriff straight in the eyes, but his own eyes kept dancing about, like drunk eyes do, then his rigid knees gave way and he slid back into the booth, a drunk grin plastered on his face. "Maybe I did have a little too much beer...but it ain't no crime to drink in a bar, is it Sheriff?" He avoided looking at John.

"No it's not Mr. Lamont."

"And Bobby here, he's my designed driver."

"*Designated,*" said Bobby.

Len waved him off.

"Mr. Lamont, drinking in a bar is perfectly fine. In fact that's exactly where I want it. But causing *trouble* in the bar *is* against the law and I don't want any trouble here. In fact I don't want any trouble in Kersey at all. You're right, I am new in Town and I want to *slowly* get to know everyone around here. So lets just say this is a little reminder to keep the alcohol in manageable levels. Remember now, no driving. If I catch you driving tonight I *will* put you in jail for the evening. Understand?"

"Got it." Said Len saluting with two fingers, his grin now gone.

"Oh, and Mr. Lamont?"

Len looked up, McCallum seemed ten feet tall and weaving, "Yeah?"

"Pay up your tab." John nodded to the others, "Glad to meet you. If you ever need any assistance just call." He gave a glance at Len. "I'm sure you all know the number."

Bobby, Frankie and Sue all nodded, smiled, and nodded some more looking like a bunch of drunken bobble-heads.

John walked through the crowd like Moses marching through the Red Sea, he gave a nod of reassurance to Evan and with his body pushed through the swinging bar panels. Grinning, he stepped out onto the porch.

"Man, I like them doors."

Thirteen

Alex's Penthouse Suite

9:10 PM

Alex propped his feet on the leather couch and clicked on his fifty two inch flat screen TV which hung between two life-size stone sculptures of a Zulu warrior couple that he and Lisa shipped home from an African safari. Alex tried to watch a re-run, but wasn't listening as Dr. Doug Ross, played by George Clooney, handsomely strutted into the patient waiting room. Alex's mind was being pulled back to the session with Butch.

He felt cold and pulled a Pendleton blanket over his legs. Was Butch telling the truth? Something kept nagging him deep in his brain, and down in his gut.

As Alex continued watching TV his thoughts left Butch's session. He was preoccupied with something else. He felt it, an uncomfortable feeling. An anxiety. Or was it dread? It was just under the surface, seeming to control his insides.

He looked at his watch, then the date. Three days from now it happened. Actually two days and twenty one hours. He was feeling it, sensing it. The time of year, the weather, the daylight. Eight years ago and it still felt real. It surprised him how fresh the emotions were. They would fade into the background of his daily life for days, even weeks. At other times he pushed them aside, pushed them down, covered by a blanket of cynicism and isolation. Unhealthy behavior for a psychologist; cutting off your own feelings while instructing your patients to get in touch with theirs.

Alex got up and walked into his home office, pulled down the *Diagnostic and Statistical Manual of Mental Disorders* and flipped to mood disorders, then the section on *Normal Bereavement.*

He read, *The diagnosis of Major Depressive disorder is generally not given unless the symptoms are still present two months after the loss.* "What a bunch of crap that is. How would they diagnose me?" He closed his eyes and scolded himself with a half breath-half snort. "Eight years... and I'm still grieving. I guess I do have a major depression."

He closed the book and left it on his desk, then walked back to the living room and stood by the grand expanse of windows that opened up over the city and the clear Denver sky.

From Alex's penthouse suite on the forty fourth floor the view was breathtaking. But for Alex it had become a common view, something he'd gotten accustomed to.

His rich lifestyle had become empty.

And lonely.

Alex pulled the curtains shut and crawled into bed alone.

Fourteen

Kersey

John bolted upright in bed as his pager danced and flashed on his nightstand. He was momentarily disoriented from a deep sleep and he still felt like a stranger in his new bedroom. He snatched up the pager, flicked it off and with sleepy eyes read the text message: *Disturbance. 204 Sixth St.*

The clock on the dresser read 1:09 AM.

With seductive ease, as if leaving a one night stand in the middle of the night, John slunk out of bed, dressed quickly and kissed his wife who had the comforter pulled up to her nose.

"Be careful."

It's what she always said when he got a midnight call.

"It's Kersey honey, not Vegas."

"Be careful anyway."

Sliding silently up to the curb in front of 204 Sixth street, the Kersey Patrol car pulled in diagonally facing the house, the engine went silent and John sat still, watching.

The lawn was overgrown. A brown Dodge Dart was pulled crooked into the driveway.

As he always did in Las Vegas, McCallum sat there for just a few wary seconds assessing the scene: A tiny two story white house. A naked bulb coated with spider webs hung in the center of the porch, it's muted rays cast shadows from the dirty Big Wheel and a bicycle laying on it's side, the kitchen light was on, little streaks of white cut through the worn print curtains. He could make out a figure moving across the room, interrupting the beam.

The houses next door were dark.

Gently, John opened the car door, slid out and listened. A dog barked across town. Then a coyote howled at the dog. Then quiet. It felt strange. Not dangerous strange, just different: No neon fog rising from the darkness, no drone of traffic that just becomes part of the daily noise, no horns honking, no jets roaring overhead.

Just quiet.

He looked upwards, the stars seemed brighter out here, sparkling against the black sky. He remembered as a kid being in the country, the sky always seemed different than it did in the city. And now he knew why: No smog.

He took a breath, then watched his exhale frost up and float away. John walked toward the front porch and instinctively felt for the comfort of his gun. As he stepped up onto the porch he pushed the big wheel off to the side with his boot, opened the bent screen door and knocked.

On the other side, a dog barreled to the door growling and jumping and scratching, then a male voice, "Git down! Git down! Down! Outta here."

Then a female voice, "Who's at the door Coby?"

John shook his head as barely audible words slipped out, "Shit. Coby Dyer's home." John immediately relaxed and rubbed his large hand over his face. He stood erect as the door creaked open and Coby peered out.

"Oh, hey there Sheriff." Coby opened the door wider and then looked down at the porch. His hair was messy and he looked like a little boy caught masturbating in his bedroom. "Com'on in."

"No thanks Coby, just step outside for me."

Coby turned to the woman inside, "I'll be right back."

"Your wife?"

"Oh, yeah, I should introduce you." He hesitated, conflicted now. "She's in her nightgown—"

"—forget it Coby. I got a disturbance call at *this* house. *What's* going on?" John smelled him. "You drunk Coby?"

Coby looked at the porch decking and scratched his scalp through thinning, greasy hair, at the same time he noticed a hole in the floor boards. Gotta fix that. He seemed to forget John had asked him a question.

John waited, but his patience and irritation was getting the best of him. Standing with one of the councilmen on his front porch at one thirty in the morning who was dressed only in worn flannel pajama bottoms, his graying chest hairs long and wild and hanging off sagging man boobs, was not what John wanted to be doing at this hour. He whispered between clenched teeth, "Damn it Coby if you don't talk to me, I'm putting you in a cell for the night and everyone in this town will know by morning. Now what is going on here?"

With that Coby's eyes grew wide, "You'd put *me* in a cell? A Kersey Councilman?"

"Coby, I don't care if you were the Mayor or the Governor. You all brought me here to police this town and that's what I'm going to do. You have five seconds to tell me what happened and why I got this call." His eyes bore into Coby's.

Coby gritted his teeth and shuffled his bare feet. he swung his head from side to side, "I got a problem with my temper."

"Turn around. Put your hands behind your back."

Coby stumbled back toward the screen door his pajamas catching on torn screen, his eyes' wide again, "What? Hands behind my back? What fer?"

"You're giving me shit Coby and I'd rather be home in bed with my wife than listen to your shit so I'm taking you in and we can deal with it in the morning." John reached around and rattled his cuffs.

"Okay...okay, John." Coby pulled the back of his pajamas free from the screen they were still stuck on. "I got these fer my birthday."

"Two seconds."

"John, just settle down..." he clicked his tongue on the roof of his mouth, then said, "I hit Jesse."

Here it comes, the confession, thought John. Then the crying. He hated wife beaters. They're all tough and mean when they smack their women around, but when the cuffs snap shut they whine and cry and blubber and plead...he just wanted to kick the shit out them.

"*Why* would you hit her?"

"Well...cause...she called me a loser." When Jesse had said it, it sounded so mean and hurtful, now it just sounded silly. Coby looked at John with feigned confidence.

John's expression didn't change and Coby's chest sunk in, his shoulders slumped forward as he turned his head away. "I'm behind on the mortgage."

Sudden Coby looked scared.

"Business been real slow, not many folks round here buying farm equipment with this drought and that damn water rationing. It's killing us here."

John knew that was true and the farmers were hurting, but it didn't condone wife beating, just the same he let his cuffs dangle from his belt. He took a deep breath and loudly forced it out his nose.

Coby watched as John looked like a bull in those Popeye cartoons snorting steam.

"I don't want to make enemies Coby, especially with the folks who *hired* me to come here." John's anger suddenly rose up, God he hated wife beaters. He let out another breath. "Coby, for the life of me, if I get one more disturbance call I'll throw you in a cell. That won't look good for you 'round here. Now I suggest you and Jesse get some counseling and get this worked out. You hear me?"

"Yes, Sheriff."

"Good. Now is Jesse alright? Does she need a doctor?"

Coby looked insulted, "A doctor? No way. I don't hurt her."

Anger shot through him again and John took one heavy step forward, "What do you mean you don't *hurt* her? If you slapped her you hurt her." Pointing his finger where Coby's frontal lobes should be he said, "Get some sense into that head of your's Coby. The last Sheriff looked the other way, I won't." He now pointed that finger at Coby's nose, "This is a warning. If you don't get some counseling, I'll recommend your removal from the city counsel. And that *will* be in all the papers. Now let me see her."

John waited and Coby just stood there.

"Now!"

Jesse peered around from behind the door. "I'm okay Sheriff. He didn't really hurt me none."

McCallum eyed her: No bruises, no blood, no swollen lip. "Are you sure? Now's the time to ask for help, Jesse."

She nodded, "I'm okay, thanks." She slipped back behind the door.

She wouldn't press charges anyway, John thought, they never do. His attention went back to the farmer, now shivering in the cold. "Don't *ever* make me come back here again, Coby. And next time you come to the door, wear a shirt."

John turned and walked from the porch, "This is like fucking sick Mayberry." He opened the patrol car door, slid in, slammed it shut and drove home.

Fifteen

Kersey Baptist Church

The parking lot erupted into screaming and yelling as teenagers ran and ducked behind cars and pickup trucks. Charles ran around a white Dodge and spied two girls huddled next to a grime-caked pickup. With a quick thrust he drenched them with a bucket of warm, sudsy water causing them to squeal and run. Charles didn't have time to laugh as a blast of cold water hit him in the back soaking him. He arched with shivers, then ran for another bucket of water.

The Kersey Baptist Church Fall Car Wash had begun.

Pastor Phillip stood at the entrance of the church parking lot next to a card table with a couple of empty five pound coffee cans on it. They were slowly getting stuffed with one and five dollar bills. By ten in the morning the fall chill was gone and the air had warmed.

One of the two Kersey patrol cars slowly pulled into the lot and parked. Both doors opened and Logan and Rhonna stepped out.

"Hey there Pastor Phillip!" Rhonna said waving and grinning like she hadn't seen him in years.

Pastor Phillip scurried up to them, "Oh! I'm so thankful you two are here. Logan, being the town deputy, can you collect the money for me?" Then Pastor Phillip leaned into Logan, "Or are you busy on some important case?"

"Oh he ain't busy," said Rhonna slapping him on the butt.

"Don't do that," Logan whispered to her through clenched teeth as he tried to stand taller to recapture his authority. With a straight face he said, "Sure Pastor I'll collect the money."

Pastor Phillip looked around the parking lot, "I just want to mingle with the folks waiting for their cars, you know, try and get some non-believers to come on Sunday."

"Anyway I can help out Pastor. It's more important for you to be savin' souls than watchin' over car wash money. I'll do the policing 'round here," said Logan.

The roar of the Harley turned heads.

Butch cautiously drove into the church parking lot stopping at the table. Pastor Phillip greeted him. "Good morning Butch." He eyed the shiny chrome, "Your motorcycle looks beautiful."

"Thanks. I washed it before getting here."

"Tryin' to save money?" Logan said deadpan with an edge to his voice.

"Hey there Butch," Rhonna smiled, her hips squirming about like her jeans were too tight. She stared at him with one eye.

"Hey Rhonna," Butch smiled back.

"Going to give rides again Butch?" asked Pastor Phillip.

With suspicion, Butch glanced at Logan, then back at the Pastor. "Yeah. If you want me to. The kids really liked it at the last car wash. I'll go slow and ride around the lot."

"I want a ride!" yelled Rhonna. "Can I get a ride, Butch?"

Logan interrupted her and directed his attention at Pastor Phillip, "I don't think that's legal, Pastor. He'd need a chauffeur's license to give rides." Rhonna tugged on Logan's jacket sleeve. "I want a ride, Loogy. Come'on, please."

Pastor Phillip countered, "Oh, Logan, it's just a ride around the lot, and it's a money maker. Money for God."

Butch looked irritated. "I ain't taking the money for the ride, Loogy, it's goin' to the church. It's charity. I don't need no license for charity work."

"Loogy, I want a ride. Please?"

Logan jerked his sleeve from Rhonna's grasp, "I'm certain it ain't legal Pastor."

Butch looked at the Pastor, "You asking me to give rides for God, Pastor?"

Pastor Phillip felt squeezed, "Well, yes, I guess I am, Butch." He turned to Logan, "That's no crime Logan, giving rides for God and receiving a donation in return."

Butch didn't need an answer. "Then I'll give rides Pastor. Loogy has no authority over God." Butch put the Harley in gear.

"Wait!" Rhonna nearly panicked. "Can I get a ride too, Butch?"

"Sure, get on."

Rhonna nearly jumped on the back of the Harley.

"No!" Logan stepped toward the bike as Rhonna snuggled into the seat, "Oh, Loogy, he'll go slow. I"ll hold my patch this time so it don't fly off."

Logan instantly looked hurt, "*This* time? What does that mean?"

Rhonna's heart beat a bit faster, "Don't worry Loogy. Butch'll be careful. It's just for fun."

A big grin swept across Butch's face. "You ready for some fun, Rhonna?" He threw a glance at Logan.

"You bet!" She squealed with excitement.

Butch gunned the engine and Rhonna threw her arms around his waist, making Logan's heart pound.

"God loves you, Butch Allee." Pastor Phillip knew Butch would collect quite a bit of cash today. Even though some folks in Kersey looked at Butch with a watchful eye and most would never allow their kids to play at his house; when it came to 'Rides for God' their kids begged for a ride and the parents coughed up the couple of bucks. It seemed that on Sundays, one day a week, folks would try and forget the tattoos and the long hair, but come Monday love and tolerance was in short supply.

Logan watched with disgust as Butch took off past the line of cars then around the church parking lot. He gunned it right past Logan and hauled down the street. He watched in the distance as Rhonna's eye patch flipped up and fluttered in the wind.

Pastor Phillip turned to Logan who was looking like a little boy that just lost his puppy to the SPCA. "It's just some good ole' clean fun Logan." Pastor Phillip glanced over at the group of people waiting for their cars and sure enough there were a couple of folks there who hadn't been to church in quite a while. "Logan will you stay here and watch the money for me? I gotta go and get me some souls for church." The Pastor left Logan in charge of the coffee cans and he quickly walked toward the Sunday prospects.

Butch rode back into the lot, gunned the engine with zealous enthusiasm and rode past the line of cars. Logan's sour expression filled his rear view mirror which made him feel quite good. He parked the Harley in the corner of the lot, Rhonna gave him a squeeze and slid off.

"Wow. That sure was excitin' " She half squatted with bowed legs, "Got my jeans all tight...and everything else." Her eye flashed at Butch.

Butch felt embarrassed with Rhonna, but felt great that he jerked Logan around a bit. "Rhonna, I gotta get ready for the kids."

"Sure. Thanks for the...," she stopped and leaned into him, "That Harley sure does vibrate." She winked at him, turned and walked back toward Logan.

Loogy would probably shoot me for that ride, Butch thought. From his side saddle bag he pulled out a small hand written sign and placed it on the seat. It read: *Ride's for Jesus. $2.00*. Within minutes kids were lining up. The first was a curly blonde haired girl about seven years old. Butch smiled, his eyes sparkling like his bike. He hoisted her up onto the seat and gently swung his leg over. He balanced the bike and kick started the engine. He felt two little hands on his hips. "Hold on tight," he said. The bike jumped forward and Butch grinned. Slowly he drove about the lot, in and out of the cars, behind the church, down the street past the two spinsters who were sitting on white plastic chairs watching the commotion. He let the engine idle and slid the kick stand down. He climbed off and looked at his passenger who was beaming with glee.

"Again! Can I go again?"

"Well, you have to give two dollars to Pastor Phillip over there, then you can get back in line."

Her smile fell away. "Two dollars?"

"It's two dollars a ride. Are your parents here?"

She shook her head. "I just walked here from over there." She twisted on the seat and pointed down the street.

Butch smiled. "Ok. The first ride's free."

Her smile returned and she held her arms out for Butch. He grabbed her about the waist and helped her down.

"What the hell are you doing with my daughter?" The booming voice startled Butch and he turned around to see Ben Womack grabbing the little blonde girls hand and giving her a good jerk. "I just gave her a ride." Butch had seen Ben Womack around town but didn't know him at all.

"Who gave you permission to give Jolie a ride?"

Butch immediately felt vulnerable, he stammered, "I just give rides to help raise money for the church. Pastor Phillip over there, he knows about it."

"I didn't give *you* permission. What if you have an accident with one of these kids? Neither of you are wearing a helmet. You got a release? Anything?"

Butch wasn't sure what to say.

"This is one big lawsuit waiting to happen."

Butch felt sick at the thought of lawyers and courts. He didn't like any of them. "She was just in line. I'm sorry."

"Can I go again Daddy?"

Ben Womack looked down at his daughter. "No! We're going home." He gave her a tug and they walked away.

"Thank you," she said and waved at Butch with her free hand.

Shit. What a way to start the morning. Butch looked at the line forming next to him: a half dozen kids were twitching with excitement, dollar bills in their hands.

He shrugged off Ben's interrogation, "Okay, you next?" he asked the little boy in line. Butch took the two dollars and stuffed the bills into the pocket of his jeans.

The lot filled with kids and cars and parents. Moms brought brownies and drinks. Others brought home made sandwiches and fresh coffee for the adults. The church lot bustled with religious zeal from the adults and sexual overdrive from the teenagers washing cars with wet t-shirts. Pastor Phillip looked on and swelled with pride.

The car wash ended at 2 O'Clock, by then Butch was dead tired of giving rides. Surprisingly, other than his run in with Ben Womack there were no other hassles. It felt good that he contributed to the church expansion fund, but he was glad it was over. He drove over to the card table and slid off the Harley.

Pastor Phillip threw his arm around Butch's shoulder, "Butch, you're rides were the most popular."

"I'm glad I can help out." He dug into his pocket and pulled out a fist of bills and dumped them into the coffee cans, then pulled his pocket inside out and retrieved a few more bills and a hand full of coins. "I guess that's it."

"This money will help with our new sanctuary that we're building next spring Butch. God willing of course."

"That sounds real good Pastor Phillip. If I can help out let me know."

"You're a good Christian, Butch. Thank you."

"What about the other pocket, Allee?" Logan said as he sauntered up. "I saw you stuff some bills in your other pocket."

Butch patted his pocket and felt a small bulge of wadded up money. He stuck his hand in and pulled out a few dollars and dumped them into the coffee can.

"Guess we gotta watch you Allee. Trying to steal money from the Church." Logan was shaking his head.

"I just forgot about those bills, Loogy."

Logan took two steps toward Butch and stared into his eyes, "Forgot huh? I could arrest you right now for stealing," -- raising his voice -- "stealing from God!"

Butch's lips disappeared into a growl, "You put one hand on me and I'll knock you cold out. Right in front of everyone." He glanced around at the small crowd gathering. "What would Rhonna think of you then? Laying on your back, bleeding all over." Butch knew he could easily take Logan, but he couldn't take the entire crowd if they jumped on him but he wasn't about to back down. "Go ahead Loogy, try and get your cuffs."

Logan trembled as his heart pumped adrenaline. He stared into Butch's eyes. "I need to see your other pockets Allee."

It took Butch by surprise that Logan wasn't letting up and it pissed him off, "Fuck you!" Butch turned then felt a hand grab his shoulder.

"Stop Allee. I need to see your pockets now!"

Rhonna had run up and blurted out, "What's happening here Loogy? Butch?"

Butch snapped his arm free and Logan stumbled and went for his gun.

Butch threw his arms up in the air, "Whoa Loogy. I aint' done nothing wrong. You got no right to put your gun on me."

Rhonna screamed, the crowd of bystanders scattered and Paster Phillip yelled out, "Logan Pike. Put your gun back in your holster. There is no excuse to draw a weapon on Church property."

Logan had regained his footing and continued to hold his weapon at Butch's chest. "You assaulted an officer of the law Butch Allee. I'm going to arrest you right now. Turn around and put your hands behind your back." The barrel of Logan's .38 was jumping about.

Butch hadn't moved and held his arms half way up. Paster Phillip defiantly walked between Butch and the barrel of Logan's gun. "What's this about?" Irritated, Logan yelled, "Get outta the way Pastor. Allee was stealing money." Logan tried to side step and the Pastor kept his body between them. "He kept some bills in his pocket. I saw him." Rhonna, scrappy and intolerant, stomped up to Logan and tried to grab his gun. "Put that away Loogy, you're gonna hurt somebody." Logan now had Pastor Phillip and Rhonna blocking his view of Butch and he began to feel the stares of the crowd gathering around again. Most of the folks in Kersey had never seen Logan Pike draw his gun and it looked kinda funny to them.

Suddenly Charles burst through the crowd and entered the ring. "What's happening Dad?"

"Loogy's accusing me of stealing money from the church."

Rhonna screamed, "Stop it Loogy. Let's go home."

Pastor Phillip crossed his arms, "I'm staying right here Logan till you put that gun away."

Butch turned all of his pants pockets inside out. "See Pastor, I put all the money in the can, I just forgot about a few bills. I wasn't stealing nothing."

"I don't believe you were stealing Butch," said Pastor Phillip. "Now Logan do as I say and put that gun away."

Everyone seemed against him at the moment and suddenly Logan felt like a sinner at a stoning. And he was the sinner. His heart pounded, he felt trapped. "Are you going to press charges Pastor?"

"Oh of course not Logan, this is insane."

Logan slowly lowered his gun, "If you aren't pressing charges then this is over." He quickly slipped his .38 into the holster, grabbed Rhonna and pushed through the crowd toward his patrol car.

"He's a nut case," Butch said as he stuffed his pockets back into his pants.

Pastor Phillip turned around, "I'm so sorry about that Butch. Logan was out of line."

Butch nodded.

The crowd thinned out as no real excitement materialized and they watched as Loogy drove out the parking lot. Butch looked at Charles who was soaking wet from the days car wash antics. "Got your bath today, huh, Charles?" Butch rubbed Charles hair.

Pastor Phillip said, "Charles, thank you very much for helping out today. God remembers good deeds. I'll see you both tomorrow in church."

"You will," said Butch as he swung his leg over the seat and sat upright. "Climb on Charles."

Charles sat on the wide leather seat and scrunched up close to his Dad causing Butch to arch his back. "Hey, you're gettin' me all wet. And it's cold too." Butch laughed.

Charles grabbed harder to soak him more. Butch gunned the bike and drove down the street toward home, his hair flying across Charles face the entire way.

Sixteen

Sunday

By 10:50 AM the Southern Baptist Church of Kersey was full. And nearly everyone in Kersey attended church: The righteous, the sinners, the newly converted and the old timers who were now praying that all that church they attended for seventy years was really going to pay off.

The stained glass windows in the sanctuary were propped opened letting in fresh air along with the smell of hay, tractor diesel and cow manure. On occasion a strong overpowering whiff of Chanel No. 5 floated off eighty-two year old Mrs. Crandel. Most folks preferred the manure.

Butch, Cindy, Charles, Margaret and Lea sat in the third row. Up front sat John McCallum and his family. The councilmen with their wives and kids all sat together, and Logan and Rhonna sat in their customary places: last row in the back – just in case Logan got paged to investigate something important.

Pastor Phillip started the service and everyone bowed their heads in prayer.

****

Aspen Grove

"You said you were a religious man. Mormon I think?" asked Alex.

"Yeah. I wasn't for a while though. I thought God forgot about me." In what became familiar anxiety symptoms Butch wrung his hands together, interlacing his fingers then pulling on them like he was trying to invigorate blood into frozen flesh.

"Why's that Butch?"

"I was brought up believing in God, then I stole that car when I was seventeen and spent some time at a youth center."

That's ironic, thought Alex, you and Charles both in trouble at seventeen.

"Wyoming started this new program sentencing juveniles as adults. They put me and two boys from each county in Buena Vista – that adult prison. That'll change ya. It aint right to put sixteen and seventeen year olds in with grown men." Butch looked away and chewed on his lip. "Violent men. Bad things happen to boys in prison." He sat silent a few moments. "When I got out I kinda drifted around, was homeless for awhile, I was really alone. I felt I had nowheres to go and I started going back to church. Not a Mormon church, but any church that happened to be around. And now I've tried to bring up my kids believing in God."

Alex looked at the clock. "We have a few more minutes Butch, then I'll let you go for lunch."

A tentative knock on the door interrupted them. "Come in," Alex called out.

"Sorry to interrupt Dr. Dalton, but Cindy Allee is here to see Butch," said Sandra, her eyes smiling. "I wondered if you would like to talk with her?"

Alex stood up, "Sure, have her come in." A biker-wife image rode into his mind: Long hippie hair, flower tattoo above a breast, tattered jeans and some sort of leather thrown into the mix along with that faint but pungent sweetness of pot.

Stepping into the office and extending her hand she introduced herself. "Dr. Dalton, I'm Cindy Allee. It's a pleasure to meet you."

Alex stood there like the town idiot, his eye's disbelieving what they were seeing. He realized he hadn't said anything, "*You're* Cindy Allee?" Now he shook her hand: Firm, soft and small.

"Yes, I'm Cindy Allee." Her smile grew a bit.

Standing before him was a professionally dressed woman, petite, mid forties, short styled hair and the confidence of a woman who doesn't put up with any shit.

"Oh, ah, I'm glad you're here," Alex stammered, "please have a seat Cindy." He motioned to the chair beside Butch.

She sat and placed her hand on Butch's knee, rubbing it, like a Mom comforting her little boy, "How ya doin' Butch?"

He nodded, his long hair moving with his head, "I'm gettin' better." He grinned and looked into her eyes, "Them voices are gone."

"Good." She looked at Alex, "So how long do you think Butch needs to stay here?"

"As long as he needs," said Alex. "He's going to be the best judge of that."

Butch looked at Cindy, "Dr. Dalton's helpin' me."

Alex could see that Butch had relaxed with Cindy there. "Cindy can we talk a bit?"

"Sure," she smiled at Alex and then turned and kept it for Butch.

He was still in a mild form of shock at Cindy's appearance. They just didn't fit. "Cindy, I'm curious how did you first meet Butch."

Her broad smile was inviting and friendly, then she seemed to blush at the question, she turned her head and looked at Butch. "I met him at the potato dock in Kersey," she said with romance in her eyes.

"Is that a restaurant?"

Butch snorted, "No, it's where you sort potatoes. Each worker got a pile of potatoes, you throw the good ones in one bin and the bad ones in another bin."

Alex blinked, his eyebrows arching, "You would do *that* all day long?"

"Yeah, eight hours of sorting and throwing. We ate a lot of potatoes back then. Mashed, baked, fried, creamed," said Butch. Cindy giggled. "We'd keep the bad ones, cut out the black spots and take 'em home for dinner. I was renting a house back then for fifty dollars a month and Cindy wanted to quit the potato dock and get a medical assistant certificate."

Alex realized he had put his hand over his mouth, like he was smothering a shriek. He'd never heard of a potato dock and never thought that a real person actually sorted the potatoes he ate so he could have nice, clean, unblemished ones to cut, chop, dice, mash or bake. He lowered his hand. "Wasn't that boring?"

Butch laughed, "Didn't matter, paid the bills."

Alex had never worried about paying the bills, he pretty much just did as he wanted and at that moment he realized their two worlds were a universe apart. His upbringing, his degrees, even his first class travels kept him isolated from the average world. Sure, he had given money to charities. Lots of it. But he had never actually went down to the soup kitchen and served meals to the homeless. He thought writing a check felt good. But maybe it didn't actually feel as good as he thought. "Money was tight back then?"

"Yeah, but we never really worried about it," Butch said, "we had each other and that was enough."

Suddenly Alex teared up, caught himself and said, "My allergies. Sorry." Grabbing a Kleenex he blew his nose and tossed it into the trash can. "Why did you want to date Butch?"

Cindy smiled, "I thought he was handsome. Other guys I dated were always talking about farming and corn and cattle, you get tired real fast of living and breathing that all the time. But Butch was different, he talked about dreams. We'd talk for hours about what we wanted and how great life could be together. On our first date he took me to Jackson lake, we sat on the bank and talked for hours, then we slept in his car."

Butch laughed, "I couldn't afford no motel." Cindy giggled like a teenager and grabbed his hand.

Alex smiled uncomfortably at the two of them, vaguely remembering hot dates at the Brown Palace. He shook it off. "What were your dreams, Butch?"

The hand wringing started again. "I wanted my own business. Like I said, fixing and repairing motorcycles and I wanted to move to the big city."

"Like Denver?" As soon as he said it Alex wished he had kept his mouth shut.

"Cheyenne. Denver's too big. Cheyenne felt good to me."

Alex nodded. "And what were your dreams Cindy?"

"To marry Butch and get my nursing certificate."

"And you did. So your dreams came true."

"I guess so."

All of this was causing cognitive dissidence for Alex and he was struggling with the spectacular chasm between these two: A cute, rich little farm girl dating a tattooed biker with an eighth grade education. This couple's way too happy. There's gotta be something else going on. The odd Norman Rockwell image sitting before him wasn't making sense and Alex felt it in his gut. Believe the intuition, he thought. He wanted to dig around some more, get them to open up, maybe make a mistake or contradict themselves. Get them to validate Alex's true image of Butch.

"What else did you like about Butch?"

Cindy thought for a moment, "Butch was sensitive. He really cared about people. And family."

Sensitive? Here it was, so easy. A bunch of crap. This guy killed someone. Alex squinted at Butch, he has "fuck" tattooed on his knuckles. Alex felt it was all a con job. The big bad scary wolf whose now a little puppy dog, and cute innocent Little Red Riding Hood. Fantastic manipulators and I'm just sitting here eating it up. What a smooth couple, had me going there for a moment. Alex berated himself for dropping his clinical guard. Butch must've smooth talked that jury right into a not guilty plea. Alex stiffened and sat upright instantly creating a distance between him and the two cons sitting before him. He suddenly felt back in control and he confronted Cindy, "How can Butch be so sensitive with 'fuck' tattooed on his knuckles?"

Butch immediately answered, "I did that myself in Buena Vista when I was seventeen. Prison screws you up Doc and I was real angry back then, I did a lot of...tattoos in there that I'm not proud of now."

"What were you so angry about, Butch?"

Butch looked up blankly at Alex, he rubbed his knees with his hands and shook his head, "I don't really know why. I just was. Maybe it was the church, or my family or the friends I hung out with. I don't know."

"Maybe the cops?" Alex knew that was a sarcastic comment but he didn't care. "How did you give yourself tattoos in prison?"

"A straight pin and some ink." He rubbed the back of his hand, "You draw on your arm or hand and use the pin to poke the ink into your skin. They let you have a pin, can't kill yourself with it."

Alex was cold, "I would think that would hurt."

"In prison you don't care. And sometimes you want to feel the hurt – to know you're still alive."

"What else did you do in prison?" Alex was fishing.

Butch thinking Alex was still questioning his tattoos said, "Well, I ain't proud of it," he rolled up a shirt sleeve, "I tattooed this."

"White Power," Alex read on Butch's left arm, "I saw it in our first session. What do you think of that?" he asked, looking at Cindy

"It's the past, Dr. Dalton. It's there for our kids to see but it's a symbol of what not to do. We've discussed it with our kids and they know that some things their Dad did when he was younger wasn't good."

Butch jumped in, "I was seventeen and I had a bad attitude and in prison that's where I learned to hate. It's scary being in an adult prison when your just a teenager. It ain't right. I got pressured into believing some things that ain't true, so I put that on my arm. I did it to keep myself safe."

"How so?"

"The kind of tattoos you have give you an identity. Part of a group...like the Marines." He swept his hair behind an ear, "The first time I saw a tattoo was on my brother. He was twenty one and I was...I think nine. He came home from the Marines and had this cool bulldog tattoo. I really wanted one. So in prison I gave myself one. It made me safe, 'cause I was part of a group."

"But you weren't a Marine. You were a member of a racist group."

"I wasn't racist and I'm not now. My weight lifting partner back then was this black dude and he had *Black Power* written on his chest in big letters. I asked him what it means and he said 'It's black pride. He was proud of being in the black race.' I liked that, so since I was white I wanted to show I believed in White Power. It's no different than Black Power or Mexican Power. But I wish I hadn't done it."

"You wish you hadn't done it because people think it's racist."

"Yeah."

"So you did it not thinking how others might see you or judge you for it?"

Butch looked confused, "Yeah, I guess."

"So Butch let me get this straight. White Power means a totally different thing to you than to other people. Is that right?"

Butch nodded trying to follow Alex's connections.

"So for example the word Fuck..." -- Butch grinned, he had never heard a doctor say a word like that before -- "...to one person it could just mean making love. To someone else it's vulgar? So why would you do it?"

"I don't know."

"So you're totally comfortable putting the word Fuck on your fingers because to you it means love."

"It don't always mean love to me. I have it on my right arm too. Want to see it?"

"No." Alex wasn't surprised to hear that and he was frustrated he wasn't making headway with Butch on how people view him. "So if you didn't like White Power on your body why didn't you get it removed when you got out of prison?"

"I couldn't ever afford it."

Alex glanced at the wall clock, "Well, that's all for today Butch." He stood, cold and professional. "I'm glad you stopped in Cindy. I'll probably be seeing you over the next few days." He shook Cindy's hand.

"Thanks Doc," said Butch.

Alex held out his hand, but Butch chopped the air sideways, straight away from his waist with his right hand.

"What's that?" asked Alex.

"That means be tough, but go with peace."

"You do that instead of shaking hands?"

"I shake hands with acquaintances. I give 'The Sign' to people I respect."

"Ah, well, thanks Butch."

Butch and Cindy walked out Alex's office and into the patient lounge.

Alex let out a breath of relief that they were gone and swiped his fingers through his hair, then he sat back into his chair and swiveled around toward his desk. From the first session Alex had written in Butch's chart:

> *Axis I: Major Depression with psychotic*
> *features.*
> *Rule out: Post Traumatic Stress*
> *Disorder.*

Alex now wrote: *Axis II: Anti-Social Personality Disorder with Borderline traits.*

Underneath that he added: *Has no insight into his own behavior or how others view him. Blames others for his problems.*

Then in red ink, as a warning to other staff reading the chart: *Possible staff manipulation.*

Seventeen

Kersey

"Hey, Charles wait up." Tommy huffed it down 3rd avenue slowed to a jog, then a fast walk. He caught up with Charles and they walked toward Kersey High School. "Got wrestling practice after school."

"Yeah," said Charles.

"You ain't excited about it?"

"I'd rather go fishing with my Dad." They walked a bit farther, Charles was unusually quiet.

"What's bugging you Allee? Almost getting shot over the weekend by Deputy Pike?"

"No! That was my Dad and Loogy's a coward, just trying to act tough." Charles stopped in the center of the street and abruptly turned facing Tommy. "Last week, did you think Len was looking at all of us in the shower?"

Tommy scrunched up his face like he had a fart trapped deep down in his bowels that just wouldn't come out, "Get outta here Allee? You a queer or something?" He walked on ahead leaving Charles standing alone in the middle of the street.

Charles jogged up to Tommy, "Hey really, I think he was looking funny at us."

"Man, quite talkin' like that Charles, fuck he's our coach. Besides he ain't a faggot he's the State wrestling champ."

"*Was* the State champ. He isn't any more."

They walked together again. Then Tommy said, "There's no way. We don't allow faggots in Kersey." Tommy thought

90

as deeply as he could. "Besides, he's married to Alisha. Can't be queer married to her. She's got them nice tits and all." Tommy eyed Charles with a sideways glance, "Maybe you're the queer, Allee."

"Shut up."

They walked the remaining few blocks to school ignoring their agitated conversation. "See ya later," said Charles.

"Yeah, see ya." Tommy waved a back hand at him and walked to class.

Between clapping his large hands, Len yelled out, "All right *girls*, hit the showers. Practice everyday all week, we have that meet in Ft. Collins on Saturday morning. Two lucky *girls*'ll ride with me, the rest get the bus."

The group of sweating, stinky teenagers broke into little groups and walked toward the gym showers.

"Allee, stay here."

Charles stiffened as Len sauntered up to him. Len seemed to be staring at him—his eyes moving up and down his body-- the same way a guy sizes up a girl in a bar. It was uncomfortable but Charles didn't move.

Len stopped, his hands on his hips, a silly grin on his face, "Charles, you have to put more enthusiasm into your moves."

Charles stared up at him and Len waited for a response but got none.

"Look Allee, you've got it. You just don't know it. It hasn't...uh..." Len's tongue searched for chew in the pocket of his bottom lip but came up empty, "...it hasn't fruited yet— you know sprouted up to see the light. But it's there. I've seen you push guys around outside of class but I'm not see'n it here. If you want to be a great wrester you need to put fire into it."

Charles bit the inside of his cheek. Tell him. Tell him now.

Len waited. "Well Allee? You understand what I'm telling you or is it too deep for that little brain beatin' off in there?"

Charles took a breath, "I don't know if I really want to do this, Coach."

Len's eye's narrowed, then a look that Charles had never seen before grew on Len's face. "Not do what? Wrestle?" Len straightened and seemed to grow a foot taller right before Charles eyes. "Are you fucking crazy? Charles you could make a career out of this if you put your heart into it. I did, look what I've done. You've got some great moves Allee," he stopped, his eye's piercing Charles eyes, "look I don't believe this of any one else on this team, but I really believe if you try hard enough you can qualify for State." Len beamed and grinned yellow, proud, like Charles was his own son.

But Charles didn't buy it. Some of the other guys like Tommy, Brian and Scooter, *they* were good, Charles could feel it when he wrestled them. They had that little extra bit of slickness, that edge that separated good wrestlers from great wrestlers. Charles was quick and he knew that, but he knew he didn't have that spark, that fire that Len referred to. Or maybe it was just simply that he didn't want to light any fires. Wrestling was fun and that was about it. And he didn't really care about making State. He's rather be home with his Dad tinkering on the Harley. And be like Len? The thought nauseated him. "I don't know." That's all he could muster.

"Look Allee, you are on this team and I better get one hundred and fifty percent effort from you." Len took a half step closer to Charles, "Got it Allee? Otherwise git outta here."

Charles swallowed and with a blank expression turned and walked toward the showers.

Len watched him then muttered softly but just loud enough, "Loser. You're just like your fucking old man."

Charles froze. All at once his armpits went wet, his heart pounded and his stomach knotted, he whipped around and like a wolf, leapt onto Len. "Take it back. Take it back!" He punched wildly and a quick jab swelled Len's left eye.

Len winced, his body folding to the right as his kidney screamed in pain. "That's it you little prick." Len grabbed Charles in a head lock, Charles' punches now landed on thick muscle, Len dropped and Charles moaned as his face met the gym floor. Len simply flipped Charles onto his back and scrambled on top pinning him with his knees and squatting his full weight onto his chest. Glaring down at Charles and through clenched teeth, "You fucking little loser!" Len felt his eye, it was spongy and stung, then he started laughing, "No one ever jumped me Allee." He shook his head. "No one, but you." Sweat dripped from his hair into Charles face. "That's the fire...it's badly misplaced, but it's there. Just like I told you so." He grimaced, the aches now coming alive across his body. "Don't tell anyone you did this or I'll suspend you...and I need you this weekend." Len let up the pressure on Charles biceps and rocked back just a bit, "Put *that* into your match on Saturday, Allee, and you'll be unstoppable."

Charles relaxed, giving in, then panic filled his gut: he had hit a teacher. His Coach. The State Champion. His mouth went dry.

"One thing Allee, if you *ever* do this to me again, I *will* hurt you. *And* suspend you." Len rolled off Charles and stood. "Go to the shower." Len touched his swelling eye. "This was an accidental elbow jab, right Allee?"

Charles felt extremely vulnerable. "Yes sir."

Len nodded, "I like that Charles. *Yes sir*, I could get used to hearing that from you. Now go on."

Eighteen

Denver

Racing from the underground garage the yellow Porsche Boxster S banked left onto Larimer street, Alex gunned it to I-25 north, and turned the radio to 630 KHOW to catch the latest controversies on the Peter Boyles show. Peter's intellectual and down-home charisma made the forty five minute drive to Aspen Grove bearable; the Porsche did too.

Aspen Grove was located in Greeley, a farming town. Alex could ever live there and since Aspen Grove desperately wanted him for Director of Psychological Services, a position he couldn't turn it down, he drove North every day but Fridays. In a Porsche, the drive wasn't so bad. But it's a peculiar drive: Within minutes outside of north Denver the congestion dies and the office buildings begin to fade in the distance, replaced with expansive fields of corn and farm houses and tractors. Cattle mill about waiting for their morning feed, and Johnson's Corner beckons with *World Famous Cinnamon Rolls*. SUV's, pickups and the occasional Humvee dominate the road. Alex noticed that the people change, too. The yellow speedster may get an occasional look in Denver, but in Greeley it draws open-mouthed stares making Alex feel like he stepped out of the movie *Back to the Future*. And in the country the men seem thinner, worn, their skin a map of wrinkles, and the women fatter. Overalls, work-boots and cowboy hats dominate along with tent dresses and the people are friendlier. If Alex ever broke down on the highway he'd rather it happen in the country than in the city. That weathered, old farmer in his rusty Ford will stop and help, while the executive in his BMW will splatter you with dirt and grime blindly unaware you're even there.

Alex parked in his assigned space and quickly walked into the front entrance of Aspen Grove. He nodded at the front desk staff not saying anything and strutted towards the patient lounge. He glanced in, Butch was there finishing his breakfast, his plastic plate on a plastic tray, coffee in a plastic cup. Butch held his plastic fork in his fist like a kid with a shovel on the beach and that's what he was doing: Shoveling the last bit of institutional scrambled eggs onto his fork, then into his bearded mouth.

Alex was curious. Why did Butch hold his fork that way?

Alex was taught to cut food with the fork in his left hand, knife in his right, then pierce the food with the tines, bring it up to his mouth -- the fork down-turned -- gracefully place the food onto his tongue, close his lips and withdraw the tines. Right handed, Alex always ate with his left -- proper eating etiquette. You don't want to look like you were raised in a barn, his Mom would scold him. Sometimes a barn or a farm or the mountains didn't sound too bad to Alex, sometimes he wished anywhere but the city.

He went to his office and before he could get settled in Sandra knocked on his door and walked in. Alex turned his chair around to face her. "Hey Sandra. How's Mr. Allee doing today?"

She nodded and smiled, "He's coming along well, he actually seems like a nice guy."

Alex grimaced. "Has anyone noticed or mentioned anything unusual about him?"

"Besides his tattoos?"

"Yes, besides those Sandra."

"No. Not really. He takes his meds, participates occasionally in group. He seems a little shy."

Alex harrumphed. "Shy? He craves attention. Why else would he tattoo his face? I think he's scamming us. Being compliant just to get out."

"Most patients are compliant to get out Alex. Only the passive-dependants want to stay."

"Stay with Mommy." Alex said.

She laughed, "Yeah, the Med-Mommy. He seems genuine to me. Remember, he was a voluntarily admit. He can walk out anytime he wants to."

Alex didn't respond. He had forgotten that.

"He's scheduled with you at ten," she reminded him. She kept standing there.

Alex nodded. "Ok."

Then there was silence. That awkward silence that two people have when they've finished talking about the weather or how their day was or some other mundane socially appropriate topic that neither one cares about. She nodded at Alex. Alex smiled.

"Anything else, Sandra?"

"No, I guess not. Coffee's ready in the lounge." She turned. She wanted to ask him, but he seemed especially heavy today. She knew better than to push his buttons, no sense in getting the cold shoulder.

Nineteen

Kersey

Cindy Allee made the best fried chicken in all of Eastern Wyoming. The Judges at the Kersey County Fair said so with a First Place Ribbon over the past four years. Her secret was passed down by her Grandmother to her Mother and then to her. She would never write it down, kept it all in her head, and someday she'd secretly pass it on to Margaret and Lea. Nearly every woman in Kersey County wanted that recipe and they all knew they'd never get it. The coating was basically the same as any other contestant: Flour and salt, egg dipping batter. Some women then rolled the chicken in more flour or corn flakes and then fried it...but Cindy's chicken had that extra kick of something that always made folks want another piece, even when they were stuffed. And no one could figure it out.

She set the plate of fried chicken in the center of the table between the ceramic bowl of mashed potatoes and a boat of fried chicken gravy. Home made buttermilk biscuits and green beans sat alone. Butch walked up to the table, closed his eyes and just smelled.

"You can eat some too if you want," she said as she placed the napkins around.

Butch opened his eyes and grinned. "Is that your Mama's chicken?"

Cindy smiled, "Sure is. Had to sneak the Frosted Corn Flakes out of the grocery store without no one seeing me."

"They'd just die at the Fair if they knew that."

Her eyes narrowed and she cocked her head, "And no one's going to be telling them."

"Not from me." Butch crossed his heart with his finger. He yelled out, "Ok kids, time to eat."

"Oh man I can smell it," said Charles as he scooted in behind the table, "County Fair chicken. I get the heart."

Lea and Margaret sat down and placed the napkins on their laps. Charles had
already grabbed the fried chicken heart and popped it into his mouth. "Lets say Grace," Butch said. They bowed their heads as Butch thanked God for all the food. As soon as the prayer was done, Charles grabbed two thighs and a leg.

"Charles!" said Butch, "Let your little sister go first. It's polite to let women go ahead of you."

Charles looked annoyed.

Margaret said, "Yeah Charles, ladies first."

"There aren't any ladies here."

"Charles has no manners," Lea said. "That's why he don't have a girlfriend."

"Shut up."

"You shut up."

"All of you's shut up," said Butch. "Now Lea what do you want?" Butch served everyone first, then himself. "How's wrastlin' going Charles?"

Between bites of chicken and buttered roll Charles said, "Ok." He kept his head down and ate fast and plenty.

"Lea, you have homework tonight?" Cindy asked.

"Nope. Did it all."

"Margaret?"

"Only some reading."

She noticed Charles obviously leaning to one side, his butt cheek off the chair.

"Charles is farting at the table," yelled Margaret.

"Shut up." He pulled a folded piece of paper from his rear pocket and threw it over the chicken to his Dad.

Butch laid down his fork, "What's this?"

"I want to go to that Dad."

Butch unfolded the flyer, read it and his eyes grew wide, he looked at Charles. "Where'd you get this?"

"What is it?" asked Cindy as she spooned herself more green beans.

He glanced at her, disappointment in his eyes, then looked back at Charles. "Charles, where'd you get this?"

"Tommy gave it to me. I want to go."

"This ain't no good."

Cindy was now insistent, "Butch *what* is it?" Her fork clanged against the plate as she set it down with frustration.

He handed her the flyer, "It's a KKK rally in Fort Collins."

"What?!" Her stare was hard and at the same time full of hurt. "Why? Charles."

A half an eaten chicken leg was in his hand, held there in mid air. "Tommy said his Pa told him that white people are going to be a minority." He set the chicken leg on his plate and breathed in some courage. "I don't want to be a minority."

Cindy's shoulders seemed to slump with the heaviness of prejudice that had just soaked the room. "I *don't* want him going to that rally." Her words directed at Butch.

"Lets talk about it after dinner" he answered calmly and continued eating.

"That's a hate rally and you know it, Butch." Cindy paced in the their tiny bedroom.

"I know. I don't want him to go either Cindy, but he'll just go anyway." Butch crossed his arms. rubbing his biceps, almost hugging himself. "Let me take him and I'll explain why this group is no good. Why it's all about hate. He'll see it for himself."

"You take him? Oh, that's all we need 'round here. If my Daddy ever found out..." she shook her head. She paced again, back and forth. "Why would Charles want to go to this?"

"Cindy, he's seventeen. He's just curious."

"Age has nothing to do with it," she stopped and glared at Butch then started pacing again. "He knows they hate black people. Does Charles hate black people?"

"I don't think so. He's never talked bad about black people. Besides there ain't no black people in all of Kersey."

She looked at him like that was the stupidest reason of all. "I just don't understand him sometimes. We raised all our kids to be respectful to everyone. Why this now? And why are you so willing to take him?" Her heart pounded from fear. Had she failed at being a good Mother?

"Cindy you know when I was seventeen I got messed up in all kinds of stuff. I don't want Charles to do what I did, I didn't have anyone to show me any thing different. The difference here is that I'll be there to help him. Show him what's right and what's wrong. He's just curious about it."

"So *you* think it's okay?"

Butch didn't want to make it seem okay, but he also knew that he got involved willingly or unwillingly in all kinds of group: From biker groups, to hate groups, to Jesus groups to no groups. If anyone knew about the good and bad of all these people it was him, and he'd rather go with Charles than have him go alone and be influenced by someone else.

"Cindy," he took her by both arms so she'd stop moving, "there's a lot of people in this town who are prejudice. He's probably picked up on some of that. You know, Mexicans, blacks, no one 'round here wants 'em around."

With a crystal clear glare into his eyes, she said, "Not unless those Mexicans are working in their yards or picking crops." She tried to move away but he held her tight.

That look always unnerved him and it was pure Cindy, intense from her core. But Butch was firm, "Cindy, I know what it's like to hate people. How it kinda eats you up inside. Let me go with him and he'll see what this group is all about.

Get it out of his mind. If we don't let him he'll just get more interested."

He didn't have to hold her now, she hugged him, her head against his chest. Butch stroked her hair, the knuckle-letters F-U-C-K and the spider web stretched across the back of his hand was lit up from the glow of the lamp. "You got to trust me on this one Cindy." He wrapped his arms around her.

"I'm scared. I don't want Charles--"

"--He's a good kid Cindy. He's just investigating new stuff."

Charles and Tommy sat in the back seat as Butch drove the station wagon to Fort Collins. He flipped on the dome light to read the directions then turned onto a gravel road with no lights. It was dark. Gnarled cottonwood trees lined the Poudre River and the only light came from the moon, it's yellow haze creating evil things in the cottonwood limbs. The station wagon bottomed out on the unpaved road rutted and worn by run off. Butch veered left into a pasture and parked in back behind some forty or fifty other cars and trucks.

He turned around in the seat, "Listen both of you. I want you to stay right with me. And if anyone asks who you are, you tell 'em a fake name. No one here needs to know who we are or where we is from."

Tommy looked at Charles. It seemed scary to be here. "Why do we have to tell 'em fake names Mr. Allee?"

"These are bad people. I know you think it's exciting and all, but if these people don't like you...you better watch your ass." Butch knew it was true, but he also wanted to shake the boys up a bit. "What name should we tell 'em?" asked Charles.

Butch thought a moment, then grinned, and nodding his head like a little kid convincing himself it was OK. "If anyone asks," he couldn't hold it in, snickering, "I'll be John McCallum." He laughed out loud and looked at Charles. "I hope he ain't here."

For a fleeting moment Charles was wide eyed, scared at the very thought that maybe Sheriff John McCallum *could* be here.

Butch said, "Charles your name is Fred Rogers. And Tommy you're Coby Dyer." Now they all broke up laughing, Charles and Tommy high-fived, and the fear of the unknown became a little more bearable.

They got out the car and walked toward the barn Charles and Tommy trailing somewhat behind Butch flanking each side, but just close enough for comfort but not too close to look like sissy's.

Streams of light snuck through cracks in the barn walls and around the door. A mans voice, loud and boisterous like a Baptist preacher, came from inside, then clapping and yelling. It seemed like thunder and lighting was ready to burst through the weathered wood.

Charles suddenly wanted to run. The whole place seemed spooky. All these men all getting together in a farmers barn in the middle of the night. Would they be dressed in sheets like in the photos he saw? Would there be a black man on his knees up front, scared, his head down and crying? He didn't know. He wanted to know and at the same time he didn't, but he couldn't turn back now.

Butch pushed on the barn door and it swung open. Charles grabbed a breath and they all walked in.

Twenty

The moon was bright and high in the night sky as Butch pulled the station wagon in front of Tommy's ranch style house and kept the engine running. "See ya tomorrow," said Charles as Tommy got out and walked toward the front door. Butch and Charles waited for Tommy to walk inside.

"You were pretty quiet all the way home," said Butch.

Charles just nodded.

"You tired?"

Charles shook his head.

"Me neither."

They sat in the car, the engine coughing to stay alive. "How bout we go over to Jackson Lake. Listen to them horned owls sittin' up in them cottonwoods."

"Sure," said Charles.

Butch put the car in gear and drove east toward Jackson Lake.

As they stepped from the truck, the yellow of the moon reflected in the oily black looking water of the lake which the Canadian geese rippled as they swam around looking for that perfect slice of liquid for sleeping. The occasional honking sounded like *shut up and go to sleep*. Warnings to each other.

It was warm for fall and Butch and Charles meandered around the lake's edge, not talking. A hoot, eerie and muffled, slipped through the darkness coming from the grove of cottonwoods. Then another answered, then the first answered back. Butch sat on the rough wild grass near the shore and Charles sat next to him. They silently watched geese silhouettes glide about, listened to the owl banter and occasionally glanced upward into the sky, the constellations were bright, etched against the night sky. Butch grabbed a flat rock and skipped it out onto the lake, the water erupted with splashing and honking.

Butch turned toward his son, "Charles what did you think about tonight?"

Charles looked at his Dad, the moon glistened in Butch's eye's. Charles never noticed the tattoos. It was just part of his Dad, like wearing a baseball cap. "If those guys really believed in what they were saying why do they hide underneath those silly robes and hats? It gave me the creeps."

Butch scratched his head, then stroked his beard. "That's a good question Charles. It's important to be thinking about stuff like that." He thought back to when he was seventeen, wishing he had asked himself those questions instead of being so easily influenced by guys on the streets. "I think they're all scared and all of 'em are cowards. That's why they hide and scare people at night." That sounded right.

They sat some more, Butch thinking about tonight's event that he never really put much thought into before.

"What do you think of black people?" asked Charles as he picked up another rock and plunked it into the water.

This was going to be a tough night. Butch had never put this much energy into social issues. A long time ago he just pretty much had made up his mind how to live his life and then just lived it. He collected his thoughts and said, "I think if God made black people, then he loves them. And white people shouldn't hurt what God loves." He turned slightly toward Charles, "If God didn't like black people he wouldn't have made them black." He was hoping this made sense.

"Do you think we're better than black people, Dad?"

"We're better than *bad* black people." Butch chuckled, but Charles didn't. "We're better than *bad* white people too.

But I don't think one good person is any better than another good person. I do know that some people are treated better than others. Like rich people get away with more stuff than poor people. And politicians don't listen to folks like us. They think we're less good than someone else who lives in the big city. They's never coming out to Kersey to ask us what we think. And that's wrong."

"Do you think white people should only marry white people?"

"Charles, you sure are full of questions." Butch smiled. "Hard ones too. I think marrying a different colored person is probably hard."

Charles sat there watching the geese stretching their wings while others had their heads tucked beneath, already asleep. "There's no black people in Kersey," said Charles.

An owl hooted.

"That don't mean we don't like 'em," said Butch. "It just means...there ain't any here. Just Mexicans."

Butch put his arm around Charles shoulder. "You know Charles, I've always liked huggin you. Since you were a little boy I always hugged you. When you went off to school, I kissed you good bye. Some men don't hug or kiss their sons. I want you to know I love you and huggin' and kissin' you is okay. And I think that's what God wants. For us to love each other, no matters if we are white or black or red."

"Indians aren't really red, Dad."

Butch laughed and pulled Charles close to his body, "I know, but that's what we used to call 'em, 'The Red-Man'. I guess that ain't right either. What I'm tryin' to say Charles is that no matter what other people think, you have to do what you think is right. I think huggin' and kissin' my son is right even if other men don't think so. And I think hating people who are different is wrong. Even if other people think it's right. You have to decide for yourself, Charles. That's why I took you tonight."

They sat a while longer, Butch still holding Charles around the shoulders. The lake was now quiet and still.

"I'm getting tired Dad."

"Yeah me too, lets go home."

They stood, and as they walked back to the car, Charles reached up and put his arm around his Dad's shoulder. "I'm glad you're my Dad."

It was dark and Charles couldn't see the tears in Butch's eyes. "I'm proud of you, Charles. And I hope you learned something tonight. I found out the hard way, that there's hate everywhere, but you don't have to be part of it."

"I won't Dad."

They pulled onto Main street about one mile off the interstate. It was a pleasant ride home. Up ahead the twin lights from a truck approached with it's brights on -- the headlights grew closer. Butch flashed his beams. The truck kept coming, seeming to speed up, the brights still on. The round orbs got brighter and larger. "Hey that trucks in our lane," said Charles. Butch flashed his lights again. The headlights grew closer and brighter, Butch could see the dust billowing up, disappearing into the darkness.

"Dad slow down—get in the other lane."

Butch veered to the left side of the road, the headlights veered too--right at them. Butch leaned on the horn and squinted to see into the other vehicle, "Shit! That's Len Lamont's truck."

"Dad! Turn off the road he's going to hit us!" Charles was near panic.

Butch abruptly veered back into the right lane -- the oncoming truck blowing it's horn sped by with dust choking the air and rocks nicking the side of the station wagon.

"He's drunk. That asshole," snarled Butch.

Charles spun around and watched as the red tail-lights disappeared down the road. "Dad, I think there's something wrong with him."

"I *know* there's something wrong with him," Butch said dead-pan. "As soon as we get home, I'm callin' the Sheriff."

****

"There's no damage and no actual proof. I just can't go and arrest him, Mr. Allee." John McCallum stood in the cramped living room of Butch's home, his Stetson nearly touching the ceiling.

"He almost hit us. Like it was a game or something. Isn't that's proof enough."

"There's rock chips on the side of the car," added Charles.

John shook his head, "Mr. Allee, I'll drive by Mr. Lamont's house, if the truck is there, then he's home for the night and I'll talk with him tomorrow. That's all I can do for now."

"That's all you *want* to do."

It wasn't difficult to sense the challenge from Butch. "It's all I *can* do, Mr. Allee. It wouldn't matter to me if it was Len Lamont or you driving that truck, I'd handle it the exact same way."

"He's going to kill somebody someday," Butch said through clenched teeth.

"Then I'll arrest him," said John. "You did the right thing though, calling me and letting me know. I'll be keeping an eye on him."

"It aint' right, him terrorizing people when he's drunk."

"Good night Mr. Allee. And congratulations to you, Charles, on making the team."

Aspen Grove

"So Charles didn't like the rally after all?" asked Alex.

"No. I was real proud of him. I told him that deep down, these people are scared and mean so they hate other people. I told him if God didn't like black people, then he won't have made them black. I told him that God loves all kinds of people and that we need to follow what God says."

Butch *seemed* genuine about his faith, but Alex knew that once these guys get into prison they start shackling themselves to God: Selling crucifixes in the prison store, sewing *God Loves You* on their jackets. Even serial killers tattoo scripture on their bodies, praying that when they die they tattooed the right God on their bicep.

Alex nodded. He used to be a faithful Methodist, went to Sunday school as a kid and even watched Robert Schuller on TV. But eight years ago that all changed. God deserted him and Alex has never forgiven him for it.

"So what happened after the rally?"

"Nothing. We talked about it a little but Charles never brought it up again. He ain't a racist, Dr. Dalton. But they tried to bring it up in my trial, saying I was a KKK member and white supremacist. They said the FBI had photo's of me at a rally. Maybe they did, from that one in Fort Collins, but when my lawyer Mark Moore told 'em to prove it they never came up with any evidence or photos."

"Why would they say that if it weren't true?"

" 'Cause they was trying to railroad me for killing Len Lamont."

"So you're saying every one liked him so much they lied for him? Even the sheriff?" Alex was suspicious.

"Either that, or they was afraid of him." Butch was confident about that.

Twenty One

The Kersey Sentinel headline read:

October 21   Len Lamont Day!

Kersey celebrates Len Lamont today.
Come join the festivities at 5:30 pm.
Participate in the parade that starts at Grandma's.
Hotdogs, Coors and soda at the Oasis bar immediately
after the parade (about 5:40). Due to last years mess,
the Town counsel kindly asks that no one marches
their hogs this year.

It was still hot for an October evening, Len was sitting on the trunk of a rented convertible, his legs swung over the back seat. His shirt sleeves were rolled up, his hair uncombed, and his scuffed cowboy boots rested on the car's scuffed vinyl back seat. He stuffed three *Coors* into the small cooler as Alisha climbed in next to him, their two boys sat between their legs.

The Kersey High School band started right in with *God Bless America* as the convertible crawled behind them. Len's car was first, followed by the three Kersey councilmen who rode on the back of Coby's tractor. Next in line, waving and blowing kisses, was the Kersey County Pork Queen, Jeniffer Spruceman. Her rein ended in December and she wanted all the exposure she could get for the remaining two months. Despite the title Jeniffer wasn't fat, in fact she was quite cute.

Being the Pork Queen for a year allowed her access to the higher up's who could giver her a job in marketing or sales or even a run at the Pork Queen State title. Behind her walked the First Place heifer followed by a group of sheep all wearing red banners that read: *For Sale I'm tasty.* A pickup truck filled with rowdy teenage boys dressed as girls throwing out candy to the little kids crept next, followed by the local fire truck blowing it's siren and flashing it's lights. Taking up the rear was another tractor pulling a flat bed filled with hay that kids jumped and played in spilling hay all over the streets.

Butch and Cindy watched off to one side.

As Len's convertible drew near Len spied Butch, then leaned over and whispered something in Alisha's ear. She giggled, glanced at Butch then looked away. Len then raised his *Coors* toward Butch and winked.

Nearly everyone from Kersey flanked Main Street as the parade worked it's way through town. Folks cheered and waved and some girls blew kisses as Len past by.

Ten minutes later they were at the Oasis bar and the three Coors were gone. Len jumped out, and keeping with his own tradition, grabbed the first girl near him and kissed her. Alisha never liked it, but the town cheered and Len usually got a good tongue sucking out of it. He strutted to the tractor and shook hands with the councilmen while the Kersey reporter snapped a photo for the next days front page.

Len jumped up on the tractor and waved his arms for the crowd to settle down, he smiled and looked about. As the crowd looked on Len spoke loudly, "As you know, every year my family and I try to do something for the needy families of Kersey County." He smiled, waiting as the crowd lightly clapped. "Well this year we've been especially blessed and we are donating one entire beef cow, cut, wrapped and ready for the grill!" Len threw up his right arm in salute and the crowed cheered and the photographer snapped some more photos.

Len jumped down, shook some hands and grabbed a beer.

Folks lingered about chatting, drinking beer and eating the burnt hot dogs that Evan had grilled. Local events were bread and butter for Evan because he was the only game in town and the Town provided him with all the food and drink. What ever was left over Evan took home, then sold it at the Oasis the next day.

"That's very Christian of you," said Pastor Phillip as he shook Len's hand. "You're a solid rock in this town; volunteer fireman, coach and a benefactor to the needy families of this community. An entire cow! I'm proud of you Len."

Butch had sidled up to Evan at the grill and they both overheard the conversation. As Evan turned the hotdogs, he softly whispered to Butch, "It's probably one of his old, lame dry heifers he's donating. I'd grill a road-kill raccoon before I'd grill his beef."

Butch took a hotdog and looked at it's black, crinkled skin as it sat in the bun. "Probably taste better than these dogs your serving here Evan."

"Hey give it back then!" Evan waved his tongs at Butch and Butch kind of ducked like Evan was really going to jab him.

Butch laughed, "I think I'll have to smother this thing with some hot chili sauce. Then choke it down."

"Damn you, Allee." They both laughed and had not noticed that Len had walked up to the grill.

"Can I get a hotdog Evan? Or do you only serve tattooed jail birds?"

"Fuck you!" Butch said as he glared at Len.

Len gave a half chuckle, "Settle down Allee, I'm just jerking your chain. Jesus Christ. Damn fine vocabulary you got there though. Hope it hasn't rubbed off on Charles."

Evan interrupted, "Len why don't you just get your dog here and go."

Len held out an opened bun waiting for Evan to put a hotdog in it. "Why do you get so pissed off Allee? I thought maybe the three of us could hang out together. Maybe you could tattoo an L on my arm like you did to Charles."

Butch ignored his comment. "That was you in the truck the other night, playing chicken." He turned to Evan, "He tried to run me and Charles off the road. I called the Sheriff." Butch now looked at Len. "Did McCallum give you a visit?"

Len just looked irritated, "Hell no Allee. You think John is going to listen to anything you have to say?" Len still had his hand out waiting for his hotdog. "Nobody 'round here gives a shit about you Allee. Now Charles...he's got potential. Must of got it from Cindy...or someone else."

Butch swallowed hard and then said, "You know Len, I was just thinking, I could tattoo that L for you? How about LL?"

"LL? Len Lamont."

"No,...Lying Loser."

The bun in Len's hand squished as his fingers clenched shut. "The only loser 'round here is you Allee. Someday I just might hog tie you and brand it into your ass." Len kept his stare, then threw the bun into the dirt and walked away.

Butch swept his hair behind an ear and laughed. He enjoyed getting the upper hand when he could, and he also well knew that Len was huge and ten years younger.

"I just don't get why everybody likes him," said Evan. "I gotta dump this hotdog."

"Why?"

Evan slid the hotdog off the fork and held it down for his dog to eat. "I spit on it."

Twenty Two

Alex's penthouse suite

Alex was restless tossing and turning in the king size bed. He was hot and he kicked off the sheets. He grabbed the feather pillow and stuffed it down between his knees. He felt comfort. A sense of security.

He laid there, still wide awake. It bugged him, and the more he obsessed about trying to sleep the more awake he became. He laid on his back looking up at the ceiling. He chanted a few hurried lines of sleep-relaxation-talk. It was useless, his thoughts raced.

He finally got up and went to the bathroom cabinet, pulled open a drawer and grabbed an opaque prescription bottle. A quick shake revealed serenity inside. Twisting off the cap he shook out one tiny blue pill, popped the *Halcion* into his mouth and drank a glass of water. He climbed back into bed and looked at the clock: 12:32 AM.

In just about forty minutes he knew the *Halcion* would pull him into a sensation of death-heavy sleep. Then, they'd start: An explosion of vivid, psychotic-like dreams splattered with wild images whirling with colors and sounds. It was like tripping on acid in your REM cycle.

It was the one thing he didn't like about the drug. Those psychotic like dreams. They felt so real...

Her screams were muffled by the dirty cloth stuffed into her mouth. She kicked and scratched and flailed about shaking her head as a wide piece of duct tape was forced across her lips.

Her cries were now stuck in her throat.

A staggering punch to her face and she collapsed onto the hardwood floor. Laying there groaning, blood seeping from her broken nose, her vision cloudy, wavy -- a savage kick to her stomach, then another to her throat--a blurred room, a wavy figure, her body broken, she convulsed, then died on the dark wooden floor choking on her own vomit.

He knelt down next to her and softly touched her cooling thigh. With her skirt knotted in his fist he forced it up to her hips and with thick calloused fingers tore open her panties. He yanked on his zipper...

"Stop! I don't want to hear any more." Alex trembled as he turned over the Polaroid photos on the detectives desk, his finger tips lingering on the backside, like he didn't want to leave her there. "I don't want anyone seeing those photos. Please."

"The only eyes seeing those are on the case, Dr. Dalton. You need to go home now Doctor. Talk with a friend...it's not good to be alone right now."

With red, scared eyes Alex looked up at the tall skinny detective, "I know."

Alex drove in a daze to his Cherry Hills home. As he pulled into the driveway he suddenly realized he couldn't go in: The yellow tape and sawhorse blockades encircled the house, barring anyone from entering.

He sat in the car, stunned, numb, not knowing what to do looking at the dark, empty home. Her spirit, her soul was still in there and he wanted to be in there with her. As a lawyer, he knew going in would contaminate the scene. He always talked about contaminating a scene. Now it was *his* scene. It sounded so cold. Emotionless. He called no one and drove to the nearest motel and checked in.

Then she was there. Lisa. Floating above him. He couldn't move, now paralyzed with fear. He felt a warm soft drip splashing onto his face...then another. Like a leaky artery, little droplets of red, glistening, moist, fell onto his face, hitting his nose and rolling into his eye.

He couldn't move. Couldn't wipe it away, his arms felt stuck to his sides. She was screaming now, "Alex! Help Me! Alex!" The fear was locked in her eyes. "Help me, please!" He tried to talk to her but his mouth was frozen. His chest heaved as he struggled to move his arms, his hands, to reach out and grab her. Save her. More droplets fell spilling onto his lips. His head was immobile, stuck to the pillow as blood covered his face. His own screams were stuck in his mouth... he felt he was going to explode....

Alex jumped when the alarm went off. He hit it and collapsed back into bed. Anxiety soured his stomach. It was the dream. The same dream. It always made him feel this way and it always seemed so real.

It *was* real.

He could never rid himself of the crushing hollowness he felt when he first saw those photos of Lisa. The look on the detectives face: Grim, professional. He just wanted to pull the covers over his head and go back to sleep. Sleep for eternity.

It happened today. In the afternoon. When he was at work. A dark anniversary. He laid in bed not wanting to get up.

Alex forced himself up, showered and got dressed. He ate breakfast, slid into his Porsche and drove into the mountains.

Twenty Three

Kersey

"Logan, get me the files on Lamont and Allee."
McCallum was leaning back in his chair sipping the
lemonade that Logan had just made.

John McCallum had spent years working the streets of
Las Vegas and was glad to be in Wyoming where his wife's
family lived. He had expected Wyoming policing to be more
laid back, less hectic; a day filled with family disputes, and
minor traffic citations. Most of all he liked community
policing – getting to know the folks and being a loyal support
system for them. But in every community there seemed to be
at least one renegade and Butch Allee was his.

John waited as Logan rummaged around in the file
drawers.

"There ain't no file on Lamont," said Logan as he walked
toward McCallum with a tattered file folder in his hand.
"Not much on Allee either when you get right down to it."

McCallum ripped the file from Logan's hand, opened it
and scanned the hand written notes inside. "This is it? You
said you had a bunch of charges and arrest records on him."
McCallum looked disgusted as his eyes moved up toward
Logan.

"Sheriff, that Allee is one slick   character. He does a lot
of stuff 'round here that everyone knows about, but he aint'
been caught too many times."

He glanced back through the folder, "Looks like he ain't
been caught *no* times," mocked McCallum. "The only thing

in here are angry comments from the last Sheriff." He shook his head to rid it of Logan's lingo and corrected himself, "From the last *police chief*. This is it? You told me, or someone did, that Allee killed someone, and he beat wife."

"No, no not me, that was Ted Rogers. He told me once that little Cindy Graff came over to talk to his wife once about Butch hittin' her and all."

McCallum's eyes bore into Logan's, "*Ted* said it? Cindy Allee never reported it?"

"I guess not, Sheriff, if it ain't in there. But it don't matter, everyone knows he does."

McCallum squinted and his lips disappeared, "Coby Dyer ever hit his wife?"

Logan's face paled, the blood running clear out of it. "No way, Sheriff. Coby Dyer?" Logan looked about the office like he was suddenly lost, he was breathing fast, then looked back at McCallum with a look of dumbfounded shock, he simply couldn't imagine such a thing. "Hey…I'm sorry Sheriff, but that ain't right, sayin' that. Coby would never hit Jessee. They're the happiest couple 'round here. Everyone knows that." Logan crossed his arms, but stayed standing there out of respect.

"Everyone knows it, huh?" McCallum was frustrated with the entire exchange, "Settle down Logan, I was just asking."

Logan uncrossed his arms.

"Sit down here a second, I want to talk to you."

Logan sat, ready for the scolding.

"I've been called twice now about Len Lamont being drunk. I know you two are friends, but you're the deputy. Now I need to know, Logan, how often is Len getting drunk?"

Logan moved about in the chair, tilted his hat back, chewed on something then licked his lips.

"Well?" John demanding an answer.

A long breath. Then squirming. "Do I have to say, Sheriff?"

McCallum sprang up like a cobra, "Logan! You are the deputy of this town!"

Logan came to attention his eyes wide.

"You have a responsibility to the law, not your friends. Now if you can't handle the law and uphold your sworn duty then you best resign." McCallum was a statue in the air.

Logan went pale, diverted his eyes, looked about the office, down at the floor, then back at Sheriff McCallum. He took a breath like he was punched in the gut, then he went tight jawed and his arms trembled.

McCallum watched as tears rolled down Logans cheeks. He slapped the desk, "Christ Logan stop that crying."

Logan jerked back to attention.

"I'm *not* going to fire you."

Logan bit his lip, blinked fast, then with a quick swipe of his hand wiped away the tears.

"Logan, Jesus Christ! You have to stand up for the law here. You have to earn respect Logan. If you have no respect people will run all over you. Shit, Logan, why do you think they call you Loogy?" He wished he hadn't said that. McCallum relaxed and settled back into his chair. "Logan, now answer the question. How often does Len get drunk?"

Logan summed up what spindly courage he had and said, "Most of the time he stays at the bar."

John rolled his eyes. *Why can't I ever get a straight answer from these people?* "So he gets drunk at the Oasis?"

"Yeah."

"Every weekend?"

"Yeah."

"And as far as you know he's never been arrested for it?"

Logan had a puppy dog look of surprise, "Arrested? No, Len's a hero 'round here, everyone..."

"...I know, I know" McCallum was thinking, trying to put all this together. Len Lamont is drunk all the time and has no file. Allee is accused of all kinds of behavior and has no file. John was seething. He hated favoritism and he hated incompetence; now he had to deal with both. He looked at Logan who was still barely holding it together. "Go to the bathroom and wash up."

Twenty Four

A few soda cans mingled with the dozens of beer bottles under the full bleachers at the Kersey High School gymnasium.

"Wrestle!" Len yelled.

Parents, teachers, farmers and friends, and aunts and uncles, and grandparents, and laborers all jumped to their feet and yelled and cheered and jeered, and just about went crazy at the first home wrestling match of the year: Kersey against Jackson Hole.

"Git 'em Charles," Butch yelled from the front bleacher.

Cindy jumped and squealed like a school girl, as Charles climbed all over Gordon Bunker, and threw him to the matt. He scrambled on top, but Gordon slid out and leaped onto Charles' back forcing him down. Len hovered, side-stepped, squatted and watched as Charles slid out. The two wrestlers sprang to their feet, squaring off. Charles burst forward grabbing Gordon around the body.

Butch stepped out onto the slick wooden floor and cupped his hands, "You gotta hurt him. Hurt him."

A father glared at Butch, then another.

"Git' em Charles." Butch's hands fought the air like a puppeteer manipulating Charles with marionette strings.

Butch stood out like a pimp in church and folks were watching him.

Gordon flipped Charles and Len dropped to the matt.

"Move Charles!" Cindy yelled, as fans rocked the bleachers.

Both of Charles shoulders were down and Len slapped the matt.

Charles bucked up while Gordon dug in his toes forcing his weight across Charles chest. Charles squirmed but wasn't moving, he dug in and pushed up with his feet but Gordon flattened him.

Len slapped the mat, once, twice, three times. "Match!"

Butch hit the air with his fist and walked back to Cindy.

Gordon relaxed, got up and raised his arm in victory, then extended his hand to Charles.

Charles took it forcing himself to stand, his chest heaved and his muscles ached, he looked at his Dad, Butch gave him a thumbs up, Charles smiled then dropped his head, swiped his fingers through his sweaty hair and walked over to the bench.

"Good job Charles," Butch yelled to him. Charles looked at his Dad and Butch chopped the air sideways with an open palm.

"I'm tellin' ya, you gotta watch that guy, Sheriff," said Damon Roundtree sucking on a *Marlboro*. A few parents were mingling in the parking lot with John McCallum after the match. "He's tellin' his boy to hurt the other raslers. You heard him."

The air was heavy. No wind. Sheriff McCallum waved away the wafts of smoke as it collect about his face. He listened.

"You ain't been here long enough to know, but just one quick look around in there and only one parent stands out from all the rest. Butch Allee," said Jack Sanders a farmer and head usher at the Baptist Church. He pushed his chew to the other cheek. "He's a loner. Don't socialize with anyone 'round here. Like a wolf, loners are." He leaned into McCallum and whispered, "When you ain't watchin', they rip you apart."

"Nothing happened in there," said McCallum, his stance wide and solid. He tilted his head back to avoid the fowl smell of Jack's breath.

"But it could," said Damon his *Marlboro* wagging between his lips ashe spoke, "remember that psycho-Dad that killed that other Dad at the hockey rink? Could happen right here." Damon's finger pointed at the asphalt. "Wouldn't put it past Allee to take a swing at someone." He kept moving the cigarette from one corner of his lips to the other.

McCallum listened and watched Damon's cigarette nervously slid about. "Have you ever seen Mr. Allee take a swing at anyone, Mr. Roundtree? Has he ever hit you?"

Damon glared, "He don't dare."

Jack spit juice on the asphalt and chuckled, "That's right. Not with us."

Damon took a real long drag and blew the smoke through his nose. He now held the *Marlboro* between his fingers and used it as a pointer toward McCallum. "I don't have to see evil to know evil Sheriff. Just open your eyes! Look at him for Christ's sake." He threw his head toward the school as Charles, Butch and Cindy walked down the concrete steps. The parking lot lights lit up Butch's flames.

"No Christian man puts the Devil's fire on his face, Sheriff." Damon flicked the cigarette and walked away.

Jack Sanders was still standing with McCallum. McCallum offered, "You're a good Baptist right, Jack?"

"Of course. Me and my family been going to church for ever."

"And Allee goes to church," McCallum said. "I've seen him there."

Jack snorted.

"Tell me Jack, why do you hate him so much?"

No one had ever asked Jack that. He shifted his stance and his eyes went from John's eyes, to his nose, to this hat, to his mouth, and back to his eyes. "Well. It's like Damon said, those tattoos. That fire on his forehead." He paused, then with new found insight said, "You don't desecrate the Lord's temple. That's in the Bible." Jack thought that was right. "And Allee, he's desecrated his whole entire body. With profanity, and an unclothed woman on his arm too, Sheriff!"

McCallum watched Jack's mouth fill with chew-juice and then watched him spit again on the asphalt. "So those tattoo's, that's a sin…and you hate him causes he's a sinner."

Jack was sure now the Sheriff done got it. "Yeah! That's right."

"You a sinner, Jack?"

Jack looked surprised. "I been forgiven. The Lord washith away the sins of the sinner."

"Maybe Allee's been forgiven too."

"You can't wash sin off your skin, Sheriff."

"Is giving yourself cancer from cigarettes and chew desecrating the body, Jack?"

Shocked and just plain flabbergasted, Jack spout out: "Hell no! These are natural plants. Grown by good farmers back in …back East. Virginia. You can't blame people for gettin' a disease from nature."

McCallum stared at him blankly.

"God Damn Sheriff who's side you on?" Jack was disgusted with the interchange and turned to walk away.

"Jack," McCallum called out.

He turned around.

"Spitting chew where people walk will get you ticketed. Just a friendly warning."

Jack stormed up to McCallum. "I vote in this town, Sheriff, and you came with good recommendations. But if you hassle the good people of this town, we'll pressure the City Councilmen to end your position." Jack suddenly looked sheepish, he never yelled at a Sheriff before. "I don't like say'n that Sheriff but tattoo's, motorcycles and bullying don't belong in Kersey."

McCallum watched Jack walk back toward his car. "Bullying by who?" he said softly.

Twenty Five

Alex's penthouse suite

6:32 pm

Alex was lounged out on the sofa reading the latest headline in the *Denver Post:*

O.J. Simpson. One year later.

O.J Simpson was still mugging for the cameras, golfing and signing autographs. Alex was amazed at the entertainers level of narcissism and bold in your face contempt for the Goldman's loss.

The phone rang.

Sipping dark sweet coffee and absorbed in the news, he let the answering machine pick up.

"Hey there, Alex." The voice was upbeat...and female.

Alex dropped the paper and grabbed the phone, "Hey Sandra anything wrong?" Sandra rarely called him at home unless there was an emergency admit or some other patient problem, but tonight he sensed no urgency in her tone.

"Relax Alex. I was just downtown doing some shopping and I thought I'd give you a call." A short pause. "Alex, I know it's the anniversary of Lisa's death."

Now a silence. Alex swallowed. No one, not even family mentioned it anymore. It was like it never happened. The American mantra: Get over it and move on.

Sandra continued, "I've never asked before, but I thought maybe you'd like some company. Want to meet me for a late dinner?"

Another silence.

"Hey you there?"

"Sure. You know Sandra, that would be nice actually. Give me half an hour."

"Great." A pause. "I'm glad."

"Me too."

He hung up.

Sitting on the couch he stared out the window and noticed his heart was racing.

With fine dexterity and practiced pressure Alex sliced the King Crab leg lengthwise with the tip of a steak knife. Then he skillfully pried the leg apart with his fingers and pulled out the sweet, thick meat in one long strip. "Perfection." He threw a smile at Sandra.

"So that's how you skin a crab," she said.

"I've never quite heard it put that way, but I guess skinning a crab will do." He presented it to her, "Westerners, that means anyone west of Maryland, use mallets. They smash everything inside and make a mess. Easterners use a knife." He cut a piece for himself, took a bite then sipped some Merlot.

"Did you read the headlines today?" Sandra quipped. "O.J. out golfing, having the the time of his life. He disgusts me." She had forgotten that Alex was a criminal defense attorney in his past life. She stabbed the long spiny leg with the tip of her knife. "Johnny Cochran pulled out all the manipulative, deceitful lies from his little bag of defense attorney secrets. It still feels like one big manipulation."

Alex winched. Was she talking about Johnny Cochran or *him*?

She sliced open the leg. "The entire trial was a joke. Even Judge Ito was mocked on Jay Leno with the Judge Ito dancers."

"I liked that part," Alex defended.

Sandra shook her head in disgust and she pried apart the shell. "If I was Ron Goldman's dad...I'd get him. I wouldn't care what happened to me." She grabbed the meat inside, pulled it out and ate a chunk.

The defense attorney blood coursing through Alex's veins pulsed. He took another bite of the firm, sweet meat. He didn't want opposing personal ethics with Sandra to spill over into work, mucking up their professional relationship. But as a good psychologist, he wanted to explore this further. "Get him? How?"

Sandra took another bite, "I'd send in a few good men." She leaned forward toward Alex, "Hide 'em on the golf course and put a bullet in his head."

Alex almost chocked on his King Crab. "Assassinate him?" Alex didn't think that it was such an awful idea; he felt the trial was completely mishandled and was played out for the camera's. He thought OJ was guilty anyway, but it surprised him Sandra did as well. He looked at her with anticipation.

"That's right, assassinate him. It would be quick, efficient and easy. OJ is so narcissistic he leaves himself wide open for revenge."

Alex nodded, "You a republican, Sandra?"

"I'm a half breed. My dad was a democrat and my mom was a republican. I go both ways." She blushed at the sexual innuendo, but Alex didn't notice.

"I've always been a republican. Lisa used to say I was a fiscal republican and a social democrat. Not many full blooded republican psychologists around. Or at least ones who can skin a King Crab."

Sandra smiled. "I knew you had other talents besides being a good psychologist."

Alex looked directly into her eyes, "I know how to survive in the wilderness too. Hunt, fish, catch a bear in a trap." He smirked, "What *more* could anyone want?"

"A survivalist, and lawyer too." She suddenly blushed. "Oh my gosh, I forgot you were a defense attorney? Right?"

His smirk vanished and he looked away. "Used to be. That piece of me starved to death...a long time ago."

Sandra had heard the whispers about his past, his career in law. "You probably thought OJ got a great defense. Got off. No consequences."

He thought for a moment, "I felt there was a little bit of truth and a whole lot of embellishment."

"Do you think he did it?"

Alex looked into her eyes. Beautiful eyes. Full of life. "I do."

"Wouldn't you want him shot? If he had killed your son and he got away with it." Alex felt his stomach knot. "I guess I would now. But not back then. When I was an attorney... I'm not the same as I was back then." His appetite was now swallowed by remorse.

They sat in silence for a short time. Sandra tried her hand at cutting another crab leg as Alex drank more wine. Then she said, "Alex, can I be frank with you?"

"No. My Dad was Frank, but you can be honest with me."

"You sure are sillier outside of work, you're so serious there."

"It's work. Serious work."

"I know. It is serious having our nosey little minds probing into peoples lives. But that's what I want to tell you. At work, I know my place with the other doctors, they don't like getting advice from an RN--"

"--fragile ego's," added Alex.

"Exactly. I can't tell you how many times I know exactly what's going on with a patient before the doctor has a clue. But, you know, the nurse can't tell the doctor what to do. So

I restrain myself. But outside work," she smiled, "I tell it like it is. I hope my abruptness doesn't offended you."

"Sandra, I like harsh, critical, blunt...and honest conversation."

"Oh, you do huh?" Now was her opportunity. "Okay, then tell me, do you ever go out?"

"Go out? Like to the grocery store? A movie?"

"Go out...like on a date. With a woman."

"A woman? Sandra, I'm gay."

Her eyes bolted from the crab, "You're *gay*? Get outta town?"

Then the big grin, "No, but not that there's anything wrong with it."

"*Seinfield*," she said.

His face it up, "You know I can watch that show over and over and never get tired of it. I still laugh ever time Newman walks through the door and Jerry says deadpan, 'Hello Newman.'"

She licked her fingers tasting the sweet crab juice on them, "I know, I love it too." She also knew he avoided her question. She wasn't sure if she should bring it up again or just let it alone.

The ease of the conversation brought back his appetite. He took a bite of coleslaw, then crab, then a sip of wine holding the stem between his fingers. "If you want to know I haven't had a date in eight years Sandra." He sipped more wine.

She stopped cutting and wiped her hands on the cloth napkin, "Why not Alex? You're a nice guy. Descent looking, I guess," she smirked, "a JD and Ph.D., it must be lonely not having anyone around." Even with the humor she felt him stiffen. "I'm sorry, Alex, I shouldn't have asked. I know this is our first time ever going out together...not that there's anything wrong with it." She smiled.

"It's okay." He looked at his crab all torn apart, legs split open, vacant between the shell. It mirrored how he was feeling. "It was thoughtful of you to call." He scratched his forehead. "Family doesn't even call anymore. To other people...it's done and over, like last years horror show. They want me to just move on, see the next movie." The muscles in his jaw flexed attempting to hold back the sudden welling of tears, he blinked, then smiled weakly, "I didn't think I was going to survive it." She held his stare. "It was the only time in my life I wanted to kill someone. It scared me. My impulses. I had a plan, I even picked out one of my deadliest big game rifles. Great scope, accurate. Easy shot out to 500 yards. I was going to shoot him in the head when they where transferring him from court to the van. It would have been easy." Alex shifted his eyes from Sandra down to the table. "Just like you said about OJ. It scared me how close I came." Sipping more wine he then added, "And there were a few times I felt like using that rifle on myself." Alex took a breath and Sandra just listened, herself being the good psychologist.

"Your heart gets sliced apart. Eventually it heals. But there's always that great big scar of memory there...and at times...it opens up wide and gushes."

Sandra placed her hand on top of his, "I'm sorry it happened to you."

"It happened to her."

Little pearls of wet formed in the corners of Alex's eyes and he chocked on a sob. He wiped away the tears that lingered on his face. "I happened eight years ago. I was a criminal defense attorney. My *job* was to make sure the rights of criminals weren't violated." He raised the wine glass to his lips and swigged a last big gulp. "I made my living by defending criminals, crooked politicians, drunks and murderers...all alleged of course. Rights of people are trampled on everyday. I defended peoples rights, I made sure the system worked and worked legally. Then I met Albert Socorro. Or rather he met me. I argued insanity and Socorro got four years in Pueblo followed by two years in a half way house, then was out." He looked away, "When I think about it now, that wasn't much time for raping his own daughter after he strangled her to death."

Sandra sucked air through her lips.

"Of course there was no follow up treatment, no medications. He was let free after serving his time and I was done with him. I did my job."

The restaurant filled but Alex and Sandra seemed to be there alone.

"What I found out later was that Albert was still psychotic and anti-social, but he was also quite lucid at times and very much in touch with reality when he wanted to be. I know all this now, but back then I didn't cared, I did my job and everyone was happy. But Albert Socorro could sweet talk a little boy into a mall bathroom, molest him and give him a special bag of candy leaving that little boy smiling when he ran up to his frantic mother. Albert did it for years. He did the same thing with authority figures. Sweet talked them, complimented them, subtly put himself down to gain their confidence and then he'd do what he wanted. It didn't matter to him what he did, take their money, kill them, he did what ever seemed justified at the moment. He targeted authority figures, and for some reason he fixated on me." He looked Sandra in the eyes, "*I* wasn't home that day. It was a Friday. I never worked on Fridays, but I went to work that Friday to finish a case review. And Lisa was home alone...and Albert knocked on the door...and Lisa let him in." Alex blinked and breathed deeply.

"Oh my God ,Alex, I'm so sorry."

"I never went back to law after that. I made a decision right then that I was finished defending the scum that crawl up from hell. I didn't care about their rights. I didn't care if they got a fair trial. It didn't matter anymore." Alex looked like this was the first time he had heard those words.

"My life mission changed. I felt this uncontrollable drive to put those fuckers away. But not at the end of it all, like a trial, but to be the first to evaluate them. I wanted to separate the deadly ones from the harmless ones, search out the manipulators from the ones with real psychological problems that could benefit from treatment. Then fight hard to keep the monsters locked up forever. Evaluate them, testify against them, and make sure they never get out. So I went back to school, earned my Ph.D. and became a forensic psychologist. That was better than jumping ship and becoming a prosecutor. The prosecutor gets them committed then walks away. I get 'em at both ends. The combination of JD and Ph.D. is a killer one."

The restaurant was silent, at least it seemed that way to Sandra. "So what happened to Albert Socorro?"

"Well he wasn't in treatment then and he isn't today. Right now he's rotting on death row. I testified and convinced the jury that Albert was very much in touch with reality when he
killed Lisa and the jury believed me."

"When's his execution date?"

Alex let out a breath, "Who knows. That part of the system just sucks."

"Should have sent in a few good men," she added.

Alex looked at her like that wasn't such an awful idea.

Twenty Six

Kersey

The phone rang. Butch hit *mute* on the TV remote and jumped up from the sofa. "Yo?"

He listened.

"What!? Who said that?" His chest heaved and a sourness quickly expanded in his gut. "Where is she now?" He dropped his head, his hair falling into his eyes. "I'm comin' down there right now...I don't care who's there." He slammed the phone on the receiver, put on a shirt and drove the three blocks to Kersey Elementary school.

The principal's office door was closed but flew open as Butch barged in. Standing together was William Corbet the principal, John McCallum, and a social worker from Child Protective Services, all three blocking the door to the next room.

"Let me see Margaret right now." His jaw was tight, his eye's angry.

"She's being interviewed by the social worker, Mr. Allee," said William Corbet. "You can't go in there right now."

"I'm her Father. Why didn't anyone call me? I need to give permission for anyone to talk to my daughter."

"No you don't, Mr. Allee," countered Francine Fish a thin, anorexic looking woman with a *Child Protective Services* badge clipped to her blouse which hung crooked off to the side. "When sexual abuse involving a child is reported Mr. Allee, *we* need to intervene first."

"What? There ain't no...sexual abuse!" He hardly could get the words out. "You sayin' it's me? Who said I abused Margaret?"

"I received a call with the report, Mr. Allee," said William Corbet his voice quavering, "So I had to call the Sheriff. Sheriff McCallum called Social Services."

"It's the law, Mr. Allee," said McCallum.

"Fuck the law! I never hurt Margaret or any of my children." He glared at William Corbet. "Tell me who said I did this?"

William nervously looked at the Sheriff, then at Francine. "It was an anonymous call."

"Anonymous? Why'd they call the school instead of the Sheriff's office?" He looked at McCallum with suspicion, then Corbet, then the social worker. All were silent. "What kind of bullshit is this?" Butch walked forward toward the door but John McCallum took one step meeting him, Butch had to look up to see McCallum's eyes.

"You can't go in there," said McCallum.

"If you don't move outta my way I'm going to take your head off."

Francine Fish gasped and put her hand to her mouth.

John took half a step backward but still covered the door. "You have my word Mr. Allee. You can talk to Margaret in a second. Just wait. If nothing happened, and I do believe you, then you don't have to worry."

"*Nothin'* happened Sheriff." Butch stared hard into his eyes. "So let me understand this, since I only got an eighth grade education you know. Anyone can call you and lie and then all my rights are gone? Is that right?"

"The law is designed to protect the children. We have to take every report seriously," said Francine Fish.

Just then the side room door creaked open and Margaret strutted out, confident and full of vigor. She spied her Dad and ran to him. Butch knelt and wrapped his arms about her. "You okay, Margaret?" He stroked her hair.

"They asked me all kinds of questions Daddy, like if you ever hit me or hit Charles or Lea and if you ever watch me in the shower."

Butch's heart sank as the words knocked the breath out of him. He threw his head upward and glared at the men and woman towering above him. He slowly stood, his biceps flexed and the tattoos expanded; blood pumped and filled the veins on his neck. He took two steps toward the social workers. "You finished here?"

"Y-y-yes, Mr. Allee," said the social worker who interviewed Margaret, she took a quick breath, "I don't see any evidence for the accusations,"

"There never was no evidence." Butch took one step closer and the social worker visibly swallowed. "You asked a seven year old if I watch her shower? You're disgusting. And you're ignorant too, she don't take a shower, she takes a bath. Did she tell you that I wash her hair. And wash her back. That I dry her hair and brush it. I get her pajamas and help her get 'em on and I kiss her goodnight. Is that okay with you Miss Social Worker? Am I bein' a good dad or a bad dad? You gonna judge me anymore?" He looked at McCallum, "You gonna arrest me for any of that, Sheriff?"

The four of them just stood there. "You're free to go Mr. Allee," said Sheriff McCallum. "Look, Butch, I'm sorry about this, but I have to follow the law. Obviously this was a false report and I'll be talking with William about it. If he knows who called this in and I find out, I'll arrest them. You can count on that. Again, I'm sorry Butch." John held out his hand.

Butch looked at it. He wanted to spit on it but instead he turned, took Margaret by the hand and walked out.

William Corbet squinted, his stare penetrating Butch's back-length hair, through the motorcycle vest, flannel shirt, tattooed skin and on into his heart, his words seethed through his teeth, "I don't think he's ever worked a day in his life. His kids'll probably grow up to be just like him."

"I do need to discuss this with you, Bill," said McCallum.

William turned and looked him in the eyes, "For the record Sheriff, I know of no one in Kersey who would make a false report like this. Absolutely no one. I'm sure his kids are protecting him. Probably scared of him I'll bet."

"Of all the people in Kersey you didn't recognized the voice?"

William was defiant, "No, Sheriff. No one I know."

John McCallum watched for any facial twitching, eye movement: a tell-tale sign of lying. Then his demeanor changed, "We're watching him, Bill. But he's not done anything wrong."

"I've been Principle of this school for ten years. I've seen kids protect their parents."

"You ever notice any of the Allee kids with bruises or anything like that?"

William walked toward his desk. "No. But that doesn't mean anything."

"Their grades okay?"

"What are you getting at Sheriff?"

John tilted his Stetson back. "It seems that folks around here just don't like Butch Allee. He rides a Harley and has all those tattoos, but I just don't get why people have issues with him."

William stood up from his chair. "It's because Allee is a non-productive bully in this community. You can't talk to the man. You see how he acted in here? Cussing, threatening, posturing. He threatened you, John. He accused us of fabricating this incident. He's not a reasonable man. He's a volatile man." William was agitated. "Folks around here have picnics, share recipes and play pool at the Oasis. You never see the Allees doing that. They don't want to participate with anyone in Kersey."

"Maybe they feel they aren't welcome."

William waved his hand, "Oh, that's ridiculous. Everyone is welcome here."

John kind of laughed when he heard that. "You need me for anything else right now? Any students cheating on tests that I can arrest."

William grinned. "No. But thanks for coming over."

"You sure now? It's been a slow week."

William sat down. "Thanks again John. See you in church."

****

Alex stared at Butch, "Did this kind of stuff happen to you a lot?"

Butch shifted in the chair, "Yeah, sometimes. Most folks in Kersey treated me ok. But some...I don't know...people don't seem to like me."

Are you kidding? Thought Alex. Butch obviously was low to empty on the insight gauge. Look at yourself. The hair, the tattoos, of course they thought you molested your daughter. Then it hit him: What am I doing? He's right... *they* judged him. *I'm* judging him.

The consultation room was suddenly silent, but Alex's thoughts pounded for attention. For the first time in years his awareness of himself was kicking in. He had become accustomed to *not* feeling, cruising in psychological autopilot. But now he was sensing an emotional tailspin of feeling and understanding. What he was becoming aware of, inside himself, he was not liking.

What have I become? He stared off, looking down and away from Butch. Do I judge people? I've never been prejudiced... no one would describe me as prejudiced. I've always been proud of being open minded. But I instantly thought...His forehead furrowed, I'm no better than they are...the Kersey people. Alex found himself sweating. He felt alone in his office... alone inside himself. He continued to look off away from Butch. He didn't know how long he was gone from the session, his gaze returned to Butch. For the first time he really looked at Butch, beyond the hair, the tattoos and the beard. He's been persecuted. Like black people. Like Jews. Like anyone in America who's different. Alex suddenly felt sick. "Butch I need to end here. I'm not feeling well."

Butch stared at Alex who was suddenly pale.

Twenty Seven

Kersey

"Yes! Yes, yes, yes...run! Run you fuck, run! God-damn!"

The insulation in the walls of Len and Alisha's house was such that sound got out and cold got in. Anyone walking by could have heard Len yelling at the TV during the Bronco's game. And no one would have cared or even noticed because all the homes in Kersey were about the same: Inadequate sealing around doors and windows; heat was cheap so it didn't matter. Wood burning stoves were the norm and folks fed their stoves with used corn cobs. The farmers gave it away by the truck load so people never really cared about insulation or heat or sound escaping into the wind.

Len was sprawled out on his Lazy-Boy recliner, six bottles of Coors lay empty on the floor next to him. Alisha was in the kitchen cleaning up after dinner.

"Hey get me another beer, will ya."

Alisha yelled back from the kitchen, "Len, I'm cleaning up, get it yourself."

"Why can't you get me a fuckin' beer when I want one? I teach those whiney-ass kids all day, I help your old man with his tractor and you can't get me a God-damn beer?"

"You've had enough...you're on duty tonight, you know." She pushed the *Ronco* Rotisserie back against the counter wall and jumped as an empty beer bottle shattered across the kitchen floor. "You bastard!" She burst into tears, "Why do you get this way?" She leaned up against the counter and cried. "Len you're drinking too much again and why are you mad at me?"

Len jumped from the recliner and stormed into the kitchen grabbing Alisha by both arms bunching them up so hard around her chest that her shoulders ached. His breath stunk of stale beer and his eyes bubbled with hate. "No one tells me what to do." She squirmed as his fingers dug deeper into her arm. "If I want another beer, you get it for me. If I want dinner in my fucking truck you bring it to me. You got it?"

Alisha sobbed and looked away. Her left bicep relaxed as Len released his grip, but then blinding pain seared her jaw, eye and nose as Len's open hand slammed into her face. Her knees gave way and he held her upright like a rag doll with his left hand, then another slap and he let her crumble onto the kitchen floor crying and chocking and bleeding from her nose.

He stared down at her, his face full of disgust, "Get me... a fucking beer."

Alisha forced herself up onto her forearms and she looked up at him. Red saliva coated her lips, mascara ran from her eyes, she opened her mouth to speak but nothing came out as her eyes looked past Len: there in the kitchen doorway stood her two little boys.

Seeing her expression, he turned around. "Git in yer room," he hissed at them. They bolted down the narrow hall and slammed their bedroom doors. He turned back toward Alisha who was still on the floor, trembling. "Now, get me a beer. You get one more chance." He waited looking down at her like she was a pitiful pig waiting to be slaughtered.

Alisha wiped her mouth with the palm of her hand and started to crawl toward the refrigerator.

"Good girl." He watched her.

She crawled on hands and knees around the metal legs of the table and chairs toward the refrigerator door, her brain was pounding. She forced herself to kneel, grabbing the door handle she pulled herself upwards. She stood, opened the refrigerator and reached inside and took out a beer. Turning she closed the door then leaned against it holding the beer in her hand.

"Bring it to me."

She was scared and didn't move.

"I said bring it to me."

Her eye's pleaded with him. She slowly wobbled around the table, her hand caressing the top of the chairs for comfort as well as support. She held out the beer for him.

"Open it."

Her bottom lip trembled, she gripped the twist-off cap between her thumb and forefinger and opened the bottle and held it out again.

He grabbed the bottle from her and took a long gulp -- his head back, his throat exposed, his adams-apple traveling up and down -- "Now get yourself cleaned up." He turned and went back to watch the Broncos game.

Forty minutes later the phone rang a funny ring that caused an excited churning in Len's gut, tonight it brought only an agitated pissed off feeling. "Shit!" Len released the lever on the side of the recliner and the chair's footrest folded in as the back of the chair shot up. He rolled from the recliner, shuffled into the kitchen, picked up the phone and listened.

The Volunteer Fire Department recording gave him the details on where a fire was. He was to respond immediately. "Shit. Why tonight? Some God-damn lunatic probably smokin' in bed." He grabbed his keys hanging on the wall then stopped. Tugging open the cabinet door next to the sink he pulled out the mouthwash he kept in there. He took a large gulp, swished it around in his mouth then swallowed it. He did this a second time spitting into the sink and stumbled to his pickup.

Two fire engines were already at the scene, the only one in Kersey and the other from Wayland. Flood lights and fire lit up the night sky, neighbors gathered and gawked across the street while a family sat on the curb huddled in blankets. The smell of burning wood, asphalt shingles, and insulation lay thick in the air. That smell also made a fireman's heart race and spiked the adrenaline.

"Holy shit! What a blaze!" Len said peering through the windshield of his truck as he pulled onto the gravel driveway. Now Len was feeling energized. He jumped from his pickup and grabbed his fire fighting suit from the back of the cab. He fumbled with the oversized trousers and fell to the ground. He struggled to stand as he pulled up the bib.

Zachery Commer ran up to him, "What took you so long? We need you in back." Zackery Commer was head of the volunteer firemen and had known Len since high school. Len couldn't get the straps latched and Zackery immediately knew. "Look at me!" Len turned away. "You look at me you son of a bitch...you're drunk aren't you?" Zackery bellowed his voice barely audible over all the commotion.

Len turned back around to face Zachary. "Fuck you! You some doctor or something? I'm not drunk. I had one maybe two beers, that's all. Now where do you need me?"

"You ain't going anywhere near this fire. I don't need a drunk firemen fucking around and getting someone killed."

Len took a step forward, "Fuck you, Commer."

Zackery laid into Len yelling and poking his finger into Len's face, "Fuck you Lamont. You've done this before. I'm wasting valuable time fucking with you. Get outta here. Jesus Christ! We need every man on this fire and you show up here drunk. You're done Lamont...you're outta here. No more you.... Get outta here!" Zackary turned in disgust and ran back toward the engine.

Len stood there watching, his coveralls hanging down, helmet in hand, "I've saved your ass so many times."

Zackery couldn't hear him as the porch cracked and thundered as it caved in, shooting blazing red embers into the sky.

Off to the side John McCallum was standing too, watching everything, his face lit by the flames that danced in the dark sky. He stood tall, arms crossed and watched as Len pulled his legs from his suit and slam both his suit and helmet into the back of the cab. Len climbed in, started the truck and backed up. He let the truck idled for a minute then sped down the road, it's taillights haloed from the smoke.

Twenty Eight

Kersey

Christmas Morning

The tiny white house sparkled with red, blue, green and yellow Christmas lights. Fresh evergreen boughs were wrapped about the porch posts and a large wooden sign, hand painted by Butch, hung on the door. It read: *Merry Christmas! Come on in!* Plastic candy canes lined the driveway, a wire reindeer coated in tiny white lights stood in the front yard and two blue spruce in the rock garden flashed on and off with twinkle lights. Inside, the tiny living room was tight with a decorated tree and presents.

Butch poured Cindy and himself some strong coffee while Charles, Lea and Margaret opened gifts.

Charles grabbed a long heavy box, ripped open the Santa wrapping and pried open the top. "Wow, a paint sprayer." He looked at his Dad whose eyes sparkled. "What's this for? Are you trying to get me to paint the house?"

"No way he can paint our house," said Lea, "it'd be a mess."

"I want the house painted pink," said Margaret. "Can we please Mommy? Can Charles color our house pink?" She beamed with hope.

Butch chuckled. "Maybe next year, Margaret. Charles, go look outside."

Charles jumped up and ran to the side window and peered out, "Oh man! Cool Dad." He ran out the front door in his bare feet and jumped down the steps while Lea and Margaret watched through the window.

Butch and Cindy stepped out onto the porch. "It's yours Charles," said Butch.

Charles jumped about in the snow dancing with excitement, "Mom, Dad, this is great! Thanks so much." Charles circled the old rusting Chevy Monte Carlo running his hands along the cold steel. "This is so cool. The paint sprayer." He yelled to his Dad, "You're going to teach me to paint it?"

"You bet Charles. Paint it any color or design you want. Except pink."

"Even flames on the hood?"

"If you want Charles. Flames, just like on my hood." Butch touched his forehead.

"How's the engine, Dad?"

"It needs a tune-up and a little work, but it runs." Butch caressed his beard remembering his first fix-up car and how he painted it with a brush and left over paint from the garage.

Charles opened the driver door and hopped in. The red leather seats were icy cold, stinging his legs and the steering wheel felt like ice. "Yeeeooooow! I love it."

Cindy set the dinner dishes into the sink as Lea and Margaret ran into the living room to watch TV. "You and Charles going to work on the Monte Carlo?" she asked Butch who was still sitting at the table sipping coffee.

'Yeah, I have about an hour before headin' out." Butch stood up and walked to Cindy as she squeezed dish soap onto the dirty dishes. His hands slid around her tiny waist. He kissed her neck, one hand moved up toward her breast.

"You have an hour, huh?"

Butch laughed, "Don't need an hour."

She turned to face him, "Charles is in the garage." She looked up into his green eyes. No matter what she did she still saw Charles in Butch's face. "You know, Charles is going to have to fight off the girls...just like his Dad."

"I'm still fightin' 'em off too." He laughed again.

It's one of the things that attracted Cindy to Butch, his laughing eyes. Eyes that were full of life, full of mischief. "You going to fight off this girl right now?" She asked.

"I'll rastle you instead...in the bedroom."

Cindy giggled, "Can we sneak in there?"

"I can sneak in anywheres," said Butch. He took her hand and they slunk out the kitchen and slipped quietly into the bedroom.

"Where you been, Dad?" said Charles as the garage door creaked open and Butch stepped in; Charles looked up through speckled goggles, his hands and face were flecked with paint.

"I was helpin' your Mom with the dishes. How's it comin?"

Charles sat on the cold cement floor, he lifted the goggles up and over his glasses so they rested on his forehead shoving his short black hair up so it stood on end like a cowlick. He wiped his hands on the kerosene soaked rag. "I wanted to finish these flames on the fender then you can draw a hood design."

"That looks really nice, Charles. Looks like real fire."

Charles beamed.

The tiny garage was stuffed to the walls with garden equipment, boxes filled with important stuff that may get used one day and now the car. Charles was squeezed in on one side with the paint sprayer. It was cold and all the windows were closed. The garage normally had that moldy, old wood smell, but now the place filled with the fumes of paint, paint thinner and sweat.

Butch squatted next to Charles, his toes curling on the cold cement. "You know after high school you could get a real good job paintin' cars for a living. Not many folks do that anymore."

"Where'd you learn Dad?"

Butch hesitated, his heart pumping a little faster. "Well...." Now's a good time as any, he thought. "You know when I told you that I was at Buena Vista?"

"Yeah."

"Well I learned how to paint cars there."

"I wish they had car painting at my school. Watch this." He pulled down the goggles and adjusted the nozzle and sprayed out a fine line of orange that flashed and waved on the metal.

Butch looked on with pride. Above the hum of the sprayer he said, "Charles you're doin' real good."

Charles looked up at his Dad through a prism of orange and blue speckles. He liked his Dad there. It wasn't intimidating or parental, it was just...comfortable. He added three more orange flames then turned off the sprayer.

"I got to clean this head then add some more red and blue. This will look so cool, Dad! When can we take it out?" His face lit up, "I want to drive it school."

"After it's all done. Do a real good job then show it off."

"Can I drive it to school? No one around here has a car like this."

Butch smiled, "Maybe."

"I'm going to work on it all night," said Charles as he dipped the nozzle into the paint thinner.

"Not past ten. If you get tired you'll make mistakes and then you'll be disappointed in the morning. It's better to do it right then have to do it over."

"Ok."

"Maybe next year you can drive it in the Lamont parade," said Butch.

Charles enthusiasm vanished. Butch couldn't read a Stephen King novel but he could read his son. "What's wrong?"

Charles looked away.

"Hey, Charles what's wrong?"

"No, forget it."

"What? You get detention or something?"

Charles looked surprised, "Detention? I've never been in trouble at school." He didn't quite know how to tell his Dad. He didn't want to disappoint him and he really didn't want to talk about it but his Dad obviously wasn't going to let it go. "No, it's not that."

"Well then what, Charles?"

He scooted around to face Butch. "Dad. I just don't feel like wrestling anymore."

Butch was relieved. "That's all? You don't want to rastle? Shit I thought it was somthing bad." Butch smiled, then realized Charles wasn't smiling with him. "Why not?"

"It's just not fun anymore."

Butch remembered how his Dad used to make him play baseball when he was younger and how he hated it. "Charles, look at me." Charles scooted around to look at his Dad who now sat on the cement floor with him. "If you don't want to rastle you don't have to. But you joined the team and you should stick with the team until the season is over. I'm not making you go, you joined on your own and I'm proud of you for that. But you can't leave your teammates without a member. Besides I like going to the matches and yelling for ya."

Charles didn't correct his Dad that wrestling had no seasons but goes on for the entire school year. "There's too much pressure."

"Like what?"

"Well, Mr. Lamont calls us names if we don't do well."

"Charles, all gym teachers call their students names. Shithead. Asswipe. Stuff like that."

Charles hadn't been called that, but maybe his Dad went to a school that was meaner than Kersey High.

"It's supposed to get you mad so you pound your opponents. And I've seen you pound 'em Charles. It makes you win. You're good at rastlin'."

Charles forced a grin. "Did they call you names in high school?"

Butch felt his heart pounding again. He swallowed. Charles just spilled his guts to him, he now felt it was time to do the same. "Charles, I need to tell you something. But I don't want you to do what I did." Charles stared at his Dad. "I've never told you this...and I'm not proud of it. And I don't want you to think bad about me." He tugged on his beard. "I didn't finish school."

Charles tried to read his Dad's face. "Did you drop out?"

"Yeah I did. I never went past the eighth grade."

"The eighth grade. Really? I wish I could drop out sometimes."

"Charles no you don't. You'll end up just like me. I'm working all the time. Workin' nights. It aint fun. You need to finish school and make something of yourself." Butch was scared at the thought of Charles dropping out.

"You get a GED?"

"Nope. I kinda had problems when I was about your age. I guess your grandparents didn't really raise me with enough discipline. So I sorta did what I wanted." Butch felt his shirt sticking in his armpits.

"But you went to Buena Vista? You learned how to paint cars there. So you didn't graduate from there?"

Butch was losing control of his breathing and his heart was jumping all over the place. For the first time Butch was afraid to talk to his son. What would he think? Would he be disappointed? Would he tell his friends?

Charles was waiting for an answer.

"Charles I did some things that were wrong." His voice cracked, "I...that place, I told you about, Buena Vista. It's not a school." He swallowed and stared at Charles. He swallowed again. "It's a prison."

Charles eyes grew wide, then filled with tears. He looked scared and disappointed all at once. "I don't believe you. You never went to prison."

"Charles, I'm sorry. It was before you was born and before I met your Mom."

"I don't believe you." He turned away, Butch's gut knotted up.

"It's true, Charles. I wasn't very good back then, but I'm not the same anymore."

"Does Mom know?"

"Yeah, of course she knows. But I'm different now, Charles. That's why I want you to stay in school, try hard and get a good job. He reached out, but Charles leaned away and he felt his heart ache. It was the same horrible feeling he had when his Dad was crying to him about throwing his life away. Butch's eyes filled with tears. "Charles, I'm sorry I never told you. I'm ashamed of it and I guess I never wanted you to be disappointed in me so I never told ya."

Charles spun around with eyes of anger, "Some of the guys said you were in prison. I called them all liars. They said their parents told them, and that you did drugs and you rode with the Hells Angles. Is all that true too?"

Butch was flustered. They're sayin' that about me? "No. No Charles, none of that is true. I *was* in prison, but you don't know why."

"Did you ever hit Mom?"

Fuck! Who's sayin' this stuff?

"Did you? Tell me!"

Butch didn't know what to do or say. He'd always ignored the rumors, but now they were here, taunting him. And it was hurtful coming from Charles. "No. I would never hit your Mom. Have I ever hit you?"

The anger in Charles' muscles relaxed. "No."

"Charles, listen to me. I'll tell you what happened. The truth this time." He took a long breath, scratched his head. "I was put there as a teenager for some petty stuff, like not goin' to school and trespassin'. Ridin the train into Denver. I did steal a car, and the State of Wyoming started this program where they put kids in with adults in adult prison and I was one of the ones they chose. It was like an experiment and I shouldn't have been there. I should have just been put in a boys home...or... somewhere's else, or my parents should have been better parents. That's why I was in prison in Buena Vista." Suddenly he felt he was there. It took him by surprise how fast the fear was alive in him, gripping his chest and stomach. "It was a bad place, Charles. There was really mean people there. I was just a kid and I had to protect myself from the men there." It was difficult for him to talk and his hands trembled. "Mean men...men who had killed people. And the guards never helped neither. It made me hateful, but I changed and..." tears spilled down Butch's face.

Charles softened and threw his arms around his Dad. He couldn't remember the last time he saw his Dad cry.

Butch bear-hugged Charles and kept talking, "I'm sorry, Charles. That's why I never read to you. I can't read real good, Charles, I never learned how. But I'm different now, I learned my lesson and I'm trying to be a good father. I'm really trying hard. I made a lot of mistakes and I never was taught how to be a good parent. I just started raisin' you like *I* wanted to be raised."

"I'm sorry I got mad at you. I'm proud you're my Dad."

Butch choked up and couldn't say anymore. Sitting on the cold cement floor they hugged each other for a few moments.

Charles slowly let go but sat close as he wiped his eyes on his shirt sleeve.

"Why didn't you ever tell me?" asked Charles.

"I didn't want to. I was embarrassed. Charles, I felt like a failure for a lot of my life. But then I met your Mom and we had you and I don't feel that way anymore. Things are good now. And I want things to be good for you too. So I didn't tell any of you kids."

Charles nodded.

Butch glanced up at the Harley wall clock. Going to work was the last thing he wanted to do right now. Just sit here with Charles, paint the car, that's what he wanted to do, but he couldn't. "I got to get goin' to work. But I'm glad I finally told you. It's a relief to me."

"Me too. I wish you didn't have to go to work."

"That's just what I was thinking. I'd rather stay here with you, but your Mom and I can't both be gone in the day 'cause of you kids. The bindery pays extra for night work and being a holiday they pay extra on top of the extra. And we need that extra money, being we just bought this house and all."

Charles looked at the Monte Carlo and his eyes quickly scanned the room, "I'm glad we finally have a garage."

Butch chuckled. "Got cold at our old place. Working on the bikes and cars in the back yard in the winter."

"Yeah, this is way better." Butch nodded. "Your Mom finally has her rock garden and I have a garage." Butch looked at the unfinished walls, the spider webs choking the corners, the smudged windows, the rafters holding odd pieces of lumber. It smelled like a garage. "I like this place too, Charles. Maybe when you get older we'll give all of this to you. Raise your own kids here someday."

"Really?"

Butch grinned, his eyes clearing, "This is our first house that we don't rent, Charles, your Mom and I want it to stay in the family. The girls'll get married and move into a house of their own, but you're our only son."

"So I get the house?"

"Maybe you will, someday. I got to get going. You gonna finish up here?"

"Yeah."

"I love you, Charles." He hugged him again.
"I love you too, Dad."

Twenty Nine

Aspen Grove

"That must have been difficult for Charles to hear," said Alex.

Butch hung is head and got that pained expression on his face that Alex had grown accustomed to. He knew it was genuine.

"Yeah. It hurt. Having to tell him that. But it's better that way. He knows where I came from and what I've done."

"It sounds like the two of you have a close relationship."

"We did, Doc. We did everything together...I always told everyone that he was my best friend. Better than a father and son."

"And now?"

Butch looked up, "It's not so good. The system screwed me when I was young and it took a long time for me to get my head straight. And now, because I was in jail for six months and when I got out I was so fucked up...I wasn't a good dad anymore Charles is in jail now. He started using drugs and got busted. Charles is the one suffering now."

"Butch you said the system screwed you, but you put yourself in the position to get screwed." Alex wanted him to acknowledge some level of responsibility.

"I'm not going to argue with you, Doc, you're right, I did some bad things. But not bad enough to put me in a prison with adults. That's how the system screwed me."

"I'll give you that Butch. It sounds like what you needed was some discipline and direction. Not prison."

"Yeah."

"And the church let you down."

"I never went back to being a Mormon. But now we go to church every Sunday. I'm a Christian now."

Alex knew the old prison saying about Jesus Christ: *Tout...until you're Out.* But Butch didn't seem to fit that mold. "Lets change the subject here a bit. When I first saw you, the voices were telling you you were a murderer. Do *you* still feel that way?" Alex sipped coffee.

"You know Doc, deep down I know I didn't murder Len Lamont, and I needed to hear the jury say not guilty. But I still killed someone. I ain't never killed anybody in my life." In an instant he was back there again, and that pained expression crawled across his face. "I still dream about it." Butch scratched at his cheek through his beard. "I can still see everything that happened."

Alex listened as Butch retold the nights events. It was the second time, but with more emotions. Alex knew that healing comes from the power of re-telling a painful experience. Like a balloon filled to capacity, then slowly, steadily the air is released, and the emotions that have been fermenting, sometimes for years, sometimes a lifetime, are quelled. Once the pressure is relieved, then the healing can start. Secrets kill people. Talking heals them.

Thirty

Kersey High School

The gym stank. It always stank. No matter how much ammonia was scrubbed into the cracked hardwood flooring it still stank. Musty, sweaty, old jock stink. It didn't matter if it was a boys school, a girls school, or a co-ed school, every gym across America smelled the same way and there's no cleaning agent or army of janitors that can do anything about it.

At 3:15 pm the wrestlers ran in jostling each other loosely attempting to line up and be serious. Len was already waiting and named each student in his head as they entered the gym. "Where's Allee?"

A few boys looked about, some shrugged shoulders. "He went home," said Tommy.

"Why?" Len's face scrunched up.

Tommy shrugged, "He said he had things to do."

Len stormed toward Tommy like a drill sergeant, "Things to do? Like what?"

"I-I don't know, Mr. Lamont. I think...he said something about painting his car."

Len nodded, his jaw tight. "Painting his car. His old man's car I'll bet." Then without thinking, "That piece of shit."

"Him or the car?" one of the wrestlers yelled out.

Len jerked around, "Both!"

Some in the group laughed, others just seemed uncomfortable. "Alright girls, get a partner we're doing

156

drills. I'm going to drill the sweat right out of every one of you today." A few groaned and Len spun around, "Hey! If you want to be pussies like Allee then get out of here." He walked down the line, the boys stiff at attention, "Who's complaining?" He looked into each teenagers eyes, "Speak up. You Frankie? You complaining?"

"No, Mr. Lamont."

Len walked, "You, Poindexter?"

"No, Mr. Lamont," Jose said pushing up his glasses.

"Well? No one's complaining? What? Am I hearing voices?" Len walked back up the line. "You think I'm a retard or something? This is a volunteer wrestling team, if you don't want to be here, go and paint cars with Pussy Charlie. I don't need you." As he reached the end of the line he said, "If you're going to wrestle then get a partner, if your not, then get your scrawny little asses out of here."

The line dissolved into groups of two and they waited for Len's instructions.

The phone rang. Cindy set the sweet potato she was peeling on the counter and wiped here hands with the dish towel then answered it.

"Mrs. Allee, this is Len Lamont. Is Charles there?"

"Oh, yes, he's out in the garage." Cindy wasn't accustomed to getting a call at home from a teacher, not forgetting what Butch had dealt with earlier with Margaret, the sheriff and the principal, she was immediately concerned. "Is there a problem?"

"Charles didn't show up for wrestling practice today and I was concerned if he was sick. Did Charles come home sick today, Mrs. Allee?"

Cindy hesitated..."I'll let Charles talk to you, Mr. Lamont, hold on and I'll get him." She quickly walked out to the garage door, pushed it open and poked her head in.

"Charles, Mr. Lamont is on the phone. He said you didn't go to wrestling practice today."

Charles was cleaning the sprayer getting ready for another color on the fender flames, he looked up at his Mom with that look that kids have when they've been caught. "He's on the phone now?" Cindy gave him that look that parents give when they're asked a dumb question by their kids who have just been caught. "Yes Charles, he's on the phone right now." She watched as Charles didn't move. "He's waiting." Cindy went back to the house and picked up the phone, "He's coming Mr. Lamont." She went back to peeling the sweet potatoes getting them ready for mashing.

The back door opened and Charles slowly walked in. He looked at his Mom, then at the phone resting on the counter, then picked it up, "Hello?"

"Hey Charles, the girls missed you today. What's up?"

"Hi, Mr. Lamont. I...guess I forgot."

Cindy shook her head and rolled her eyes.

The other end of the line was silent.

Charles was silent.

Len waited.

"Mr. Lamont?"

"I'm still here, Charles, like a wet dream you can't roll away from. You know Charles, I'm just wondering when you're going to stop lying to me and tell me what's going on?"

Charles swallowed. "I really forgot--"

"Forgot!? You've been coming to practice for months and now you suddenly forgot. Don't hand me that shit Charles. We have a regional match with Colorado in one month. I need you and I'll expect you to be at practice tomorrow. Got it?"

"Yes sir."

Len hung up but Charles held onto the phone his eyes staring at the back of his Moms head, "Ok, Mr. Lamont. So no practice till next week? That's too bad. Ok, thanks for calling." Charles hung up.

Without turning around Cindy said, "Charles if you don't want to wrestle you don't have to. No ones forcing you to."

No one at home, he thought. "I'm goin' back out to the garage call me when dinner's ready."

"Ok sweetie."

Thirty One

"Oh my God! What a view!" Sandra said not censoring any girlish enthusiasm as she stood in front of the window in Alex's living room. She had heard he had money but she never really knew how much. Now she was certain.

"I guess it is pretty nice," he said. "You kinda get used to it.

"Get used to it? How could you? Its so...breathtaking."

Alex wasn't sure how to answer her subtle confrontation. "You want something to drink Sandra?" She turned now standing against the backdrop of the black sky and city lights. Alex now really looked at her, not as a nurse or co-worker but as a woman; a sexy woman at that. Turquoise fetishes danced above her breasts, her hair was pulled back accenting the line of her jaw and the straightness of her nose. Her hips were neatly packaged beneath a black skirt. She stood taller than usual, her Margarita boots adding an inch or two.

"Some red wine would be nice."

He stared at her. "You look...very un-nurse-like tonight Sandra."

"Oh, wow, what a compliment Alex." She pursed her lips. "You don't need to be uncomfortable with me."

"That sounded silly didn't it? I'm not used to complimenting a fellow worker." That seemed cold. He decided he should just shut up for now. Alex wasn't used to complimenting a woman at all. Not since Lisa died. He used to tell her how beautiful she was, how 'turned-on' she made him feel. Comfortable compliments. Now he says stuff like this. "Sandra, I'm just a little rusty at this, I'm sorry. Now what was it you wanted to drink?"

"Red wine."

"You don't like white?"

"I never have, it tastes too much like alcohol to me. Red tastes like...well it's much smoother, there's more flavor..."

"Bouquet." Alex added, then wished he hadn't corrected her.

"I just like red better. It's easier to get drunk on."

Alex raised an eyebrow and went to the wine rack for a bottle. He walked in holding two goblets of wine and saw that Sandra was still looking out the window.

"This is so beautiful, Alex." She turned and took the goblet from him, holding it up for a toast, "To life." Her eyes twinkled.

"Can't argue with that, To Life." Their glasses tinked together and they each sipped.

"Mmm, that's a great wine." She deeply inhaled as she swirled the wine in the glass.

"New Zealand merlot. I have a case shipped in four times a year." Why did I say that? Twice in five minutes. Am I trying to impress her? Like a stupid teenager? "I'm sorry. I didn't mean to sound so uppity."

"You have too much money Alex." She peeked over he rim of the goblet. "So what other extravagant things do you do?"

She waved him off, "I'm just pokin' at you a bit Alex. You're kind of stiff tonight."

Stiff? That was an understatement. How about scared or panicked? That would work. Hell, the last woman in his penthouse was the cleaning woman. He couldn't remember the last time he had a real woman at his home. Or any guests at all. He was full of secrets, he shared with no one. He remembered what he was thinking when listening to Butch: Secrets kill people.

"Sandra, I'm just not used to having-- "

"—are you uncomfortable because we work together?" She took a step away.

"No. No, that's not it. I'm just not used to having *anyone* up here. I guess I've become something of a loner."

"Well that's too bad. You have all this great stuff and no one to share it with. Sounds lonely to me." She noticed his sad expression. "How come shrinks can't cure themselves?"

With a snicker he said, "You're assuming shrinks need curing."

Sandra laughed out loud, "Are you kidding? Of course they do. Isn't that why you guys get into psychology? Because you have problems?" She immediately knew how that sounded. "I'm sorry, Alex, I didn't mean how that came out. I'm shooting off my mouth trying to lighten things up and I put my big foot right in there."

"More like a green and red boot." He smiled.

She glanced down at her new cowboy boots, "Yeah, my boots." She looked him in the eyes, their gaze connecting for just a few seconds and Sandra blurted out, "Oh what the fuck, Alex, lets get this over with." She stepped forward and planted a long, soft kiss on his lips.

To his shock he kissed back.

Their mouths separated just a few inches and she licked her lips. "That was real nice Alex, I hope you didn't mind."

"Actually Sandra, I've been wanting to do that for a year...I just didn't know how."

"I love new students."

"I love new teachers."

Still holding wine goblets, they kissed again. Then Alex said, "Actually, after we had dinner together I've been thinking about my motives."

"I called *you* Alex, they were my motives."

He leaned back a bit. "No, my motives. The real reasons I got into psychology?"

"Oh, *those* motives," she said with a bit of disappointment.

"What I'm...uncovering in myself isn't real nice."

"Why are you telling me this now?" She tried to be light hearted, "Don't you want to make-out some more? Review a few old lessons?"

"I do. But I opened up to you, at dinner. After all these years, finally I actually started looking inside myself. Lets sit down." Alex walked over to the circular leather couch and sat. Sandra sat next to him pulling her leg up and under her other leg, keeping her boot off the leather.

"Since Lisa died, I guess over the years I've just isolated myself and went on this war path of revenge." Alex turned toward her, "But you know what really's been battering me?" He didn't expect an answer but waited just the same. "Butch Allee."

Sandra scrunched up her face. "Butch Allee? That wild man at the center?"

Alex was nodding, "Yeah, *that* wild man. Though after you get to know him he's really not a wild man at all. You noticed that before me. He's tame...traumatized actually. Deeply scarred about killing that wrestling star from Kersey." Alex opened the safe on his locked-away thoughts. "When you see him for the first time and you know he smashed someone's skull in with a rock, you think, 'Of course he killed someone, probably didn't bother him a bit.' But the fact that he killed this man, even though he was found not guilty and set free, it's still eating him up inside... like a guilty ravenous cancer. Like his soul was murdered. That's what made him psychotic. That's what brought him in. Guilt. And guilt only comes from someone with a conscience. That conscience is killing him."

Sandra hadn't sipped any wine, she had let kissing go for now and just listened to Alex.

"If it had been me? I wouldn't have one bit of guilt. I'd be boasting. I'd probably write a article on the Cleansing of Revenge."

"Narcissism," said Sandra.

Alex was animated, "Correct. I have it, Butch doesn't. Lack of guilt creates monsters...anti-social personality disorder, myself excluded of course, but guilt creates pain and pain propels people to make change. That's what got me thinking. Am I that cold? Is Butch Allee that sensitive? He looks like a killer and he's not. I look like a mild mannered doctor... and I'm not. After Lisa was murdered, I was homicidal. I just wanted...I *needed* to kill Albert Soccorro. I had detailed plans in my head, I fantasized about it, dreamt about it. I was obsessed with this feeling that when I did it, I'd do it right. Not make any mistakes. I was that close. Then after some time, I thought, no. Don't kill him, send him away for life. That would be my revenge. Who'd ever think I was capable of these ideas...these plans. Nothing is what it seems." His heart pounded and he could feel his chest heaving. He had disclosed probably way to much. Especially on a first date. "You probably want to leave now."

"No. It's exactly what I wanted to hear."

His eye's squinted and he bit the inside of his cheek.

Sandra started right in. "I knew you were lonely. Even through all that Kevlar coating I knew you were sensitive. But you keep everyone out. The staff can feel it at work. I didn't know much about Lisa, but I've been in mental health for years and I don't need a Ph.D. to know when someone's depressed. Even if it's the doctor. I could see you struggling and that's why I gave you that book." She stared into his eyes. "Your more like Butch Allee than you admit."

"How's that?" He couldn't wait to hear this.

"Your guilt is killing you."

The wind just got knocked from him but he didn't show it. She was right. So fucking right that it scared him. "So if you knew all this, why come over here and hang out with me?"

"Because you're a babe." She smiled, "I admit it, I'm shallow." She laughed now
and drank the wine.

"I like shallow girls." He didn't feel like disclosing anymore; he already said way too much and way too fast. But it felt okay. "Thanks for listening to my craziness, Sandra."

"Anytime, Alex. I mean that."

He smiled at her. "Would you like to watch a movie?"

"Sure. Is there a theatre close by?"

Alex reached behind the couch and grabbed the remote on the table. He pushed a button and the large viewing screen slowly scrolled down from its hiding place in the ceiling. At the same time, a projector behind them slowly lowered then clicked into place.

Sandra watched with amusement. "You really do have too much money, Alex, but it's so much fun."

"How about Young Frankenstein?"

"I haven't seen that in years, I love it."

Alex pushed another button and the movie started.

Sandra scooted closer. She felt his arm wrap around her shoulders pulling her close. "Be careful of my hump," she said, "It moves around."

Alex laughed. "How 'bout those knockers?"

"Alex, I never knew you noticed."

"It's...it's in the movie...Dr. Frankenstein's at the door..."

"...I was just teasing. Quit worrying Alex, I won't sue you if you want to bang my knockers."

They both laughed, but Alex laughed with nervous excitement.

"I guess through all these years, I never tried to figure you out," Alex said.

"Stop trying to analyze me. Lets just have some fun."

He liked what he heard and nodded. He smiled at Sandra and said, "I am having fun." She leaned into him and kissed him again. Through his lips he mumbled, "A lot of fun."

"You ain't seen nothing yet, Doctor."

Thirty Two

February 18

Kersey

Butch had the bedcovers pulled up over his face leaving only scraggly locks of brown graying hair hanging out. He was deep in sleep, exhausted from strenuous work at the bindery that had been especially tough last night. At six in the morning he stumbled into the house, skipped a shower and just crawled into bed next to Cindy.

Rhythmic breathing and dreamy fantasy had taken hold when, without warning he was tackled in bed. A sudden bouncing weight was on top of him, he stirred from the deep sleep, then the covers were ripped from his head, he startled, then a scream, another bouncing body and a jab in his stomach with a foot, a heavier weight landed on his back with fingers clawing at the covers, yanking, pulling. Then giggling and laughing and as the sheets were yanked from his bare chest. "Happy birthday to you, happy birthday to you, happy birthday to Daaadddy. Happy birthday to you," all three kids sang.

Butch tried to pull the sheets back over his body, but the kids wouldn't let him. He laughed and sat up in bed, rubbed his eyes, ran his fingers through his hair and smiled broadly, "Wow, my birthday already? I forgot."

"Oh Daddy, no you didn't," said Margaret who was fighting for cuddle-room next to Lea in the double bed, Charles snuggled under the covers. They looked up and watched as Cindy walked in holding a birthday cake with lit candles.

"Make a wish!" squealed Margaret.

The kids watched as Butch leaned over toward the cake. "I wish--"

"Don't tell us it won't come true," said Lea.

Butch chuckled, closed his eyes, paused to make a wish and blew out all the candles. "We havin' cake and ice cream for breakfast?"

"Yeah!" All three screamed in unison. Even Charles got excited about that.

"What did you wish? What did you wish?" said Margaret.

"I'm not supposed to tell," Butch said crossing his arms pretending to be seven.

"It's okay to tell *after* you blow out the candles."

Butch laughed, "Oh it is, huh?" He grabbed Margaret and Lea in a big hug and kissed them both on their faces. "I wished for three smart, good looking kids and a sexy wife."

Lea's expression was one of disappointment, "That's what you wished for? You already have that, Daddy."

"Well then, I got my wish." Butch winked at Cindy. "Ok, take the cake into the kitchen and Charles you cut up some pieces for all of us. I'll be there in a second." Margaret jumped from the bed and quickly swiped a finger through the icing, stuck it in her mouth and ran out the door.

"Hey no fair," yelled Lea running after her. Charles took the cake from his Mom.

"Be careful," she said.

"Hurry up Dad or we'll eat it all," said Charles as he walked out the bedroom.

"You better save me a piece."

"Don't eat any 'til we all get in there," scolded Cindy.

Butch dropped back into bed, grabbed a pillow and snuggled up to it. "I wish this pillow was you."

Cindy grinned. "That was a nice wish are you sure you got the last part?"

"Of course, I wasn't sure about the *first* part," he chuckled.

"Hey! All the kids look like you, of course they're good looking," said Cindy.

"And they all are smart, so they must of got that from you." Butch winked at her.

Cindy sat on the bed. "Forty six. I can't believe I'm married to such an old man."

Butch grabbed her and pulled her next to him. "An old man who feels eighteen." His hand slid up Cindy's tee shirt.

She squirmed, "I thought you wanted cake and ice cream with the kids?"

"How 'bout I eat the cake and ice cream off your belly?"

"I'll yell for 'em to bring it back in here." Cindy playfully slapped his chest. "Get out there, they have presents for you." She put her arms around his neck and kissed him, his beard always felt scratchy but comforting, "I love you. I'm glad you were born today."

Butch's eyes twinkled, "Me too."

Cindy got up and Butch rolled out of bed, slid on jeans and a pulled on a shirt and bounced into the kitchen. "Where's my birthday breakfast?"

Butch and all three kids ate cake and ice cream, then piled the dishes into the sink. "I'll open my presents after you get home from school. I'm taking the night off work and spending it at home," said Butch.

"Great, Dad," said Charles "we can paint some more of the car. See ya'." Charles kissed his Dad goodbye.

"Love you, Daddy," said Lea. Butch kissed her, then she ran for the door.

"You're the best Daddy ever," said Margaret giving him a big kiss and a hug.

Butch felt warm inside.

Margaret let the screen door slam shut while Butch turned to Cindy, "We was one man short at the bindery last night, so I'm beat. I'm going back to bed for a while."

"It's your day honey, you can do what ever you want. I've got to get ready for the clinic so I'll get my clothes out of the bedroom and you can sleep the day away."

Butch crawled back into bed and slept part of the day away. He ate cake again for lunch, then watched an old John Wayne movie on TV. The kids got home about three. Charles and Butch spent a few hours putting the finishing touches on the hood of the Monte Carlo. Then dinner came and went. Margaret and Lea went to bed and Charles asked to go over to Tommy's house, since school was closed the next day.

"Hey Charles, you want to go with me and get some paint thinner so we can start on the trunk tomorrow?"

A mixture of disappointment and conflict slid across Charles face, Butch read it immediately. "Oh you can go see Tommy, I'll get it for you." Charles beamed, gave his Dad a hug and ran out the front door.

"Cindy, I'm running to town you need anything?"

"Nope, I'd go with you but the girls are fast asleep."

"Remember when they was really young and we'd lock our bedroom door, slip out the window and have breakfast at Grandma's alone?"

Cindy closed here eyes and shook her head, "That was bad."

"Nah, they just thought we was asleep."

"Go." She said.

He smiled, slid on his coat from work and went outside.

It was cold, the air bit at his nose and ears, but there was no snow. Butch started up the station wagon and drove into town about half an hour away. He got the paint thinner, then sat in the car just warming up. Then it occurred to him, I didn't get my drink. The *Oasis* bar gave away a drink of choice on your birthday; an unwritten ritual and only the locals knew to ask. Butch turned the corner and drove down the street to the *Oasis*. He waltzed through the swinging doors and hunkered up at the bar as Lynyrd Skynard blared from the jukebox in the background. He scanned the place: A couple other men at the bar, a few folks in booths and two playing pool.

"Butch Allee!" Evan grinned, "Don't see ya much in here, what gives?"

"A birthday drink, Evan. How about a Black Velvet."

"Birthday? What are you...forty..."

"Six."

"Forty six. You got it Butch. That's all you want?" Evan laid his palms on the bar. "On birthdays I'm usually pouring the best stuff in the house or a strawberry daiquiri for the ladies."

"You want me drinking a daiquiri in your bar?" Butch grinned through his beard.

"I'd have to kick your ass out before someone else did." Evan laughed at him as he poured the drink for Butch and laid it on the bar. "Happy birthday, old boy."

"Thanks, Evan. Any new tattoos?"

Evan leaned on the bar, "Oh man, Butch, I got a great lookin' American Flag on my back. Got it in Cheyenne from Juan at The Pigment Palace." Evan turned around and pulled up his shirt.

"Man it's beautiful." Butch slowly sipped the Black Velvet. "That's a good choice Evan. Nice and big too. I need to get me a flag, but I'm running out of skin."

Evan lowered his shirt and turned back toward Butch. "You got me there Butch." Evan quickly scanned his bar: No one seemed to need him a the moment. "Which one is your favorite?"

Butch rubbed his arm, "I have a couple. An eagle on my chest--"

"Flyin' over the mountains right? I've seen it when your ridin' your bike."

"Yeah, I like that one a lot. I got a 'C' on my shoulder, when Charles was born. That ones important to me, and of course my flames."

"I like that fire too. Never in my whole life have I met anyone else with a fire tattoo on his forehead. I really like those spider webs on those big paws of yours. Hey you ever been up to Sturgis?"

"No, never have Evan, but I bet it's fun."

Evan leaned into Butch's face, "You and Cindy, and me and Joleen should ride up there together. It's a blast, a weekend of drinking, tattoos, bikes and tits. Nothin' like it on earth." Evan's eyes spilled with anticipation. "It's hot as hell and dusty...dirty like you never seen before." Evan glanced both ways down the bar then back at Butch, "Ever bang a vag full of sand?" He didn't wait for Butch to answer, "We call it rough ridin'." Evan laughed out loud.

An annoyed voice behind them interrupted their fun, "Evan! Are you going to quit gabbing and get us another pitcher?"

Evan looked up and Butch turned his head; Len Lamont was walking up to them, his face tense.

"I thought that was you, Allee? No one could miss that hair."

"Len, leave my customers alone." Evan straightened up and tried to look authoritative.

"Just get us a pitcher. Sometime tonight would be swell." Len turned and went back to the booth.

Evan watched him. "You know for a volunteer fireman, coach and a father he sure gets nasty when he drinks. Most the time he's a nice guy, but put a couple in him..." Evan shook his head. "He's been sittin' over there with his brother and Alisha just puttin' 'em down. Hell, I think he alone pays my mortgage here."

Evan brought Len his pitcher and checked on other customers, made a few drinks and served them, then walked back behind the bar.

Butch tilted his head back and swallowed the last drip from the glass. "Thanks again, Evan. I'll have to let you know about Sturgis. Got to get permission from Cindy, you know." Butch chuckled and Evan made a face like *Good Luck*.

Butch got up from the bar stool and felt a presence behind him. "Going so early Allee?" Len stepped in front of Butch and blocked his way. "Don't see you in here much. In fact don't see you hanging around town much either. You too good for us? You and all that Graff Farm money?"

The smell of alcohol was heavy on Len's breath and Butch could easily smell it. He felt uneasy with this conversation.

"I haven't had a parent-teacher conference with you lately...thought you might like to know your boy hasn't been attending wrestling practice." Butch stood still "I've been wondering why he isn't disciplined better."

Len was easily five to six inches taller and more than sixty pounds heavier and stood just a little too close to Butch. Even so Butch's gaze never left Len's eyes.

"How I discipline my kids is none of your business. Now would you move so I can go home?"

Len put his right hand on the bar blocking his exit, "You know, Allee. Last year Charles was a tiger, unbelievable, he ripped the competition apart. And this year?" Len snickered, rubbed his nose with his index finger and looked at the floor like he was embarrassed. "This year...Charles is a cat all right...a big pussy."

Butch's face grew tight, "Don't--"

"—a pussy. Did you hear that, Allee? But should I expect anything else? Look at his old man." Len leaned his body forward while still holding onto the bar, "You're nothing but a long-haired, tattooed, loser. That's my boy, Charles is going to be just like you...a big fucking loser." Len's demeanor changed. "You know what, Allee? I think you could use a little discipline right now."

"You're talkin' about my son." Butch stood his ground while breathing the stale air that Len exhaled. He had no desire to get into a fight with Len Lamont, who was drunk and huge, but he wasn't sure if he could walk out of there without one.

"Len! Get back to your booth and let Butch go home," scolded Evan, a safe distance away.

Len slapped the air with his hand, dismissing him. "Charles could be really good if he only got some decent encouragement at home. You're wasting great wrestling talent Allee, don't you understand that? Can't you get that through your thick empty skull?"

Butch felt threatened and not many men made him feel that way. His right hand slid into the pocket of his work jacket and his fingers felt cold metal, a tool from work.

"You *want* him to grow up to be just like you? A fucking loser?" Len took a step closer.

In desperation Butch pulled the box cutter from his pocket and held it between him and Len. "Get outta the way Len. I'll use it if I have too."

"Oh shit," said Evan, and he went for the phone.

"Len stop it!" Alisha grabbed her husbands shirt sleeve and yanked on it at the same time seeing the box cutter in Butch's hand. "Oh my God. Stop this both of you." She glared at Butch, then her eyes pleaded with Len. She pulled on his arm again but being just about five feet tall her impact was minimal. "Len stop. Please. Listen to me. Please. Come on back to the booth with me." She turned back to Butch. "I'm sorry. He's drunk. Don't pay any attention to him."

Len's brother, Gregg, walked between the two men and with authority said, "Len end this now. Get back to your seat."

Butch had slipped the box cutter back into his pocket and Gregg never saw it.

"Come on." Gregg grabbed Len's shoulder and was able to turn him then guide him back to the booth.

Butch let out a breath. "Evan I'm outta here. Thanks." Butch chopped the air sideways, his hand perpendicular to the floor. Evan did the same while talking on the phone and Butch left.

When he got outside he stood there feeling his heart racing. He took a couple of breaths, "Shit! What a birthday present." He rubbed his face with his hands, "That's why I stay home."

****

Charles pulled the half-painted Monte Carlo towards his house and Tommy snuffed out a cigarette in the ashtray.

"It's almost one in the morning, your Mom's going to beat your little ass for being out so late," chided Tommy.

But Charles wasn't listening. "Who's truck is that in my driveway?"

Tommy peered through the windshield moving his head side to side to get a better look. "Who's ever truck it is, he's on your front porch."

Charles pushed up his glasses and squinted at the figure standing in the porch light, his back toward them, one arm leaning against the porch beam. "Who would be at our house at one in the morning?"

They watched the man stumble down the porch step, walk over to the side of the house, open the screen door and with his fist bang on the locked wooden door. The outside light now caught the features of his face.

"It's Mr. Lamont!" said Charles.

"Shit, it is. He was pissed at you for skippin' practice."

"What's he doing here now?" said Charles. "He's going to wake everyone up."

"He must really want you at practice, Allee. Jesus Christ, comin' to your house to tell ya."

Charles fished in his pants pocket, "Here's the front door key go inside and get my Dad."

"What? Me? Your Dad'll kill me wakin' him up."

"Just do it."

"What if your Mom's naked?"

Charles gave him a look.

"What are *you* going to do?" asked Tommy.

Charles watched as Len leaned up against the inside door. "Shit I don't know, talk to him I guess."

They both got out the car and Charles headed for the side of the house while Tommy ran to the front porch.

Len saw Charles walking toward him, he let the screen door slam and headed right for him. "Hey Pussy." Len's long strides covered the distance quickly.

The intensity of Len's posture sent a jolt of fear through Charles and he froze in the middle of the tiny yard. Before he knew it Len grabbed him by the shoulder, spun him around and gripped him in a head-lock. Pain exploded in his face as Len's fist smashed into Charles nose, his glasses flew off somewhere and blood splattered across his face. Charles felt his knees weaken. Len released his grip and Charles crumbled onto the frosted ground.

"Get up pussy! Is that what I taught you?" Len leaned over and in one huge grasp grabbed Charles's coat and pants simply hoisted him up off the ground. "Stand up you little fucking loser. Stand up!"

Charles staggered upward, weaved, his vision was blurry from blood, pain, and no glasses. He was stunned from the assault and eked out: "Hey, Coach what --" He didn't finish.

"You need this, boy." Len slapped him in the face, the same way he slapped Alisha. "No discipline at home. What you need is a *real* Dad. One who will set your scrawny ass straight." For a second time Len hauled off with another punch to Charles's bloodied face sending Charles stumbling backward and falling against the hood of Len's truck, he slid down the grill onto the dirt driveway.

Butch jumped and kind of yelped as Tommy shook him awake. "Charles's gettin' beat up outside, you gotta get out there!"

"What?" This was no birthday surprise. Butch sprung from the bed and parted the curtains looking out the window just as Len picked Charles up off the ground. Butch grabbed his jeans, slid them on and bolted outside screaming, "Get your fuckin' hands off my boy."

Len spun around. In the moon light Butch could see Len's eyes looking wild and angry, the fear Butch felt at the bar jumped alive inside him.

"You're next you tattooed freak." Len came at him.

Sleepy and scared, but knowing he had to do something, Butch quickly scanned the yard and took two steps toward Len. He bent down, grabbed the hose with the lawn sprinkler and swung it in a circle above his head. The sprinkler head sang and sparkled in the porch light. Len was almost on top of him as Butch's sinewy muscles give it one last spin like an old fashioned slingshot, and the metal sprinkler head smashed into Len's temple.

Len drunkenly screamed and doubled over grabbing his face, the blood was seeping through his fingers and dripping onto the grass.

Behind Len, Butch could see Charles who was now standing next to the truck, he yelled, "Get inside and call the cops."

Len, still bent over, charged towards Butch. His head and massive shoulders caught Butch in the belly and forced him backwards. Butch stumbled, nearly falling, he pawed at Len's shirt, pulling it up and over his head all the while feeling the deep, solid punches in his chest and then exploding pain in his kidneys. Butch's hands were groping about Len's body, pulling his shirt further over his head trying to impede Len's blows.

Len was grunting, his breathing heavy and loud; he ripped off his shirt and threw it to the ground. He was big: muscles forged over the years of wrestling, farming and construction. The sight of him sent terror through Butch's battered body.

"Get off my property!" Butch yelled out.

Charles was now on the porch opening the door and running inside. Cindy was at the window already calling 911.

Butch tried to move closer to the house, but Len caught him, knocking him backward onto the gravel driveway. They rolled around until Butch was on his back in Cindy's rock garden, small rocks and dead weeds dug at his skin. With his massive bulk, Len pinned him to the ground, his fist slammed into Butch's face--the pain rocketed into his eye and through his brain. There was no way out from the crushing weight of Len's body.

Groping and reaching upward, Butch grabbed at anything: hair, an ear, an arm, clawing for a hold all the while trying to avoid another devastating blow. But Len seemed superhuman, intensely strong, drunk and wrestling-fast, he simply grabbed Butch's frantic hands and crushed them in his own. Desperation welled in his gut and for an instant he saw Len's eyes, cold, intense, brimming with rage, his breath white in the night air, heavy with beer and cigarettes. Instantly Butch knew Len could kill him right now, right here in his own front yard.

Butch flailed his arm to the side, his bare skin instantly stinging against the icy cold earth in the garden, his fingers searching, clawing at dirt, dead flowers and weeds. His finger tips felt it: A rock. With frantic, grappling fingers he loosened the decorative rock from its shallow hole, griped it tight and swung it fast and hard up against Len's forehead.

Len belched out a low groan, grabbed his face and his massive body weaved, teetered and like Goliath collapsed into the dirt.

Butch rolled away from Len's body, scrambled to his knees and stood up. He dropped the rock onto the ground. He watched as Len struggled to his knees. Like a monster in a cheap horror flick, Len straighten and towered upward like a beast that wouldn't die, his breath snorting in the cold night air. He was shirtless and looked huge. Len slowly rolled his head, his eyes trying to focus. He took an awkward step, then stumbled backward toward his truck.

Butch was exhausted. Smoking, beer and his forty-six birthday was working against him. He bent over and rested his palms on his knees, his chest heaved, his face throbbed and his kidneys were killing him. He was twice as old as Len and hadn't worked out in years, a rush of relief warmed him as he watched Len lumber away.

Len grabbed the door handle on the passenger side of the truck. He flung it open and partially climbed in.

Then Butch saw it: Len's rifle was waiting in the rack on the back window.

Len reached for the rifle, but Butch was already there and grabbed him by the pants pulling him back outside. Len struggled, holding onto the seatbelt, resisting what ever energy Butch had left in his body. He lost his footing and slid down the side of the seat, Butch grabbed the truck door, swung it open and slammed it hard into Len's body. Len shuddered and tried to stand. Butch slammed the door again against Len's shoulder causing him to slid down the seat, his arm stretched out, his hand holding firmly onto the seatbelt, Butch slammed the door again. This time the metal frame smashed into the side of Len's neck and head. Len couldn't hold on any longer and his body spilt onto the ground.

Butch backed away and looked up as headlights blinded him; he stumbled backward, half running, toward his house

A car sped onto the front yard, onto the grass and stopped. Gregg and Alisha jumped out. As Len stood up and leaned against the truck, Gregg ran toward Butch.

Butch, unsure of what to expect, waited and Gregg cold cocked him in the face. Butch crumbled to the ground and Gregg kicked him in the stomach.

Charles then stepped out onto the porch, "I got your gun, Dad, I'm going to kill him."

"No!" yelled Butch, weakly holding his hand up into the air.

Gregg got a quick glimpse of Charles holding a rifle and he left Butch on the ground. He ran back to Len who had pulled himself up against the truck, he put his arm around his brother's shoulder and lowered him to the ground. Alisha was at Len's side.

Butch stumbled up the porch stairs, blood coated his face and beard and was smeared about his chest. He took the .22 rifle from Charles and holding it with the barrel pointed upwards yelled, "Get off my property. All of you."

A second set of headlights lit up the tiny yard as Sheriff McCallum pulled up.

Thirty Three

McCallum stepped from the patrol car and quickly assessed the scene, "Damn brawl" he said under his breath.

Cindy was on the porch with a warm wet cloth cleaning up Butch's face. Gregg and Alisha were next to Len.

"Put the gun down and don't come off the porch, Butch," McCallum ordered.

"They was trespassing and beat up Charles," said Butch.

McCallum walked toward Len who was now standing again.

Len took two or three wavering steps and wrapped his arm around the Sheriff's shoulders, "I'm real sorry to get you outta bed, John." Len's breath coated his face.

"You've been drinking again?" McCallum gritted his teeth as he removed Len's arm. "What's going on here?" He glared at Gregg and Alisha, Len leaned his bulk against the patrol car hood. He's so drunk he can't even stand up, thought McCallum. He looked back toward the porch and walked toward the house. "Butch, set that rifle on the porch."

Butch did as he was told.

"What happened here?"

Butch was trembling from cold and fear: "Tommy woke me up and said Charles was getting beat up, I looked out the window and I saw Lamont beating up Charles and I went outside and Lamont started beating' on me, we wrestled around in the garden over there and I hit him in the head with a rock. Then he tried to get his gun outta his truck and I hit him with the truck door. Then Gregg came and beat on me, then you came. They was trespassing Sheriff and I was defending Charles."

There was no blood on Butch's face now and Sheriff McCallum took no notes. "Who's is that?" He pointed to a Coors on the porch.

"It ain't mine," said Butch. "It must be Lamont's."

Anger boiled in McCallum's gut. All he was doing lately was dealing drunks. "Stay here." McCallum walked from the porch and strode toward the other three. "Gregg turn around you're under arrest."

"What? Me? What for?" Gregg went wild, he started jumping about like a bantam rooster in a cock fight. "Arrest that fucking asshole," he pointed toward Butch. "We didn't do nothin'."

"Do as I say, Gregg."

"Fuck, no way you putting cuffs on me, John." Gregg tried to run toward the porch but McCallum grabbed him and wrestled him to the ground all the while Gregg struggled to get loose.

"Stop fighting me, Gregg, you're getting yourself in deeper." With McCallum's size he simply overpowered Gregg, twisted his arm behind his back and slipped a cuff on, followed by another. He literally picked Gregg up off the ground and threw him into the back of the patrol car. John was breathing heavy as he grabbed the patrol car mic, "I need an ambulance at 210 Fourth Street. Alcohol intoxication and possible head injury." He stepped from the car, "Alisha what are you doing here?"

She was obviously flustered and seemed to babble about, "John, no, ah, Len..." she put her hand to her mouth, "is he going to be alright, John?"

"I called an ambulance, now tell me what happened."

"Well, I don't know exactly." She looked about. "Len was, no we was all in the kitchen, Len said he was going to check on the calves out back--" she suddenly went pale, "Oh no! My boys are home alone."

McCallum shook his head he couldn't believe what he was hearing. "I'll call Logan to go check on 'em. Then what happened."

"Well, we were at the *Oasis* and Butch threatened Len with a knife, then we went home and we was all drinking, Len went to check on the calves and then we heard his truck drive out the driveway and we followed him here." She started to cry, "Oh my God, then Butch was hittin' him and then hittin' Gregg and Charles had a gun...and I was afraid they was going to shoot us. I didn't do anything wrong, Sheriff." She was babbling and crying, not making much sense. "Why is Gregg arrested? I'm not bein' arrested am I, Sheriff? I didn't do anything wrong."

"Go home, Alisha. I'll take care of things from here."

"No, I don't want to leave Len. Are you goin' to call Loogy to
check on my boys?"

"You should go home, Alisha."

The ambulance pulled up and they quickly examined Len who was now sitting on the hood of the patrol car. He was slurring his words, but was talking and answering the mini-mental status questions that ambulance crews routinely ask. They loaded
Len onto the gurney and slid him into the back.

"I want to go with him," said Alisha, and she climbed in. Gregg remained in the back of the patrol car as McCallum walked back to the porch where Charles, Butch and Cindy were waiting. He looked about the yard: A sprinkler and hose, a chain with a metal ball on the end Butch sometimes used for hand starting a Harley, the Coors bottle on the porch. Nothing else really caught his eye. "I'm arresting Gregg for trespassing, it seems that Alisha backs up your story that Len came out here drunk but she said you beat them up."

Butch was aghast, "How could I beat up them two? You see the size of Lamont? No way. They was beating on me. He started on Charles first, then me."

"I don't see any blood on you. Turn around."

Butch held out his arms and turned. McCallum didn't make any comments as he eyed tattooed skin. No signs of any cuts or bruises.

"Cindy just cleaned me up," said Butch.

McCallum looked at Charles, "Why did Len come over here to see you?"

Charles pushed up his glasses, "I don't know. He called me a name and grabbed me in a wrestling hold and hit me and was yelling at me for not going to wrestling practice."

"Len came over here at one in the morning because of wrestling practice?"

"Yeah, he just showed up and was banging on the doors. Tommy'll tell you the same thing."

McCallum shook his head. "Alisha said you pulled a knife on Len at the *Oasis.*"

"He threatened me there. You can ask Evan. I pulled out my box cutter that I use at work, but nothing happened."

"Butch I need you and Charles to stay around here for a few days untill I sort this out."

"I wasn't going anywhere's anyway, Sheriff," said Butch.

McCallum walked from the porch, got into the patrol car and drove off.

Butch, looking scared and turned to Cindy, "They're going to railroad me on this. You watch."

Thirty Four

Gossip in Kersey spreads like the smell of cow manure on a windy day especially when word got out that Len Lamont lapsed into a coma and was airlifted to Denver General Hospital. He was put on life support for two days.

Len Lamont died on the third day. The surgeon found he had a brain bleed that went undiagnosed on that first day. Sheriff McCallum received notice from the District Attorney who was now involved. McCallum and Logan went to Butch's house.

McCallum was distant and cold as Butch stepped out onto the porch. "Butch Allee you're under arrest for assault and second degree murder in the death of Len Lamont. Put your hands behind your back and don't make a scene."

Butch went pale. "He died? When?"

"Today," spit Logan, "from the beating *you* gave him."

"What?" Panic splashed across Butch's face. He looked at Cindy, his eye's wild, he was seventeen again, scared, the inside of a jail cell shot into his mind. "I told you," he whispered, " I knew it."

Tears erupted from Cindy as she watched a nightmare start to unfold.

"Charles's gettin' arrested too," said Logan with summed up authority. "I knew we'd get you two someday."

Butch's heart broke open, "Charles? Charles didn't do nothing." His eye's pleading with McCallum, desperate now. "He was defending himself." Butch knew what the future held for boys in jail.

McCallum motioned with his head for Butch to turn around.

"John. Please. Don't put cuffs on him, he's just a kid. Arrest me. Put the cuffs on me, but please don't put 'em on Charles."

Logan jumped in, "He's goin' to whether you like it or not."

McCallum shot him a look and Logan shrunk a bit.

"Butch I have to, he's being charged with accessory to murder. Roy Parker the DA is filling the charges."

Cindy screamed, "Accessory to murder! Len Lamont came here and beat up my son and my husband and you're arresting us?" She could feel her heart beating out of control. "You son of a bitch! How can you do this?"

John glared at her, "They killed a man, and they're being charged by the DA, don't interfere with this."

"You've been against us from the beginning. Now you finally got what you wanted."

McCallum ignored her.

"Who's Roy Parker?" asked Butch.

"He's the District Attorney for this county. He's pressing the charges against you because you killed a man."

"It was self defense. It's because it was Len Lamont ain't it? Tell the truth Sheriff."

Logan yelled out, "Charles. This is Deputy Pike get in here."

Cindy let loose and gave Logan a quick shove in the chest, "Shut up you little insignificant ass. Don't you yell in my house."

Logan reached for his cuffs and John's jaw clenched. "Stop."

Charles slowly walked into the living room. He had never seen his Dad being arrested before and he remembered their conversation in the garage.

"Please let me talk to him," Butch said to McCallum.

John released his grip on Butch's wrists and Butch walked up to Charles.

"I heard it all," Charles said to his Dad.

"Charles. We'll take care of this. Don't you worry. Mom will call Grandpa and get a lawyer." Butch swallowed. He was near tears but held it back as he struggled with the words: "They got to put cuffs on you."

"I know."

"I'm sorry, Charles, you didn't do nothing wrong. Remember that. Always remember that, no matter what happens you didn't do nothing wrong."

Butch watched and almost broke as McCallum tightened the cuffs on Charles skinny wrists. He wanted to scream and cry, but he stayed strong. He knew if Charles saw him cry he'd see weakness and Butch needed to be tough so Charles could be tough too. Butch shoved it all down, deep down.

Logan's face sported a huge grin as he watched Butch and Charles standing there cuffed in their own living room, both looking scared. He leaned close to Butch, "The truth will set you free, Allee...or make you pee when they hang you."

"Fuck you." Butch wanted to spit in his face but he didn't.

Sheriff McCallum led Butch, and Logan led Charles out the door and into the back of the patrol car. Logan climbed in the passenger side and John went back toward the porch. It had been three days and the Coors bottle was gone. John picked up the ball and chain that was still laying in the yard, threw it in the trunk, then he drove to Kersey County Jail.

News spread quickly of Len Lamont's death. The TV stations started their morning broadcast with the story from Kersey, even NBC gave it five seconds of air hyping up the State Wrestling Champion angle. They had to, otherwise it was just another hick-town murder.

Butch and Charles were fingerprinted, photographed, and before being sent to two different sections of the jail

186

Butch looked deep into Charles eyes, "I love you...be tough. You gotta be tough."

The steel door creaked open and Butch hesitated, a sharp shove from behind sent him forcefully into the cell. He held back tears, but they weren't for himself. If anyone here saw him cry he'd be a goner. Butch sat on the lower cot and a groggy voice came from above, "Get the fuck off my bed asshole." Butch leaned over and looked up at a bald, wrinkly faced man, his mug stuck over the edge. "You hear me, get off my bed you louse-filled fuck. I've been here for nine months and these are my beds."

"So you get both. Where do I sleep?"

"Where the others slept, on the floor fuck face." The man rolled over with a grunt.

For just a second Butch sat there, then slid off the cot and stood up. He didn't want to, but he knew what he had to do. He reached up with two hands, grabbed the mans shirt and jerked him from the cot tumbling him down onto the floor. The man cringed at the sight of Butch, but didn't say a word as Butch beat him. He was old and stupid and took the beating with no resistance.

When Butch was done, he grabbed the man by his bloodied shirt and jerked him upward so he could look right into his eyes. "That is your bed, up there." He pointed. "This is my bed, down here. Now when you go to the showers tomorrow, you be sure to tell everyone this is how Butch Allee says Good Morning. You got it?"

The man was shaking, and he just nodded as his mouth was too bloodied to talk.

Thirty Five

The juvenile section was on the north side of the Kersey County Jail. Charles was seriously scared as he awkwardly hobbled down the hall; legs shackled and his wrists handcuffed. He had never seen the inside of a jail before.

The guard stopped and opened the steel door to a cell with four cots in it. Three boys, each sitting on their own cot, waited like vultures. The guard bent down and unlocked the leggings, then sent Charles into the cell. The door clanged shut. "Turn around and put your hands against the bars." Charles did as he was told. The guard unlocked his handcuffs and pulled them through. "Hey guys, here's the Len Lamont killer for you." The guard chuckled and walked away.

Charles looked about the cell. There were three boys with shaven heads and tired looking eyes. Tired of being locked up, but certainly not sleepy.

The older looking of the three jumped down from the top bunk and sauntered up to Charles. "Skinny four-eyed dick like you killed Coach Lamont? How's that possible?" He eyed Charles like he was the new wolf in their territory; he circled him as Charles stood still. "What you do, stick him from behind?"

"There aint no way he killed Lamont," said the other boy on the bed.

"Unless he tricked him," added the other.

"Yeah, like that old lady." In a mocking, child-like whiney voice: "Please help us find our cat, Mammy, he went under your car. Bam! Whacked her on top the head." He laughed hysterically.

The first boy poked his finger into Charles chest, the force made Charles lean back. "You goin' to say anything, four-eyes?"

Charles swallowed, he had heard the stories of life in jail; especially for young boys, boys with glasses, boys who are small and thin, boys from good families. They're never come out the same. His Dad's voice echoed in his mind, *Be tough.* Charles stood his ground. "I didn't kill him. I was just defending myself."

The larger boy laughed, "Defending yourself? Len Lamont. Wyoming Wrestling Champ. And *you* done him in? You must really be one-mother-fucking-tough-son-of-a-bitch."

The second boy jumped down.

Charles glanced down the hall: No guards, no one. He held out his hand, "I'm Charles Allee."

He never saw it coming, the boy in front hit him so hard it sent Charles stumbling backward into the cell door. The inside of his head rang and before he got his senses the three of them crowded him with their bodies, hitting and kicking and spitting until Charles was on the floor, unconscious, his breathing labored and he gurgled blood.

It took less than one minute.

Finished the three boys hopped back up into their beds and returned to their comic books. Charles didn't move for two hours until a guard came by to get them for lunch.

Thirty Six

The long strings of yellow tape looked like a boundary line for a cheap yard party, but this tape had *Crime Scene* and *Do Not Enter* repeated along it's entire length.

Cindy pulled the station wagon up to the curb in front of their house. She couldn't get into the drive way because of the tape. John McCallum, Logan and another deputy stood on the porch with the front door wide open. She stepped from the station wagon and ducked under the flimsy, but legal boundary.

McCallum saw her and marched toward her. "You can't come in here Cindy." He pointed at her as she continued to walk toward him. "Cindy. Stop! You can't come in here."

"This is my home."

McCallum blocked her way and handed her a legal paper.

"What's this?" She quickly scanned the document.

"It's a search warrant. We're here to search the house."

"For what?"

"Evidence." McCallum stood his ground and tipped back his cowboy hat.

"Evidence? We're the *victims* here. Don't you realize that? What evidence are you looking for?"

"A bat."

"Oh, my God. A bat? There's no bat here. We don't even own a bat."

"You stated to the 911 operator you saw Butch hit Len Lamont with a metal bat. And we're going to find that bat."

She replayed the events in her head. "I was hysterical. Len Lamont was beating up my husband in our front yard at one in the morning. I thought I saw something shiny. Maybe I said a bat, but I don't know what I actually saw."

McCallum just stared at her. "I have a search warrant from the DA to go through your entire house and we're going to do it." He looked back toward Logan and the deputy. "Go ahead."

Logan let out a whoop and stormed into the house. The other deputy followed.

"Cindy, get on the other side of this crime scene boundary. Now."

Her look was grim, intense. "What's the matter with you, John? You know this was self defense. You thought so that night. What's happened?"

McCallum didn't answer.

"Butch was right. You're going to railroad him on this. You're a disgrace."

McCallum turned and walked back to the house where Logan and the deputy from Cheyenne county were legally tearing up the place.   McCallum looked around the tiny house as Logan pulled up the couch cushions. "Stop a minute. We're looking for a metal bat. But if we find anything else it's allowable as evidence so be on the look out."

"For knives, brass knuckles?" said Logan, just itching to rampage again.

"Drugs, Logan. I don't care about knives. Drugs. Anything that can show that Allee was using." He nodded for the go ahead and let 'em loose, McCallum didn't participate and waited outside.

Logan and the deputy flipped over the couch and slit open the bottom.

Nothing.

Each cushion was gutted with abandon glee.

Nothing.

They grabbed the flower pots sitting along the window ledge and dumped each one on the carpet. They yanked the larger ones down from the ceiling hanging by hardware chain spreading dirt, flowers and ceiling plaster all over the floor.

Nothing.

They moved into the kitchen.

They ransacked the refrigerator, poured out all the milk and juice, opened up the ice cream. "All's they got is chocolate? I hate chocolate," said Logan.

He left it on the table.

They pried open the Tupper-Ware and scattered the food out onto the floor.

Now the cupboards.

The two of them tore open the flour sack and the sugar and the pancake mix. Bags of cookies, rice and noodles were thrown about.

"I guess we better open all the cans in the cupboard," said Logan. "Never know what Butch might hide in one of those secret cans with those false bottoms."

"Where you can hide some weed," said the deputy.

Logan grinned at him, "Yeah, maybe some heroin."

Logan laughed a lot as they opened every can in the cupboard. Some they shook the contents out into the sink, others got dumped on the floor or onto the counter. Some they just opened and didn't shake out anything at all.

When they were finished the kitchen looked like a black bear had ransacked a cabin.

"Shit. Nothing here, except this mess," Logan said standing in the center of a garbage filled kitchen. "Well, we ain't finished yet."

They went into the bedrooms.

McCallum had started searching the bedrooms and had opened all the drawers scattering shirts, pants, underwear, bras, panties, pajamas all over.

The second bedroom was already gutted. In the middle of the floor was a little heap of white and pink and blue panties with flowers on them, little socks, skirts and jeans. Blouses were torn off hangers and a couple training bras were scattered about.

Charles's room had the posters ripped off the walls, books lay open on the floor and clothes and papers were everywhere.

They turned every bed upside down. Logan pulled out his official deputy folding knife that had *Deputy Pike* engraved on the blade. He held it high and stabbed it into the foam, slicing downward. "Cuts like butter." He was giggly with pride.

He disemboweled each mattress, leaving gapping holes with white foamy flesh hanging out. "This one must be Allee's," he said. With psychotic glee he stabbed the mattress repeatedly. Stabbing and slicing until sweat dripped from his face and soaked through his uniform.

They found nothing.

The deputy from went around taping his night stick on the floorboards making sure that what echoed back didn't sound hollow.

The hours turned into a day. The day turned into night and they finally left.

Two days later the yellow tape came down.

The kids were at their Grandparent's home and Cindy went inside. She stood in what was left of their living room, at first not recognizing anything. She didn't walk about. She couldn't move. She stood frozen to the spot looking at the aftermath of law enforcement's duty. She was sick to her stomach and crumbled down onto the floor sobbing.

Thirty Seven

"Sell the house. Get a second mortgage, do something but get the money." Butch was shaken and near tears when he heard the news from Cindy about the beating Charles had. Everything he had tried to protect Charles from was now happening. It was like his own life was being reenacted, only this time Charles took his place. The difference was that Charles was innocent.

"The doctor said he'd be OK."

"Fuck those doctors. They're jail doctors, they ain't going to say nothing else. They all protect each other in here, Cindy. We have to get Charles outta here."

"His bail is fifty thousand dollars."

The dollar amount was staggering to him. He'd never had fifty thousand dollars in his entire life. "Get the money from our house and get him outta here."

She withheld how the Sheriff and Logan had destroyed everything inside their home, knowing it would tear him apart. "The house is all we have, Butch." She looked at him as he hung his head. This was a nightmare.

"I know. The house took so long to get, but I don't care, jail will kill him. I've got a public defender I'm meeting with today, I'll ask him how we can sell the house or get some money out of it."

Cindy had always handled the bills and she knew what the house was worth and how much equity it had. How would she tell him? It hurt just to think about it, yet say it out loud. "Butch. If we take the equity out of the house for Charles..." her lips trembled as she looked into his eyes, desperate eyes, scared eyes... "we won't have any money left for you to get out."

For one second Butch hesitated. "I don't care about me. Just get Charles out of here."

Cindy broke down, and Butch couldn't even touch her.

****

Alex sat mesmerized, not blinking, his lips parted in a silent gasp.

"Charles actually got beat until he was unconscious? How is that possible in the juvenile section? Where were the guards?"

Butch was agitated by reliving the horrible events, his eye's locked onto Alex's. "You educated people don't have no idea what it's like in there. The guards don't rule a prison the prisoners do. If the guards don't like you they can spread all kinds of rumors to get you killed. Guards are like...paid thugs." Butch leaned back and crossed his arms.

Alex had heard the stories, but in the past he really didn't care. He had never done time, not even overnight in jail. No DUI's or a disorderly conduct. He unconsciously shook his head. There's thugs everywhere, he thought. Cops came to mind so why not prison guards. He knew a few attorneys who were thugs. "So what happened? Did you get the money to pay for Charles bail?"

"Yeah, that's how we lost the house. We pulled out some money, Charles got out of jail, and then Cindy couldn't pay the mortgage because I wasn't working for six months while I was in prison. When I got out I was so messed up I couldn't work then either. I never realized how hard it was on Cindy. She never told me. She said she didn't want to burden me with it."

Alex watched Butch's lip quiver.

"I tried to go back to work after the trial but I stayed alone in my room for a month. I couldn't sleep. I wasn't eating. I kept seeing Lamont on top of me and me hitting him with that rock. I wasn't making any money. The bank wouldn't give us a break and foreclosed on us. Everyone was against us because so many people liked Len."

Butch looked sad, his heart heavy. Alex wasn't even seeing the tattoos now, just feeling this profound sense of loss that Butch was re-living. It seemed to be a breakthrough in the therapy...for Alex.

"It was the only house I ever owned and they stole it from me." Butch then forced a smile, "If you rent though you don't have to worry about roof leaks or stuff like that."

Alex forced out a smile.

Thirty Eight

Kersey

Everything looked normal as Charles walked toward the Kersey High school steps, the only difference was his usual buddy's now avoided him, stared at him, pointed. Tommy didn't even walk with him. Charles had already missed over a week of school and he was anxious to some normal routine back.

The town's people and the school staff were still in mourning over the death of Len Lamont. The newspaper headlines painted Butch as a murderer and Charles as an accomplice; the running story was that Butch had set up Len in the bar to get him to come to the house so he could kill him. The town was severely divided between a lynch mob and the small fraction of people still supporting the Allee's.

Charles started for the steps and Mr. Corbet meet him there.

"You can't attend school here anymore, Charles." Mr. Corbet stood two steps above Charles looking down at him.

Charles heart thumped heavy, "Why not?"

"Give this letter to your Mom. You'll need to find schooling somewhere else." William Corbet turned and walked back up the stairs, leaving Charles standing there in shock.

"This is an insult," said Cindy throwing the letter onto the table. She picked up the phone and dialed out. "William Corbet, please...Cindy Allee..."

She waited.

It seemed like minutes.

"I don't care if he's in a meeting get him out to talk to me or I'm coming down there right now."

She waited some more.

"Mr. Corbet this is Cindy Allee, would you please explain this letter to me."

She listened as he talked, her heart beating faster, her mouth was pursed with anger.

"It's State law? But it's your discretion."

A few short seconds of hopeful listening.

"You won't! You..." She slammed the phone down.

"What did he say Mom?"

She looked at him. Then swallowed. Then sat down. "Mr. Corbet said it's Wyoming State law that if a minor has been charged with a felony he can be barred from school." Her hands trembled. "This is America. What happened to innocent until proven guilty?"

"It's Kersey, Mom."

"It think it's...it's still America!"

No one ate breakfast and Cindy was sitting in the living room with the television on but not watching. Her whole world was collapsing about her and she didn't know what to do or who to ask for help. Her own Dad's words echoed in her head. *Don't marry him, Cindy.* The phone rang and she jumped.

"Mrs. Allee?" A female voice asked.

"Yes."

"I'm Mary Greenville. I'm a substitute teacher at Kersey High and I've taught Charles a few times. I heard about this mornings incident and it's unfair. If you want me to, I'm willing to come to your home and tutor Charles till this is all over."

Cindy teared up. "Really?" The voice on the other end of the line sounded soft and comforting. Exactly what Cindy needed right then.

"You've been through a lot and if Charles wants to go to school he should be allowed to. Is that okay with you Mrs. Allee?"

"Of course. Yes. That is so kind of you, we'd be so grateful." She hesitated, "I don't know how much I can pay you though."

"Don't worry, we'll work it out later. Tell Charles I'll get his school work together and I'll be over on Wednesday."

Cindy jumped as the front door flung open with Margaret screaming, "Mommy! Mommy, is Daddy a killer? Mommy! Where are you?"

Cindy ran from the kitchen, tears already in her eyes, she knelt and grabbed Margaret and buried her face in her thick hair at the same time whispering into her ear, "No honey Daddy's not a killer. That's not true, honey, that's not true." Between biting her lip and breathing she held back the tears, "Who said that?"

"The kids at school they said Daddy killed a teacher. Is it true?"

"Daddy's in trouble, but it wasn't his fault."

"Then why's he in jail?"

How would she explain this? An emotion she hadn't experienced before seeped in and for the first time she felt it. Rage. Intense rage at Len Lamont who came over here and ruined their lives. One deep breath and the tears and fear vanished. "Margaret look at me." She gently separated herself from Margaret but kept hold of her arms. "Listen very carefully honey, Daddy had to hurt a man because that man came to our house to hurt Charles. Daddy protected Charles, he would protect all of us. But some people think what Daddy did was wrong and that's why he's in jail right now. But he's not wrong. He'll go to court and talk to a judge, and I believe Daddy will be home soon. Real soon. Don't you believe what those kids are saying, they're wrong. Daddy was just protecting Charles." She dried Margaret's tears and gave her a kiss. "Does that make any sense to you?"

Margaret nodded her head, "I just want to hit those kids."

I want to hit their parents, Cindy thought. "Margaret. Don't hit anyone. If any one says that again to you, you tell them that he was just protecting your brother. Go on now and change your clothes, honey."

Over the next week Cindy attempted to make life as normal as possible for the kids. She needed to be strong, she was now Mom and Dad rolled into one, the only wage earner and a shield against what was out there.

Suddenly Margaret and Lea had no friends to play with. It proved to be much more hurtful and overwhelming than Cindy could ever have imagined.

Thirty Nine

"Everyone ready? Lets go or we'll be late," said Cindy.

Charles, Margaret and Lea ran out the front door and piled into the station wagon.

The white steeple atop the tiny church pierced the blue sky, a warm welcoming beacon above the rows of corn stubble. Cindy remembered how she, Butch and all the kids were baptized there, in the traditional way: A tank of water and a total dunking by Pastor Phillip. She relaxed and confidently drove into the parking lot. It was already full. Then she remembered their pledge of monthly tithing for the church addition. She'd have to talk to the Pastor about putting that off for a while. At least until Butch got out and started working again.

Pastor Phillip, warm under his church robe, stood at the open door greeting his flock as they filed into the sanctuary. The air outside was cold.

Cindy, with the kids right behind her, walked toward the small group of church friends lingering at the steps. She was ready for some support.

"Hi Louise, Mark," she smiled at the group. Two of the couples turned away and walked up the steps, some mumbled a perfunctory "Good Morning" but stabbed her with their eyes. Before she knew what was going on she was the center of attention: Folks walking around her staring, women and men dabbing their eyes with tiny hankies. Where was the support? The Christian open hand? Was this a mistake? She hurried the kids up the few steps of the

Church and there stood Jack Sanders. "Good Morning, Jack," Cindy said. She watched him move his chew from one side of his lip to the other. Her eyes moved about his face, his expression didn't change and he was silent. He blocked the door with his body, a guard of God. He stared at her. His lips pursed like he was going to spit. Cindy could feel the presence of others behind her, waiting to go inside and worship. "Jack can we get a bulletin please," she asked. The bulge in his lip slid to the other side, she could see his tongue moving around. He stared into her eyes, took a small step to the side and Cindy and the kids walked in.

Church is where the needy get comfort. But this morning there was no comfort to go around.

They settled into back row, Cindy felt deeply alone. Butch should be here with her. They should be sitting in the third row, next to the aisle with the Jensen's on the other side and the old deaf man behind them who continually rubbed his shined shoes together squeaking them through the entire sermon. The McCallum's were here, the Councilmen and their families were all sitting in their customary places. She never sat in the back of the church before but for some reason she felt she belonged there.

Pastor Phillip started the service. The welcoming came and went with no mention of Butch or Len. The singing and the passing of the collection plate; done as usual. Then the sermon. What would Pastor Phillip preach today? How would he address his congregation after this horrible incident? Cindy read the topic in the church bulletin: *Noah's Ark*. But this was printed weeks before Len's death and Butch's arrest.

Pastor Phillip stood, walked up to the podium and looked out over his very somber and intense congregation. He was silent for a moment, then said, "We are faced with challenges everyday. No one among us can escape these challenges from God...and Noah was no exception."

Cindy's mouth dropped open.

"God told Noah he would send a mighty flood to drown out the land and all mankind and all animals. He commanded Noah to build an ark of immense proportions..."

Cindy couldn't breath. She was choking back tears, choking on disbelief and felt deathly alone. She caught her breath and looked about. Was everyone here in denial? Weren't they upset with this absurd Sunday topic? There was a tragedy in the community, wasn't Pastor Phillip going to address this? She sat for a few moments listening to Pastor Phillip read the scripture of Genesis 7:1.

He wasn't even going to try and pull the community back together. Surrounded by past friends, she felt alone and isolated. She readied the kids and they all got up and walked out.

No one tried to stop them.

Forty

Monday Afternoon

Cindy loaded the last sack of groceries into the back of the station wagon and started for home. She now bought their food on credit cards instead of writing a check and the amount of credit she had left was low.

"We going to see Dad today?" said Lea.

"You bet," said Cindy, trying to create enthusiasm from nowhere. "Visiting hours are after three and we can only talk to him on the phone through the glass, one at a time. I know he'd really like to see us."

The hardest part was trying to keep the family in some arena of normalcy. But how can the kids be normal when their Dad is stuck in jail and they can only talk to him for a few minutes through a dirty glass window? It isn't normal for anyone.

As the station wagon rounded the corner, her eye caught something unusual - on the left side of the street right near their house. Cindy leaned forward straining to see what was up ahead. A black-gray billow of smoke twisted upward and outward toward the trees. Someone's burning leaves, she thought. But it's so black.

She slowed the car. A thick, smoky cloud batted by the breeze, twisted about. As she drove closer: "Oh, no," slipped through her lips, "our house!"

She gunned the station wagon up to the front yard and slammed the brakes. The street was empty. "Our pickup!" She jumped out yelling, "Charles, help me." She ran toward the side of the house where Butch's Dodge pickup was parked, plumes of smoke were sliding from the truck's underside, up the side panels and billowed into the sky.

Something was sticking out from under the pickup between the wheels.

She was frantic, "Charles, can you see? What is it?"

Charles was already on his belly looking under the truck from a safe distance.

"Can you see what it is? Is the car going to explode?" She grabbed the hose and turned it on.

"Mom, it's a lawnmower," said Charles. He jumped up from the ground and grabbed the handle that was sticking out.

"Don't! Charles do you think that's okay? Be careful."

Cindy felt some relief that it was a lawnmower on fire but at the same instantaneous moment didn't know if what she saw in the movies of cars exploding to pieces was actually true. She didn't want to find out. "Let me squirt it."

With one powerful yank the lawn mower rolled out from under the car, flames still shooting from it's oil and gas engine.

"Someone's trying to blow up our truck, Mom."

"Get inside, Charles, take the girls with you." Frantically she sprayed the lawnmower engine. "Those bastards." The force from the water splattered her hair and face and dress with soot and greasy oil, but the flames easily went out. Pencil lines of smoke grasped at the air. She threw the hose dow and stormed into the house.

A firm knock on the front door and Cindy bristled. "Come in."

Sheriff McCallum walked into the house.

"The place looks different than the last time you saw it, doesn't it Sheriff?"

After some awkward silence, McCallum spoke, "Tell me from the beginning what you saw and what you did."

Cindy recalled the events all the while hating to have to talk to McCallum.

"Did you see anyone near the scene as you drove up?"

"The scene!? It's all just a scene to you isn't it? You don't care about the people or a person's home. It's just a scene." She was struggling. "You're suppose to serve and protect the *people* of this community. Not scenes."

McCallum was motionless. Expressionless.

Cindy knew none of her ranting mattered. "I thought it was odd that no one was around when all this smoke was all over the place. Do you think that's odd?"

McCallum took a breath. "Cindy, unless someone comes forward and gives me some information I'm not going to be able to do much."

"Not going to be able to do much?" Her look intense, "Or don't *want* to? In this tiny little town you can't find out who did this?"

"I'll have Logan do a little digging around. If we find out who did this, I'll arrest them." He looked directly into her eyes. "Cindy, I will."

"Logan." She shook her head. "Someone's harassing us and he's all I get?"

"We'll do our best, but I can't pull clues from the air."

"Did you find any clues on who tried to run Butch off the road? Any clues on why Len Lamont came over here, drunk, at one in the morning to beat up my son and shoot my husband? Any clues when you ruined our house in your search, Sheriff? Or are all the clues hidden up your ass?"

Charles held in a giggle as he listened in his room.

McCallum's jaw tensed and he just looked at her. "I can't discuss the case, Cindy, but your implications are wrong. I'm fair and honest with everyone."

"Fair and honest? I know you don't like us and you singled out our family since you came here--"

"-- I have not." He towered over Cindy and without meaning to looked down at her, "When I came to Kersey this place was out of control, kids drag racing in the streets, drunken brawls, drugs. I was brought here to enforce the law and clean up this town. Now I've tried to give everyone a fair shake. You know very well I've never once arrested your husband since I've been sheriff. The tattoos and hair, it doesn't mean anything to me."

"The tattoos and hair? What does that have to do with anything? Why'd you just bring that up?"

McCallum was feeling trapped and misjudged, "If I arrested everyone who looked odd to me, half this town would be in jail." He immediately knew that didn't come out right. "Look, if we come across anything you'll be the first to know, Cindy." He walked from the house and Cindy slumped onto the couch.

She missed Butch so much. This whole thing was a nightmare. How could this have happened? We stayed to ourselves. Didn't bother anyone. She held in the tears, "I don't know how long I can take this," she said through a heavy breath.

Cindy was getting dinner ready while the kids were outside playing. The knife she held in her hand was forcefully brought down onto the carrots, cutting each one into angry slices, ready for butter, sugar and a good boiling. She tried to focus on the kids, their schooling, keep them preoccupied so they didn't dwell on the reality of their current lives. Her thoughts were interrupted by a knock on the front door.

Now what? Cindy looked from the kitchen and saw Paster Ned Phillip on the porch. Her anger drained and relief replaced it. She quickly wiped a tear that held onto her eyelash and she walked to the front door wiping her hands on a dish towel.

"Hello Pastor Phillip, come on in. It's really nice to see you."

He stepped into the house, "Thank you, Cindy. Did I catch you at a bad time?"

She cocked her head, "Right now there's no good time, Pastor." She noticed his eyes divert, he looked anxious and uncomfortable.

"Can I have a word with you? For just a few moments?"

"Sure. Let's go in the kitchen."

They took a seat at the table, Pastor Phillip sat upright and stiff. "Can I get you something to drink? Coke, water?"

"No thanks, I'm fine." He shifted in the chair, "Cindy, you attended service yesterday." He stopped.

She waited for him to continue, her eyes searching. "Yes?"

Pastor Phillip took a breath, "Cindy. You know that the McCallum's and the Councilmen attend the church. Friends of the Lamont's too, and with whats happened..." he swallowed, "the incident in your yard..." Sweat broke out on his forehead. "I think it's better that you and your family find another place of worship." He abruptly stood. "I'm sorry, but I feel it would be better this way." He turned to leave.

Cindy stood, her mouth open with no words coming out. This was insane. She stared at his back as he walked toward the door. She couldn't believe what she had just heard. "Wait!" Her voice was loud and commanding in the small kitchen. "You came here to tell me to stay away?" She rushed around him blocking his hasty exit, "Is that what you're telling me? To stay away from our Church?"

She waited for his reply her eyes burning into his.

He stood silently.

She saw the sweat beading on his forehead, his hands trembled. "Well?" she demanded. Diverting his eyes he tried to walk around her, but her steps cut off his retreat. "What happened to love thy neighbor? What happened to Christ's unconditional love?" Her breathing quickened.

He swallowed and gripped the cracked, worn leather Bible tighter to his chest like a Shield of God.

"You hypocrite. Len Lamont came to *my* house. Drunk. And beat up my son and his father protected him. Len Lamont is the guilty one, he caused all of this and you're telling *my* family to stay away?"

"I'm sorry, Cindy."

"I'm disgusted with you. You're no leader of God."

Pastor Phillip's eyes grew wide. "Now Cindy, hold on a minute."

"I don't need you or your church or *your* God."

Accused, he stood frozen to the spot.

"I want you to know *Ned* , my God is *not* the same God you believe in. My God doesn't judge and reject people. But maybe you're just a lost, misguided soul. Maybe I should be praying for *you*." She punched her finger at the Bible against his chest, "You hide behind the Bible because underneath it you're..." she held back. "Get out of my house!" She threw her hand toward the door and Pastor Phillip scurried out.

Cindy watched the screen door slam shut, then she looked upward, "Why are you doing this to us?"

Forty One

Kersey County Jail

Balancing the pad of white lined paper on his knees Butch wrote:

> Charles your free. Stay free!! No matter what happens to me my life iş already been more fulfilling than most men's life. I have a son who has and still does love me enough to trade places with me if I'd ask him to, but I never would ask because even though I'm in here you are out there and one day you'll meet a lady as great as Mom. And what about friends? Does anyone really need them? You're my friend Charles. And my family is my best friends. Our family is prove of that. Son I love you with a very special love the love I know God had for his son. I know money or nothing else can buy this love and respect I have for you. But always remember we are right in what we did. What we had to do. McCallum will lose his job. Parker will be punished. It's not easy for you right now but it will get better you will be totally free. Don't worry about school, you can study and get a GED. Pray. Right now school is only trouble. Talk to your Mom. She is the best Mom in the world. I know what a Mom should be and that's Cindy. I've never seen a more giving Mom. Thank God for her. I do.
> Love you son. Forever and always
> Dad

Butch climbed onto his bunk and laid down.

"Allee." The guard hammered the bars with his baton; an annoying, commanding sound that Butch never forgot and never got used to. It always seemed like the guard was wishing he was hammering a skull instead of a steel bar. "Get up, you're being moved."

Butch rolled out of bed grabbed his toothbrush and toothpaste, his Bible, a couple photo's of the family and the letter he had just written to Charles and laid them on the bed. He then stood by the door.

"Turn around."

Butch turned and held his hands behind his back. The guard put on the handcuffs, then opened the door and marched Butch to a different section of the jail. "Your new home, Allee."

Butch walked into the six man cell, had his cuffs removed and looked for an empty bed. There were already four men claiming territory leaving two beds available. Butch took an upper bunk.

Four days crawled by.

The monotony of each day was setting in: Wake, wash up, breakfast. Wait or read or write letters, lunch. Exercise for an hour. Wait, dinner. Wait, bed. The next day, it was the same all over again and in the constant company of four strangers.

By the fifth day Butch was familiar with his cell mates. Jimmy was fifty-two, a skinny white man who had that "old man nose" with skin that looked like a road map. He was an alcoholic and repeat drunk-driver offender. Thirteen arrests in four years to be exact. He missed his grandkids and sometimes wept at night.

Palo was forty-five, a disgusting, fat, Mexican who rarely bathed and was constantly complaining about how bad the treatment of Hispanics in America was. He monotonously reminded everyone that every strawberry the *Gringo's* ate were hand picked by a Mexican. Then he'd laugh, "and we never washed our hands after shitting in the field." His long black mustache hung over his lips and food was always hiding in there sometimes dropping out when he rubbed it. Palo was convicted of raping two teenage sisters. He denied it, but bragged about raping six or seven other girls that were afraid to finger him. "All nice, tight teenagers," he would say, boasting he never had to rape any bitch over the age of twenty.

Chico, also Mexican, was twenty-nine, a gang banger and was convicted of assault, drugs and a drive by shooting. He was quiet and kept to himself. .

And finally Carl T. Thirty-nine, a truck driver, mostly white with some Navajo and Spanish thrown in. He killed his wife because of adultery. Used his double barrel shotgun: One side for her, the other side for his best friend. He buried them in the back yard underneath a truck load of snow. When spring came the crows were feasting and raccoons were everywhere and the neighbors called the police thinking Carl T was building a trash dump. They were dead wrong.

Butch was the new guy, kind of famous with all the newspaper and TV coverage.

They sat around playing cards. "Hit me two, ass wipe," said Palo, holding his cards close to his belly so no one could see them.

"You sure you want two?" Butch said looking funny at Palo.

"You deaf, freak? I said two, now give me two or I'll give you two of my fingers right up your ass." Palo glared, then a smile cracked across his face.

Butch did what Palo wanted and threw out an ace and a three of spades onto the seat of the plastic stool.

Palo tipped his cards slightly outward so he could glance down and add them up. He was constantly re-adding because he couldn't remember what he had. He licked his lips and a flake of mashed potato fell out, he stared into space, blinking. "Fuck man, I'm over." He threw down the cards and crossed his beefy arms.

"Over by how much?" asked Carl T.

"You add them up retard."

"Carl picked up the cards and added them in his head, "Over by ten. You owe the Pussy ten cigs."

"Fuck." Palo reached into his pocket and counted out ten cigarettes then tossed them with reservation into the "Pussy Box."

"Chico?" asked Butch.

"I'm staying."

"Carl T?"

"Ah, give me one, Butch ole buddy." Butch threw down a Queen of Hearts and Carl T giggled.

"Okay lay 'em out," said Butch.

"Dang it," Carl T drawled, "Chico won."

"Twenty One you jail birds, I get the Pussy." Chico took the box of cigs and refilled his pocket.

They were so into the game they hadn't heard the guard walk up.

"Move back." The guard commanded.

They all stood and moved from the door eyeing the young black boy waiting to be put in to their cell. The guard unlocked the door and the boy walked in. He turned around as the door clanged shut, was un-cuffed and then stood still.

The guard grinned looking at the six of them, "Look like we got every nation of the Yoonited States in there." He turned and walked down the hall.

The young boy, not much more than nineteen, just stood still, his eyes focused on the floor, his hands were at his sides.

"What's your name?" asked Palo.

The boy looked up, meek, his face was filled with fear, "Joshua."

"What you in for Bible Boy?"

He was silent.

"Hey! I'm talkin' to you slave boy." Palo walked close, he sniffed the air. "I smell sweat. Sweaty fear. You ain't never been in here before, have you?"

A tear dripped down Joshua's cheek and Palo saw it. "Hey boy, don't be scared. Daddy's here." He threw his arm around Joshua's shoulder and walked him over to the empty cot. "Here's your bed. Your new home." He sat next to the man and whispered something in his ear.

Butch walked toward them, "I'm Butch," he said holding out his hand. Joshua took it and Butch felt clammy sweaty first timers fear. He looked at Joshua, into his eyes, the fear was deep. And that look scared him. It was probably the same look Charles had, but instead of a welcome he got the shit beat out of him. The image chocked him up and he immediately felt protective of Joshua. "If you want, I'll tell you the routine."

"Outta here, Allee," said Palo waving him away with a fat hand. "I'll help him, we don't need no Harley Hag buttin' in our business, do we Josh-oo-aa?" Palo man-hugged him from the side making Joshua look like a broken doll.

"I'm right above you if you need anything," Butch climbed up to his bunk and waited for dinner.

"Lights out," the guard called and the main switch darkened all the cells. Butch closed his eyes knowing tomorrow would be a repeat of today. He fell asleep to the sound of men talking, laughing, singing, some yelling out, some screaming, some weeping. Prison music.

The next morning Butch stretched out his arms and rubbed his face. He sat up in his bunk and groaned as he stretched his back. The steel springs wrecked his spine. He swung his legs over the edge and peered below, Joshua was on his side curled up like a baby. Butch jumped down. The others were already awake.

Palo was at the sink yanking and pulling his shirt over his belly, his hair wild and his eyes sleepy. He splashed water on is face and said, "He said I'm too big, wants some vazoleen next time." Palo threw a nod toward Joshua. No one paid attention, except Butch.

"What did you say?"

Palo grabbed his crotch, "He cried like a baby when I gave him my bottle."

Butch immediately felt sick. He stepped over to Joshua and turned him over.

Desperate and frantic Joshua grabbed Butch's arm, clawing for comfort. The intense reaction startled Butch, he recoiled. "It's okay, it's okay." Joshua's right eye was bruised and swollen, his lip split with dried blood caked around it, terror pulsed through his face.

"Oh, fuck." The words slipped from Butch's lips.

"He wants some more," laughed Palo, "Give it to him, Tattoo Man."

Butch shot his head around, staring at Palo while Joshua gripped his sleeve. "What did you do?" But Butch already knew and the image of Charles rushed into his mind and tore at his heart. "You fucking animal." Joshua couldn't hold on as Butch rushed Palo. But Palo was ready for him and swung low and up, catching Butch in the chin. Butch stumbled backward, stunned, ringing pierced his ears.

Palo's street savvy brutality erupted and he pounced; slamming his fists into Butch's chest, neck and face.

"Fight! Fight!" Voices erupted up and down the hall. Men gripped the bars forcing their faces between the steel rods straining for a look, "Fight!"

Welts quickly appeared on Butch's chest and neck. Evidence, he thought, now you'll get it. He grabbed Palo by the throat and rammed him against the cement wall, Palo burped out a groan and gasped for air as Butch squeezed tighter, leaning his body into Palo's fat belly. He flexed his triceps and forced the palms of his hands into Palos throat.

Then from nowhere a shocking pain radiated down Butch's neck and shoulders, his deadly hold weakened. He felt another shattering blow between his shoulder blades and then a screaming pain on the back of his knees. Butch stumbled and fell. Looking up from the cement floor he saw four guards, weaving and blurry.

"Get those cuffs on him!." He heard one say. "Hands and ankles."

Butch laid there as two guards cuffed him, they forced him up on weak, wobbly legs, then practically drug him down the hall.

Butch was weak and disoriented with pain as they opened the solid steel door, they un-cuffed him and shoved him inside. His knees gave way and he stumbled and fell onto the floor, his check scrapped against the cold cement.

"See how you like solitary, Allee." They laughed as the door slowly shut, the bolt slid across steel and their footsteps clicked away.

Butch laid on the cold cement, hurting, alone in the dark.

He didn't know how long he was in the room. He had felt around the walls searching for a switch, finding it, but it didn't work. He felt about like a blind man: The room was small and rectangular. His fingers found the cement ledge with a foam mattress on it, a sink and a toilet. That was all there was. He laid down on the mattress and waited, falling asleep, waking up, the darkness thick with no evidence of time.

He jumped as a slot in the door opened and a flash of light shone through. "Breakfast." A voice said.

He suddenly realized he'd been in there for at least twenty four hours. A tray was slid through the slot and Butch grabbed it.

"Is there a light for this room?"

"Your light isn't on?" the voice asked.

"No. How long am I going to be in here?"

"The guard must have forgot to turn on the switch. I'll get your light on. How long? You'll have to ask your attorney." The slot shut and once again darkness fell all around him. Suddenly the bare bulb lit up and Butch squinted. Now he wanted to turn it off.

Slowly, his eyes adjusted and he saw the stark cement walls of his six by eight foot room. He picked up the plastic fork and wolfed down dry french toast.

Forty Two

"We're going with the *Make My Day Law*," said Mark Moore, the public defender assigned to Butch. "Self defense all the way." Talking into the grimy phone gave him the creeps as he looked at Butch through the plexi-glass. "I, tried to get you back into a regular cell, Butch, but they're saying you started the fight and you're a danger to others. With the notoriety of this case, they're going to make an example of you."

Butch felt whipped. "I told Cindy they was going to railroad me on this and it's happening."

"I've got Dan The Man diggin' up dirt on anyone involved. He's an investigator who works for me. He'll want to talk with you, Cindy and the kids too. He's the best around, if there's rotten meat buried somewhere he'll find it."

"He can talk to anybody in my family, we've got nothing to hide."

"I also spoke with Sheriff McCallum and Logan Pike. They don't like you one damn bit. Word has it that you egged on Len Lamont to come over to your house and finish the fight that started at the *Oasis*."

"That's bullshit. If I wanted him to come over, why was I in bed asleep?"

Mark nodded, "That's a good point. It sounds stupid. Want to hear another stupid thing? McCallum's saying you hit Len with a ball and chain. That thing you use to start your Harley."

Butch gripped the phone tighter, his knuckles turning white. "That's wrong. I told McCallum I hit Lamont with a rock from the rock garden. I didn't hit him with nothin' else. Except the sprinkler when he came at me."

"I don't think a sprinkler would kill him. There's also the 911 tape. Cindy called in saying someone had a bat."

Butch looked confused. "A bat?"

"Yeah, I haven't heard it, but I read the notes from the prosecutor's office and Cindy plainly says 'a metal bat.' I'll have to listen to the actual call, though. What's said in a conversation during an exciting or upsetting time can be a whole lot different than what's written in a transcript."

"I don't own a bat. We never played ball or anything like that."

"Maybe that sprinkler you swung about...that could shine in the porch light and look like a metal bat." Mark shrugged his shoulders. "You're sure you've told me everything. Nothing left out?"

"Yep, I didn't leave nothing out. I was at the Oasis, Len hassled me and called Charles a pussy. I got scared and I did pull out my box cutter, but that was it. Talk with Evan who owns the bar he'll tell you the same thing. Then Len came over to our house at one in the morning and tried to beat up Charles and I hit him in the head with a rock. He tried to go for his rifle in the truck and I hit him with the truck door."

"Well, that rock is what killed him. I'm sure of it."

"Len was so drunk he had trouble standing up. He sat on the hood of McCallum's car."

Through the smears and scratches of the plexi-glass Mark watched Butch's demeanor. He sure seemed genuine. Then he said, "Lamont was so drunk he couldn't stand up?" One eye twitched.

"That's what I thought, and I think McCallum thought that too."

Mark shook his head and let out a breath, "Probably had a concussion, and starting out intoxicated anyway, he probably just looked drunk the entire time." Mark was thinking, shifting pieces together that would later be an issue in the trial. "I know he's huge, but if he was so drunk why couldn't you beat up that son of a bitch?"

"It was like fightin' a bear. Him being a rastler, he just put his weight on me and I went down. Smoking don't help either. I just didn't have no energy and I was woke up in the middle of the night. Mark, I was scared for my life, that's why I hit him with that rock."

The fingers of Mark's left hand rested on his lips, "Ok. That's all for now. I'll be in touch."

"Well, what do you think?" What happens next?" Butch wanted an answer. He needed one. It was the only thing that could get him through the solitary.

"It's self defense. It's clear and bare bones. Nothing else matters, what happened at the bar, the alcohol, your history, his history...it's bare bones...Lamont came to your house and tried to hurt or kill Charles. Then he went after you and you protected your son. That's it." He shook his head, "I have no idea why Parker is pushing this case...he's going to lose. He's up for re-election, I don't know why he thinks this would help. I'm going to put in a dismissal, but I'm sure it'll be rejected. For now, we wait."

"Wait?" Butch couldn't stand the word. It made his skin crawl to have to go back to the isolation room. Wait? Then what?

"That's all I can do for now, Butch. I'll get things going and try to get this pushed as fast as I can." Mark shook his head. "But I know the courts...they're in no hurry. Get one case through and there's another behind it." Mark Moore stood.

Butch reluctantly accepted his word. "Okay. But get me outta this solitary if you can." Butch hung up the phone.

The guard walked Butch down the hall. It was good to see other people, even if it was just for a few minutes. As they approached his cell his heart jumped into his throat and his hands shook. "Can I get a book from the library?" he asked the guard.

"No. Library day for you is *never,* Allee."

Butch felt his chest tighten and he gasped through his mouth; each step took him closer to four walls with no sun light, no sounds, no talking ... nothing. He stopped, frozen to the spot.

"Lets go, Allee."

Butch swallowed. His mouth felt thick and tacky, his breathing trembled.

"I *said* let's go, Allee. I'll use the taser on you and we'll keep you here till you rot."

Butch took one step. Then another. Against every fiber of his body, he walked to his cell door. The guard shoved him in and bolted the solid door behind him.

Forty Three

Solitary Confinement

He was finally given a stubby chewed on pencil and a few sheets of unlined blank paper. He'd been on suicide precaution while in solitary and no inmate is allowed even a pencil -- fears that he might stab himself in the throat or something. Butch crossed off today's date on the homemade calendar he had drawn on a single sheet of paper: One month.

If he *could* be happy it was because he could write a few letters home and at least sketch a bit.

> Dearest Loved Ones!!!!
> Finally got a pencil to write you's with. I hope and pray to be home with you's soon. At times it seems I dig down to find strength to go on and theres none left. I turn to Jesus and it helps but at times I still ask why Lord why? I'm sorry to be so depressing but I need a shoulder to cry on sometimes, to stay strong but at times it's overwhelming, the pain and I wish I could end it all. Then I think of you's and I know I have to keep on keeping on. For you's as much as for me.
> Love you deeply,
> Dad
> Butch

It was all he could get out. He shuffled to the basin and splashed water on his face letting it drip down into his beard and onto the floor. He didn't dry it. He walked to his cot, "One, two, three." He turned, and with arms outstretched, walked heel to toe back to the basin, "One, two, three, four, five." *Would it be less if I did it backward?*

Butch had grown accustomed to talking to himself out loud, the actual sound of his voice was comforting. He turned around and toe to heel, backward, counted "One..two..three," he stumbled and lost his balance. "Fuck. I'm getting weak." Two times a week for twenty minutes in that silly little gym was nothing: the worn and mismatched weights, the ten by ten foot room, a bare light bulb in the ceiling, the stink of sweat. But Butch looked forward to each session because it got him out of this little damp cave.

He sat on the cot, laid down and placed his hands behind his head. He closed his eyes for awhile. Then opened them and stared at the stone ceiling. He took a long, deep breath and held it, counting in his head: *One, two, three, four...*he shut his eyes and his muscles relaxed, he felt his heart beating. *Ten, eleven, twelve...* his biceps twitched. The pressure built slowly, steadily in his chest, expanding through his ribcage. It felt heavy. He never understood why holding your breath made your chest feel heavy and tight, but it did.

*Twenty five, twenty six, twenty seven...*He pursed his lips and squinted his eyelids forcing himself to hold it. *Thirty eight, thirty nine...*he didn't know if he was actually counting seconds or just counting, but everyday he tried to beat his last time.

*Forty two, forty three, forty four, forty five...*his thighs and calves tightened, his knees locked, he flexed his pecs and forced his lips tighter fighting the urge to gulp and relieve the pain.

Sixty two, sixty three...his skin shaded red, it felt like he was going to explode from the inside out, *seventy six...*" Uhhhhh." Air rushed into his lungs and saturated his blood, the pressure vanished and his face returned to it's normal color. He breathed deeply a few times.

"Tomorrow...eighty." He laid on the cot for awhile and fell asleep.

Solitary was insanely quiet and the sound of metal sliding across the track woke him. He peered at the slot in the door which was now open, life on the outside peeked in, "Dinner, Allee."

Butch rolled from his cot and grabbed the plastic tray coming through. "Thanks," he peered up and through the narrow opening. "What's the weather like outside?"

"Cold and snowy, Butch, better in here where it's warm and dry." The man on the other side always told Butch it was nasty outside and better in here. Inmates on good behavior were rewarded with chores and Butch was on his route. "You're still in the papers, Butch. The most famous guy we got in here."

Butch didn't know who this man was or what he looked like except for a slot-size peek of humanness, but he'd recognize his voice anywhere. "Parker's telling reporters you and Charles set the whole thing up to get Lamont. He said it's a plain case of premeditated murder."

Butch was still holding his tray as he knelt on the floor, looking at the attendant's empty belt loops and protruding belly. "Wasn't no murder. Lamont came to my house at one in the morning. I was sleepin'."

"Hey, they had a good picture of you in the paper lookin' mean and everything. I brought you a copy." He slid it through the slot.

Butch chuckled, then the thought of him looking mean worried him.

"Did you hit Lamont with a bat?"

"No, I don't even own a bat." The bat issue gnawed at him. "I never liked baseball and I never played baseball."

"Parker said you hit Lamont with a metal bat, then hid it. They're goin' to dig up some farm or something lookin' for it."

"He can dig up all of Kersey but he won't find no bat."

"McCallum was interviewed too, said you intimidated folks. Beat the snot out of people who gave you a hard time."

"I never beat up anyone. In Kersey that is. I did some stuff a long time ago, in my twenties. But McCallum, he don't have no arrest record on me either, he's just a liar cause he's friends with the Lamont's"

There was a silence.

"Gotta go, Butch, talk to you tomorrow. I gave you an extra biscuit."

"Hey, thanks. Oh, here's a letter, can you get it mailed home for me?"

"Sure can."

Butch slipped it through the slot. "What's your name?" The slot closed shut, the outside world now gone.

Butch set the tray on his cot and opened the folded *Westword* newspaper. He read the headline, bold and large, *That's my boy. By Karen Bowers.* The lead in read, *Ex Biker Butch Allee wanted his son to be just like him. Police say he got his wish.*

He read the headline again feeling like it was someone else, some crazy man until he looked at the two photos at the bottom. One of him, looking straight at the camera, long hair and flame tattoo exposed for all to see. And one of Charles, short brown hair and glasses, looking scared and very un-tough. He missed Charles deeply, their time together talking and painting the car. He looked at the headline again. How can they get away with sayin' this? I sounded mean right from the start.

It hurt him that a reporter he never met was saying these lies about him. Authority pushing their weight around not caring who they hurt.

He flipped to the next page. There was his home with Christmas lights decorating the roof line. He wished he was there right now sitting at the kitchen table, smelling the aroma of Cindy's chicken. The kids laughing or fighting over a TV show. It all seemed so far away now.

Near the bottom of the page was a photo of Len and Alisha; their heads together, like in a honeymoon magazine, both smiling, looking great. He turned back the page to the photo of him, looking mean and angry and Charles looking scared. Then back to Len and Alisha.

"That ain't right." Butch felt the prejudice again. "They's making them look so good and me so bad." He couldn't read anymore. He folded the paper in half and laid it on the floor and ate dinner sitting on the cot. After dinner, he laid back thinking about what the attendant had said and the headline in the newspaper. He fell asleep worried about the bat.

Forty Four

"I sent a complaint to the warden after reading your letters describing the treatment by the guards and what happened in the cell." Mark Moore held the jail phone with a handkerchief. "I'm doing everything I can to get you into a single cell, Butch, but my hands are tied. They said you started the fight and that guy you choked is filing a complaint against you. I don't see you getting out of solitary anytime soon, except on a good behavior recommendation from a guard. That's not going to happen."

Butch listened to Marks reasoning, he nodded and chewed on his lip. It sure wasn't fair, defending this kid and now being punished in solitary for it. He was feeling powerless and the prison system seemed against him. Everyone seemed against him. There was no way anyone here would give him a good behavior recommendation.

"You Okay?" Mark asked. "You look a little...tired." Is all he could describe.

"I don't like what they's saying about me in the newspapers."

Mark grimaced. He'd hoped that Butch hadn't seen any newspapers, but since he had he said, "Look Butch. The newspaper agencies want to sell papers. They can print anything they want as long as some yahoo says it or believes it. It doesn't have to be true, just an accurate quote. Don't pay any attention. Just remember what I tell you. You're innocent. You have to keep that in your head. "

"It's hard remembering that. Everyone says I'm not. I always thought that newspapers told the truth. But I read what they is saying about me and it's not true."

"Look at me, Butch. No one else matters except me and what I say. You and I know the truth. You have to trust me on this."

Authority figures and trust never went together in Butch's mind. Authority is what got him here and authority figures were dishing out lies about him in the newspapers. He couldn't trust any of them and now Mark was asking to trust *him*. A lawyer. He didn't know how much trust he had left, but he also knew that Mark was his only hope. He studied Marks face, his eyes. Butch could size up folks pretty fast. "Ok."

"Good." Mark swallowed and tapped his chin with his finger. He realized Butch was getting hit hard with the real world, and the real world hurts. It hurts worse when it's about you. Unfortunately, in America, perception is reality, and when people looked at Butch, their perception was cast in cement. Bad cement.

Mark said, "I need to talk to you about the autopsy. The medical examiners report said Lamont died from blunt trauma to the head. He wrote in his report that the wound didn't match a wound from a metal bat. But he didn't know what might have caused the wound." Mark shook his head, "Didn't know what caused it? County medical examiners...they should stick to cows and goats."

"I told the truth, Mark. It was just a rock from the garden. I've been tellin' the truth over and over but everyone believes something else."

Mark was nodding like it was a nervous habit. "I know, Butch. They have their own fucked up theories, but those bastards need to prove it. Prove that you set Lamont up and had that bat ready. In court we'll be ready for 'em. Don't worry."

"They took my Harley starter."

"Yeah, the examiner said the ball wasn't the right size compared to the wound. Maybe he is on our side. I just don't understand why they keep focusing on that bat." It bugged him. Did the prosecution have some evidence they weren't revealing? Did they know something that he wasn't privy to?

"Did they dig up that farm?"

Mark laid down the phone and wiped his forehead with the opposite side of the handkerchief that he held the phone with, then covered the phone again and picked it up. "They dug up *two* farms. Made a fucking mess up there with all that snow and mud and old corn stalks. I was there. You hear what they found?"

"No."

"One of the backhoes...dug up bones. Shit, what a God-damn zoo. They got all excited and rumors were flying that you killed someone else and buried him at one of those farms."

Butch went pale.

"It was so damn funny! Watching reporters in their London Fog coats scrambling around trying to get a look, slippin and fallin in the mud, photographers snapping pictures for tomorrow's front page. After I left I was told that McCallum, and, what do they call him? Loogy? They raced over. I know they were thinking 'We got that son of a bitch now.' McCallum was probably dreaming of a pay raise." Mark chuckled, then realized he was the only one of them laughing. "Hey, you look like you just seen a God-damn ghost." Mark paused. "Ah, shit, I'm sorry Butch, I got carried away there. It was nothing! The bones were from a deer probably two or three hunting seasons ago"

Butch breathed easier and some color crept back into his face. "You had me real scared there Mark." Butch chuckled at his own dread.

"Parker and McCallum are sticking to their story that you hid a bat somewhere and they're crazy-assed determined to find it. It's all from that phone call with Cindy telling that 911 operator about a bat and then Tommy in his interrogation confirming from inside the house he saw a bat."

"Tommy said that?" Butch couldn't believe that Charles's best friend would lie to McCallum. "It's that sprinkler head they saw. I know it. That's what they saw."

"Well, the medical examiner didn't mention that at all and McCallum never took the sprinkler head as evidence. The fact is he didn't take anything as evidence 'cept that Harley starter. He grabbed the wrong fucking piece of evidence. He's a fucking idiot."

"He didn't take the rock?"

"Hell no."

"I showed him the rock."

"I know, that's what you told me from the start. It isn't any good now."

"Did he get that beer bottle that Lamont was drinkin' from that night? He left it on the porch."

"McCallum didn't take anything."

Confusion crept across Butch's face. "Why not?"

"Hell if I know, Butch. But it works in our favor."

"It's cause they're stupid."

Mark looked at Butch. Suddenly it was clear...the reason for all this mess. "You just might be right. They're all stupid."

Forty Five

The graying, stained canvas, stretched over the clumped cotton batting, was the only comfort for Butch as he stretched out and clasped his hands behind his head. The bed probably hadn't been cleaned in years and it smelt of unwashed skin, greasy hair and sweat. When Butch slept, he tried to keep his face off the canvas. The meeting with Mark this morning helped his worry, but solitary mangled his thoughts; screwed up his reasoning. And there was nothing to do in solitary except think. Ruminate. Going over and over again the sickening events that caused him to be here. He knew in his heart that he was innocent, but try to convince twelve people of that. Especially since he was a loner in Kersey never getting drunk or partying with the local boys. He was a father with responsibilities, not a twenty something show off. Besides with working twelve hour night shifts at the bindery all he wanted to do in the daytime was sleep and spend some time with the kids. To keep his thoughts sane he kept reciting what Mark said, 'No one else matters except me and what I say. You and I know the truth.'

Butch slowly drifted off to sleep.

He awoke to the sound of the door slot opening. He took his meal, ate, and then sat on the cot staring at the newspaper laying on the floor. The article about him was there for everyone in the Rocky Mountain region to read. It pulled at him, upset him. He grabbed the paper and struggled through a few paragraphs sounding out the bigger words.

Out loud he read: '*Butch's return ... signaled the beginning of his reign as the unofficial town bully. "When he's upset, he rages,"* He skipped a few lines. *"...people refused to make complaints because of a fear of him.'*

"That's a lie." Butch responded.

A few paragraphs down he read, '*Charles Allee III spent most of his formative years as the son of the town tough. ... he found release for his adolescent aggressions on the wrestling team.... He could be difficult to handle and was often in trouble for "mouthing off," says one parent, who, like many others in town, will speak about the Allees only on the condition of anonymity. Charles also had a reputation for intimidating younger smaller kids.'*

He was close to tears reading that about Charles. He knew Charles better than most parents know their kids and Charles never bullied anyone. Charles was a good kid, he had raised him right. How could this reporter write this? She never talked to us. He just couldn't believe this was in a respected newspaper. He felt betrayed. Further down the page the tone changed and he read about Len. *"...to me, he was a Gentle Ben," says another firefighter...I never saw him mad." ... (he) "was known to toss a beer or two or three, but he didn't have a reputation as a drinker.'*

"What a crock of shit that is." He felt sick to his stomach reading it but continued, skipping over parts. What caught his eye next made his heart sink and he struggled to hold back tears.

A benefit dinner and farm auction has been organized to help Alisha Lamont....

The rage boiled over and tears for his family spilled, he tore the newspaper into pieces, balled it up and threw it into the corner. "No one's giving us a benefit dinner."

"Lights out." The yell echoed down the short sterile hall. "Lights out."

Butch set his Bible on the stool, then heard the bolt on his door being unlocked. The cell door creaked open and a guard stood there, the hall lights radiated from behind him so Butch couldn't make out the guards features in the partial darkness of his cell. "So you're the famous Butch Allee?"

Butch remained on the cot as the guard stared at him.

"Been in the papers a lot lately." The guard cocked his head. "You are one wild lookin' fuck."

Butch didn't move but cast his eyes away from the light.

"Just to let you know, Allee, Len was my wrestling coach a few years back. I went to State." A soft slurping sound followed his words as the guard sucked on chew. "I still wrestle pretty damn good, Allee... and with a night stick and my electric cattle prod here," he patted his holstered stun gun, "I'm pretty damn hard to beat. Not to mention my .45."

Butch's heart raced, the tone from the guard was ominous. He knew what guards could do to a prisoner. There were some who were honest and hard working, but the bad ones were bad. Worse than a street thug because they beat you under the guise of the law.

"I'm just hope'n... no, pray'n that you give me just one little reason to come in here and wrestle your chicken shit ass." He rolled his chew to the other cheek, "Just one reason, Allee, and I'll show you what bein' a real man is all about."

Butch hadn't said a word.

"You hear me, Allee?"

Butch turned his head and looked at the guard, "Get outta my room."

With his tongue the guard stuffed the chew into the worn pocket of his lower lip making sticky sounds with his spit. "Me bein' responsible, I thought I should let you know that I got word that Cindy's goin' to leave you. She's taking the kids and moving back in with her parents. Can't say I blame her."

A few moments of silence dragged by.

"Tell me somethin' Allee. When you fuck a girl like Cindy, and six or seven months later she squeezes out this baby, is it born with all those tattoos on it? Like parents passin' on some genetic mal-fer-mation, like AIDS?"

"It's nine months" Butch said quietly.

"What you saying, Allee?"

He waited.

"Charles got AIDS, Allee?"

Butch breathed through his nose, don't do anything he thought. Don't do anything. Don't say anything.

"Saw Charles' picture in the paper. What a little four-eyed puke he is. You must be real disappointed. Raisin' a family of girls."

Butch stayed silent.

"Come to think of it, he don't look nothin' like you. Cindy must have fucked around a lot back then."

Butch blurted out, "What do *your* kids look like?"

"Fuck you, Allee." The guard took a step forward. "Remember, just one little reason." He turned and pulled the door shut, slid the bolt over and locked it.

With relief, Butch went to sleep.

Even in his sleep Butch's eye's fluttered at the words: "Where's the bat, Allee? Where's the bat? Couldn't do it with your bare hands. You had to use a bat?"

Butch rolled over and stirred.

"Ooooooohhhh. Butch Alleeeeeeee. Big bad scary killer." A voice filled his cell and Butch bolted upright in bed.

"Where's the bat? Got Charles to hide the bat for you?"

Butch looked about. He was wide awake and what he thought was a dream wasn't. He heard the words...a voice he'd heard before.

"Wake up murderer."

The door slot. It was coming through there. Then a flashlight beam peeked through and waved about in the dark space. "Your wake-up call, Mr. Allee. You awake?" The

234

voice was sarcastic and provoking, "I got breakfast, Mr. Allee. Lets see, you ordered pancakes, bacon, eggs over easy and nice hot fresh coffee. Got some *Johnson's Corner* cinnamon rolls for you too. Oh, look here, you wrote on your room service order you wanted some nice, sweet pussy. Sorry Mr. Allee, I already ate that." A forced laugh. "Couldn't resist Cindy's nice sweet pussy. She's awful lonely. I went up to see her...the bitch came onto me. I told her 'No. No, get off me woman!' But she wanted a real man, gave it right up. Uhmmmm ummmm...good." The guard smacked his lips a few times then slammed the slot shut and walked away laughing.

Butch looked at his clock: 12:30 in the morning.

Butch awoke again as the light beam flashed into his eyes. He covered his face with his hand, "What do you want?"

"You're mine Allee, get used to it."

It was 1:30 AM. Butch pulled the flat pillow over his head and tried to get back to sleep. But the guard came by about every hour or so and woke him up.

Sleep deprived and yawning, Butch woke at six, the usual wake up time. His body felt heavy and his mind thick as he sat up in bed. He smelled something foul and pungent. He looked about and when he stepped out of bed his toes squished into something cold and wet. It immediately reminded him of his childhood, walking barefoot through the cow pastures. He turned on the light and was revolted, then scared. Streaks of spit and clumps of chewing tobacco littered the floor of his cell. He shook his bare foot and a soggy mess of tobacco flew off. "Shit. They'll say I snuck this in." He was suddenly terrified of the chewing tobacco, of punishment.

Going for the toilet paper he slipped, stumbled, he grabbed two hands full of toilet paper, dropped to his knees and feverishly wiped up the brown, slimy clumps. He hated the smell and breathed through his mouth. Sweat dripped from his face as he wiped up the floor, the brown juice soaking the toilet paper and coating his fingers. He threw the mess into the toilet, then went over the floor one more time making sure the tobacco was all gone. There was nothing he could do about the smell, hopefully it would just vanish.

They were going to get him. He knew it.

Forty Six

Sweat rolled down Roy Parker's chubby, pale face as he huffed up the few wooden steps to Sheriff McCallums office. The wind chill was near twelve degrees but he dripped sweat like he was vacationing in Florida in August. Between gulps of air he talked out loud to himself, "I've got to win this case," -- a gasp of stinging air -- "or I'll end up back in the public defenders office somewhere." He stopped on the porch looking like a huge, nylon cloaked bear; his mouth opened wide, his chest heaving. He leaned his bulk against the porch post; of all the people to be killed, had to be Lamont. Any other country fool and this wouldn't be happening. He gulped again. He had to win this case.

The pressure on Parker was enormous: The media coverage, the newspaper articles, and Butch Allee looked like a killer and Len Lamont looked like a winner. A dead winner, but a winner all the same...and people love a winner and people hate it when *their* winner goes down. To his benefit the public and the media were on his side. And Butch Allee was a biker from Hell. All of it made the case look like a slam dunk. Parker was counting on it.

He pushed open the front door of the Sheriff's office and stopped in the living room. Without saying a word he peeled off his down parka, stuffed his rag-wool gloves into the pocket. He was impatient. "In all that searching you never found a bat?" He pulled off his earmuffs and laid them on John's desk. "Are you sure you got the location right from that kid? What's his name? Terry?"

"Tommy," John corrected as he stroked his chin, he couldn't get his eyes off Parker's matted earmuffs. They were probably the only set of earmuffs in all of Kersey and they were sitting right there on his desk. Disgusting. The soggy wool with Parker's body secretions were probably stripping away the lemon-shine on his newly polished oak desk.

John looked at Parker, "*Tommy,*" he emphasized, "was scared, he changed his story a few times...I don't know." John wasn't hiding his frustration as he mumbled out loud, "I hate interviewing kids...they can't keep their stories straight."

Roy looked across the tiny room and critically examined Ted and Fred, both were drinking coffee and finishing off *Dolly Madison* powdered sugar doughnuts. Coby Dyer was pouring a cup of coffee and Logan was fumbling with another package of the powdered breakfast.

Roy never liked going to Kersey, the town gave him the creeps: Too small and too much familiarity with everyone's business. He ignored John's comments and watched Logan fish a pen knife from the pocket of his uniform and slice the bottom of the doughnut package trying to lift up the lid. On the stool was another *Dolly Madison* package, empty, the lid torn, ragged and forced up backwards. What an idiot, he thought.

Fred popped the last bit of doughnut into his mouth and washed it down with coffee; powdered sugar circled his chapped lips. Ted grabbed a paper towel, mouthed the end of it like a doting Mom and handed it to his brother, "Wipe off yur mouth, Fred. You eat like a six year old." A silly grin spread across Fred's face and he obediently did as his brother told him wiping off the white powder with Ted's saliva soaked paper towel.

Roy felt sick. He was looking at his prosecution team.

"Loogy, get Mr. Parker some coffee," demanded Ted.

Roy waved his hand, "I'm fine." They probably re-used the grounds, he shuttered at the thought. "That kid Tommy, he's friends with Charles Allee, right?"

"They've been friends for quite a while," said John. "I know the kid, he's okay."

"And he was there that night?"

John looked at Roy with surprise. "*Yes*. Tommy was there that night. You recall that bit of information?"

"Yes, yes I knew he was there...just making sure. What exactly did he tell you?"

John pulled his notes from his file drawer.

"I need copies of those."

John nodded and read from the scribble before him, "He said he 'saw a flash and then Lamont went down onto the ground.'"

"That's all?"

"I asked him, 'What did the flash look like?' He said, '*Charles* swung this silver thing and I remember it made a pinging sound and I thought it was a bat.' I looked at him and I said ' So *Charles* did it? Not Butch?' Then he got flustered and he nodded his head yes, and I said again, 'Are you sure? Was it Charles or Butch?' Then he looked surprised and nervous and he said 'I meant Butch...Charles is Mr. Allee's real first name. Not Charles Jr, but Mr. Allee.' He's looking all around and then says, 'you know Charles Jr. and Butch have the same name...both are Charles...I meant Butch.' Butch must've had a metal bat cause it made that sound. Butch hit him.'"

Roy stared at John. "Well that's clear as day. He'll be a mighty big help. That call from Cindy, she clearly says 'it looks like a metal bat.'"

"That's from the transcribed 911 call. You *have* read it, Roy?"

"Look John, I need more information, more leads on Allee. Everyone here knows him. We got that rag of a coroner's report that I'm going to discredit. Even though *you* didn't find the bat, I still think it's the murder weapon. And we have motive, Allee being at the *Oasis* and picking the fight with Lamont. But I need some dirt. What happened to that FBI file on Allee at that Klan rally?"

McCallum squirmed, "It's the CBI, and we don't have any evidence that he was a member or participated in the Klan. He was seen at a rally once in Ft. Collins with his son. That's about it for the Klan angle."

"I know he did stuff," said Logan as powdered sugar floated down from a mouth-full of doughnut.

"Hey Loogy, you need to clean that up," said Fred nodding toward the white dust now coating the floor and flecked onto the toes of Logan' s boots.

"I will."

"People's goin' to step in that and track it all over the office."

"Fred! I'll get it swept up."

"Will you two shut up," said John.

Their postures shrunk like scolded little boys and Logan went to get a dust pan and broom.

Out loud John sighed, he was embarrassed by the entire interchange

"I need some hard evidence," said Roy. "Anything. Did you check out California?"

John nodded, "Yes. He has that stolen car incident and some pot possession, he spent some time in Buena Vista, but that's it. And that was a long time ago. Since I've been here, he's not done anything unlawful."

"Why was he at the *Oasis* that night?"

"He went for his yearly birthday drink."

"A yearly drink? And this all happened on his birthday?"

What a miserable birthday present, John thought, but didn't say anything.

Roy huffed, disgusted like he missed the last piece of pumpkin pie. "We need to sway that jury that this is one bad guy. Just look at him, who the hell injects ink all over his body and is an upstanding citizen?"

They all nodded, like that's certainly enough evidence right there. All except John.

"He intimidated people 'round here," said Coby. "Tried to rule the town."

"So did Len Lamont," Roy shot back. "But that's no reason to be murdered."

Coby continued, "When people heard that motorbike comin' they jumped off the street. No one knew what Allee would do to ya."

Logan was sweeping up the crumbs and chimed in, "He came right at me and Rhonna one day, laughin too. Rhonna couldn't see him on account of her eye, I had to pull her right outta the way."

Fred was wide eyed, "She didn't *hear* him comin'?"

Logan thought for a moment, "I think her hearins' gotten a bit bad over the years."

"Whoa, Loogy, Rhonna's turnin' into a deaf mute," said Fred, eyes wide.

Loogy straightened up. "She ain't neither."

"She can't see, and now can't hear," said Fred.

Ted interrupted, "Fred...you dummy, that isn't right. A deaf mute can't hear or talk. Rhonna would be a deaf blind girl."

"Hey--"

"What the hell are you all talking about?" interrupted Roy.

Logan responded, "My wife got her eye poked out--"

"Enough!" John slammed his palm on the desk. John rarely lost his temper but it seemed easier to do since he came to Kersey. He looked at Roy, "It's got nothing to do with what we're dealing with here."

"He almost hit me once," Fred quickly added.

John shot him a look and Fred took another doughnut. "I have to say this, Roy. I had more run in's with Lamont

241

than with Allee." John was uneasy in the room of Allee haters, but he was going to be honest. "Len drank an awful lot and got in trouble. When he drank, he got mean."

"Did you ever arrest him?" asked Roy.

"No."

"That's all I need. He was a good upstanding citizen. Hell, Len Lamont Day! What town has that?" Roy breathed deep like he couldn't quite get a full breath from the weight around his chest.

"Never arrested Allee either," said John.

Roy let out a loud *harumph*. "So what are you telling me? We've got nothing? His eyes pierced John's. "Look, I have to prosecute this case. The town... the entire country knows all about it, hell it's been on national news. And I *will* win, there's no way I'm letting this tattooed Hell's Angel walk." Roy wiggled up from the confines of the chair. "The fact is Len Lamont is dead and a Hell's Angel KKK lover killed him with a bat. Case closed." He grabbed his ear muffs.

John pursed his lips, "Mark Moore is going with the Make My Day law. Len was on Allee's property and opened the screen door."

"Moore! He's just a scrawny public defender."

Roy slipped on his ear muffs and again lost a few confidence points with John.

"I know what Moore is doing, going with Breaking The Close. You know what that is?" Without waiting for an answer Roy continued, "It means your home is secure and anyone opening a door breaks that security: Breaking The Close. Even if you don't walk into the house, it counts. But I'm going to argue that an *outside* screen door is *not* breaking the close. A front door or side door is different, the screen door is a secondary door. Hell, that stupid law goes back to the colonial days and they didn't even have screen doors back then."

"When *was* screen invented?" asked Logan, looking at John for guidance.

John dismissed him. "We still have to get around the self defense argument."

Roy shook his head, "You pull a knife on a man in a bar and when he comes to your home you hit him in the head with a bat, then slam his head in the truck door and he dies, that's not self defense, that's murder." Roy stuffed himself into his coat. "Call me John if you dig up any other information."

Refusing to address anyone else, Roy turned, went outside and trudged down the steps and squeezed into his Lincoln.

John was uneasy. Roy seemed way too confident with so little evidence.

Forty Seven

Solitary

Two months later

Dearest Loved Ones
Sitting here being real, as your husband + your Dad I have
to be real. If I'm found guilty of this I want us all to be
ready for it, to deal with it as God's children. If I'm found
guilty PLEASE, PLEASE, PLEASE look to God for
comfort. I will still thank him because of you four, my life
on this earth is complete. Charles thank you for being the
son my Dad wanted me to be. Lea thank you for being not
only Margaret's big sister but showing Charles and me
what a big sister is really about. Your beauty and charm
and your caring that no diamond can compare to. Margaret
my baby girl. How I look up to you as my angel from God.
I want to keep you as my baby girl as long as I can. Your
more precious than any ruby. Cindy I can remember asking
God for a hot rod a motorcycle and a little boy. He
replaced the hot rod with you, he replaced the motorcycle
with Lea and Margaret. This is one of the many reasons I
thank him and trust him. He gave me what I needed not
what I wanted. I will always thank him for giving you to
be my wife and the mother of our children. Your brighter
than any star and more beautiful than any rainbow. Thank
you for being you. Thank you for three great kids. You're
the mother of mothers you're a wife beyond a wife you're a

friend a lover a teacher and a prayer answered. I'm what I am now thanks to you more than anyone. I can cry without worrying thinking you'll think I'm a baby.

I have everything. Love you all deeply truly and forever. Thank you God.

Butch

Dad

"The Lord is my Shepherd I shall not want. He maketh me lie down by green pastures, he leadeth me beside still waters, he restoreth my soul, he leads me into the path of righteousness for his names sake. Yeah, though I walk through the valley of the shadow of death, I will fear no evil for you are with me. Your rod and your staff they comfort me..." Butch stopped. He couldn't remember the remainder of the verse and flipped open the Bible and read, "You prepare a table before me in the presence of my enemies. You anoint my head with oil. My cup runeth over. Surely goodness and mercy shall follow me all the days of my life and I will dwell in the house of the Lord forever." He closed the Bible and let it rest on his chest.

He fell to sleep.

Startled, he bolted upright, the Bible slid off his chest onto the concrete floor. He felt his hair being tugged on, yanked, like a sister would do when you're a kid. His eyes darted about the room. Then again, the painful yank at the back of his head. He swatted backward with his hand feeling only air. Another tug and he slapped the air like there was a bee around his head.

Then he saw it, floating in front of his face. He cringed and scooted backwards on the cot till the cold wall of concrete smacked his bare back.

Fingers rhythmically waved in front of his face, each finger slowly bending forward. An index finger, a middle finger, then the next one and the next one, curling into a fist, then a quick jab at his face, Butch ducked and jumped from the cot. He spun around...and saw nothing.

"Killer!" The Voice echoed in the damp, dark room. *"Murderer!"* Butch stumbled across the room, flipping on the light fearful of what he might see.

He spun around. His little room was empty. Now silent.

With his back against the steel door, his heart was pounding, his armpits wet. He tried to calm himself and breath normally.

He waited. He listened.

He chuckled at himself. "Must have been a dream." He laughed, "That was so damn real." His posture softened and he walked to the basin and threw cold water on his face and beard, then slid his wet fingers through his unwashed hair slicking it back.

"You're evil Butch. A sinner, the Devil."

Butch whirled around and gripped the edge of the sink, his head turning left then right his eyes examining every corner of the concrete cubicle.

"The guards. It's the guards fuckin' with my head."

"You're the Devil."

He ran to the door dropped to his knees and wedged his ear to the slot.

Nothing.

"Murderer."

It was *in* his cell.

It had to be the guards, those fuckers. They must be piping it into the room. He cupped his hands on the cold steel, his mouth buried into his palms, "Stop it. Stop tormentin' me!" he yelled through the slot. "Stop!"

The Voice expanded in the cell growing louder, angrier, *"Murderer. Killer. Murderer. Killer."* Then a woman's scream.

Butch pounded on the door, "Stop it! You fucker's stop it." He pounded until his fingers went numb. "God-damn you! Go to hell, all of you!" Then one swift punch with his left hand and his knuckles cracked, the skin split wide open and blood dripped onto the floor. He winced in pain and slid down the door onto the floor. "Stop it, stop it, stop it." He sucked his bleeding knuckles like a pacifier as he sat there cowering, forced to listen to the Voice: *"Murderer. Evil. Killer."*

Butch rocked, his eyes staring into nothing, the back of his head rhythmically banged against the cold steel door. Now he chewed on his knuckles, his breathing fast, staccato, babbling, "I did it. I'm guilty." He stared not blinking, mumbling though his hand, "I'm guilty, I killed him. I'm guilty. I'm goin' to Hell."

The voice eased to a whisper.

Cindy hated walking past the row of visitors talking on dirty, outdated jail phones; their tones of anger, hate and sorrow all mixed together so no one can actually make out what was being said.

As she walked down the narrow hall she looked at the large black numbers painted on the wall above each window. *Eleven.* That was her assigned seat. She pulled out the worn metal chair and sat. The narrow ledge that knew thousands of elbows was smeared with dirt and grime collected on top of a weeks worth of tears. She didn't touch it. The seat on the other side of the plexi-glass was empty for now and she picked up the gray colored phone that was once white, and waited.

"Oh..., my God." Cindy said, the phone now lowered past her jaw. "What's happened to you?" She watched Butch drop into the plastic chair. His hair was matted and hung into his face, his lips split and sore, the knuckles on his left hand swollen and angry and dark with bruises.

She gripped the phone because she couldn't grab him, "Butch, what's happened?" With the critical eye of a nurse's aid she scanned his pasty skin, sunken eyes surrounded by deep dark caverns. He looked ten years older! Wide eyed she looked up at the guard standing behind Butch, her look questioning, accusing, then back to Butch.

"I gotta get outta here, Cindy. Get me outta here." Tears filled his eyes and he licked his lips, hungry for the freedom on the other side of the glass. Hungry for Cindy.

She whispered into the phone, "Did the guards do this to you?" His eyes looked vacant. "Who did this Butch?"

"I'm evil, Cindy. I did it and I'm going to Hell. They said so, they told me so." He scratched at his scalp through unwashed hair, then his fingers lingered on the grooves in his face.

Cindy stared, Butch was going crazy right in front of her.

"I'll call the doctor here. I'll get Mark Moore to call the doctor. Has he seen you?"

Butch nodded and slowly closed his eyes like he was thinking about what Cindy had just said, "I think I do need a doctor. I can't take it in solitary. I'm...so lonely." His lips trembled. "I'm praying to God everyday Cindy. I need to see the kids. I need to see them." His breathing was shallow, labored. He was hunched over like it was too much effort to sit upright. "I'm prayin' for God to kill me."

Her heart sank. In all the years she knew Butch she never heard him talk like that before.

"I'll get a doctor for you baby." She didn't want him to see how scared she was. "You'll be all right Butch. I'll get Mark Moore to get you a doctor."

"I need to see the kids. Are the kids OK? Charles?"

"Yes, they're all good, they said they love you and miss you."

Butch gritted his teeth. He ached for the touch of Charles, Lea and Margaret. His large, tattooed hand covered his eyes, resting on this face. He held it there. One deep breath held back the tears.

She didn't know what else to talk about. Everything would remind him he wasn't free, and he seemed so fragile, and she had never put those two images together before. "I'm praying for you, Butch. God is good Butch. God will help you through this. Just keep praying."

He lowered his hand to look at her. "I'm praying too, Cindy. I read the Bible...but God tells me I'm evil. I keep asking for forgiveness but ..." his voice trailed off and both hands now rubbed his isolation worn face, trying to wipe away the hopelessness.

The guard walked up and stood behind Butch, "Your session's over."

Cindy bolted from her chair, "Over? It hasn't been fifteen minutes. He needs to see a doctor. Look at him."

The guard couldn't hear Cindy and didn't pay attention to her anyway. He poked Butch between the shoulder blades. "Hang up."

Like a child Butch did as he was told, stood and followed the guard toward the locked steel door.

"Get him a doctor. Did you hear me?" She was frantic, "Did you hear me? Get him a doctor." She banged her fist on the plexi-glass and watched as the door slid open and Butch followed not even turning to wave or throw her a kiss. "You fucking assholes! He needs a doctor."

The visiting-room guard rushed up to her, "Cease that now, you need to be quiet and your time is up."

"Fuck you." She turned and ran from the room.

****

"Those were the darkest days of my life, Doc."

Butch looked like he was reliving solitary all over again. "Your defense attorney, Mark Moore, he couldn't get you out of there? Out of solitary?"

"He tried, but I think Sheriff McCallum and Roy Parker kept me there."

It's possible, thought Alex. Especially in a small town, but Alex felt contempt toward the guards. There was no logical reason or excuse to keep a prisoner psychotic. A psychotic prisoner could plead insanity at the time of the crime. They certainly wouldn't have wanted that. But if McCallum and Parker felt they had the case sewed up, then keeping Butch psychotic was...punishment.

"Did you ever see a doctor?"

Butch shook his head, "Not until just before the trial."

"How long did you hallucinate in there?"

Butch was silent and Alex saw him swallow. Fidget. It was obvious Butch didn't want to go there.

"Weeks."

Alex felt the breath punched out of him. "Weeks? You hallucinated for weeks? Alone?"

Butch chewed his lip and slowly nodded. His fingers anxiously wrestled each other.

He was probably mistaken, thought Alex. Time is warped when you're psychotic. Minutes seem like days and a day of hallucinating could feel like a week. "How did you know it was weeks Butch?"

Suddenly the anxious movements were gone. "You questioning me?"

"No. No, I was just curious how you knew it was weeks?"

"I kept a calendar and a journal. I wrote crazy things in it. It was weeks."

Alex couldn't imagine it. He knew the psychic pain of psychosis makes some people commit suicide. But it depended upon the type of psychotic episode. The psychedelic world of a manic psychosis with it's grandiosity and power is enjoyed and welcomed by some patients. But persecutory hallucinations and delusions were different. That's a dark and scary craziness, the kind that creates sadistic monsters from the nice, quiet neighbor boy next door. Or the Voice that tells you to saw off your right hand because you masturbated and you obey. Or it convinces you

you're guilty and sinful and evil. Maybe that's what McCallum and Parker wanted. For Butch to just kill himself.

But how could they allow him to stay psychotic for weeks? How was that possible? The prison and county would be legally exposed to medical negligence. But who would believe a Butch Allee type? A "Tattoo Man?" No one. That's why they kept him in solitary. No one would know and know one would care.

Alex felt disgusted. Even he believed that the most hardened criminal deserved medical or psychological treatment. No one deserves to be kept psychotic. It's inhumane, immoral. It's what they did in Cold War Russia and Iraq. Not in the United States. Not in Small Town USA. But here he was, sitting right in front of Alex, living proof that it was going on right now.

Alex felt personally uneasy. He could remember how, as an attorney, he manipulated situations, words, and meanings, played loose with the legal system or called in favors; stepping in and pulling strings to get information he wanted or to make unwelcome information vanish. The prosecutors did it too. One big manipulative circus: Who could outsmart the other and win. He felt the heaviness of his past game playing.

His attention diverted, he played a scenario in his head: If I was the prosecutor would I get Butch put in solitary? Force him to crack and confess? His answer troubled him.

For a brief moment he felt far away from that other world. He was better than that now.

Or was he?

Forty Eight

Aspen Grove

Two Days Later.

Alex felt Butch was ready to hear this. "We've had a number of sessions together and I have a pretty clear picture of what happened and how it's affected you. And you know what I think?"

Butch's face was a mixture of expectation and apprehension.

"I think, you know in your *head* that you're innocent. You *know* what you did was right." Alex leaned forward, closer to Butch. "But you haven't accepted it...in your heart." He watched for the inner acknowledgment that Butch got it.

It didn't come.

Butch looked confused. "How do I do that? Get it to my heart?"

No one had ever asked Alex that before. Alex paused and looking thoughtful. "Well, Butch." Alex shifted in the chair. "Let's put it this way. When was the last time you rode your Harley?"

Butch scratched his head, grinned, then said, "I haven't since I went to jail."

"So, over a year ago."

"Yeah. It's sitting in the garage. Haven't even changed the oil."

"Have you and Charles finished painting his Monte Carlo?"

Pain erupted in his eyes. "He finished it alone."

Alex was nodding, gentle nods of encouragement for Butch to keep thinking and start feeling.

"When was the last time you went out to dinner with Cindy?" Butch looked away and Alex thought he was going to cry. "Do you see where I'm going, Butch?"

"Kinda. I haven't done any of those things since I was arrested."

"It's deeper than that." He wanted Butch to feel it. To come up with the "Ah-Ha" experience that is so rewarding in therapy: The Golden Ring of Awareness.

"I'm not sure what your getting at. Doc."

"Butch. You haven't been living. Even though your free, you're still in solitary."

Alex felt it before Butch. He found himself shaking, little tremors in his hands, then his arms. His breathing quickened and his eye's uncontrollably welled with tears.

"What's wrong Doc?" There was concern all over Buch's face.

"I don't know." Alex bolted from his chair. "Give me a second, I'll be right back."

Alex raced down the hall and into the men's room. Fumbling with the faucets he turned on the cold water and splashed it into his face. The cold constricted the blood flow easing the tremors in his hands and fingers. He glanced into the mirror: The pained expression he had seen so many times on Butch's face was now on his own. He dipped his hands back under the cold flow and drenched his face again, his fingers lingering on his forehead, his cheeks, his lips, then he rubbed his eyes. What the fuck? Breath.

He again drenched his face hoping the panic and puffiness of crying would wash down the drain. Where did this come from? He gently slapped his face, twisted his neck about, breathed deeply a few times. Minutes went by. Then he walked back to his office.

Settling into his therapy chair he said, "Sorry about that Butch. Sometimes I get these...little asthma attacks."

Butch said, "You know Doc, I guess I need to get back to my old way of doing things. Riding my bike and taking Cindy out."

"That's exactly right Butch. Start living again." The anxiety jumpstarted in his gut.

"Thanks Doc."

It took every bit of strength for Alex to sit there, controlling the tremors. He had opened the door of awareness, maybe for Butch but more for himself, and he could not close it again. Alex managed to squeeze out: "That's all for today. I'll see you tomorrow." Alex did not stand up.

Butch nodded and looked at Alex with an expression that read: You okay, Doc? But he said nothing. He chopped the air, turned and went to his room.

Alex sat there, alone.

For an hour.

In solitary.

Forty Nine

Aspen Grove

Alex was wearing blue jeans and a brightly colored Pendleton shirt, he smiled at the front office staff and walked down the hall feeling upbeat and refreshed. The staff were shocked that he was here and that he had actually greeted them this morning. "I heard he's seeing Sandra," one of them whispered.

Alex knocked on room # 4. "Come on in," Butch answered and Alex pushed open the door.

Lounging on the bed, Butch was naked from the waist up and was struggling to make his way through the Bible. The room felt sterile and plain. Just like a hospital room. It was the first time Alex ever noticed how bland the room actually was.

"Hey Dr. Dalton, what are you doing here?" Butch swung his legs off the bed and laid the Bible on the side table. "Isn't it Friday?"

Alex had never seen Butch without his shirt and the menagerie of tattoos surprised him: The eagle flying over the mountains on his chest, the naked lady, white power, various words, spider webs on both elbows, daggers, skulls, blood drops. It was like Butch was permanently wearing an old faded psychedelic shirt from the 70's.

Alex smiled. "Yeah my day off, but you have a pass for a few hours this morning. Want to get out of here?"

Through a trimmed beard, his teeth shown white, "Sure, but I don't got anywhere's to go."

"Can I take you for a ride? I want to show you something."

"You and me?" Butch grinned. "Never been out with a doctor before. Let me put a shirt on."

They walked out the front door of Aspen Grove. "Do you read the Bible a lot."

"Yeah, it gives me hope."

Alex nodded and walked toward his parking spot.

"Holy shit Doc, that your car."

Alex wilted and quickly looked about hoping by some miracle a staff person had left their keys in one of the Toyotas or Subaru's. No such luck. "Yeah that's my car, but that's not what I wanted to show you." Alex beeped the Porsche open. "Go ahead and get in."

"I ain't never been in a Porsche before." Butch was as giddy as a teenage boy and slid in. "Man, this is nice! All this leather. You sure are lucky, Dr. Dalton."

Alex hadn't expected that response, he just took the Porsche for granted and he now felt embarrassed by his own excess. He knew that when a patient enters into your world all kinds of transference can happen. He'd been isolated in his own world for so many years he had forgotten how his own "normal" isn't normal to others. He was quickly realizing how much of his life he had allowed to slip away.

He closed the door and the engine purred into action. I hope I didn't screw this up, he thought.

Through callused fingertips Butch felt the leather's softness, "The last car I had was a station wagon. Wood paneling on the side and everything."

Alex looked over at Butch and made an attempt at being sincere, "That sounds nice."

"Yeah it was, good for us and the kids. On trips they could play games in the back, eat and drink while we drove."

An image of chewed gum on leather seats and Dumm Dumm suckers stuck to door handles shivered Alex. He backed out the parking lot. "What kind of trips did you take?"

Stroking his beard Butch looked out the window. "We use to go camping out to Lake McConaughy in Nebraska. Do some fishing. Couple times we camped out in Rocky Mountain National Park to see the elk."

Alex nodded. His last trip was...before Lisa's death. He never really went anywhere after that, just skiing up at Breckenridge. Alone.

Alex gunned the Porsche and headed towards Greeley.

"We ain't done much though since all this happened."

Alex nodded.

"You got kids Dr. Dalton."

Alex shook his head, "No."

"You married?"

Alex again shook his head.

"I'm getting too personal...it's none of my business."

"No, no that's okay Butch. My...." He stopped. He was still the doctor here and unnecessary disclosure could muddy the therapeutic waters.

Fuck it, he thought. "My wife was murdered a few years back."

Alex felt Butch's stare. No words of condolences, no 'sorry', nothing. They drove for a mile or two. The air in the Porsche always seemed sweet and expensive, invigorating, but as Alex breathed it now it seemed stale and thick, heavy.

"Is that why you were assigned to me? To figure me out. Why I killed Lamont? Because your wife was killed. You think all killers are the same?"

Shit! God damn it! "No, Butch, no that's not it at all." This was not were Alex wanted this to go. Regret filled his gut, like a inexperienced therapist fresh out of school. What the fuck was he doing? Was this little trip and conversation for him, or me? Butch had folded his arms across his chest. "I wasn't assigned to you, Butch, and after working with you these past few weeks, I do believe you acted in self defense.

But you're paying the price of killing another person even if it was justified and the right thing to do. But you still killed someone, and it was someone who was important, at least in some peoples minds, and now you're suffering. That's why you're so depressed. My wife was killed because someone was...trying to hurt me. She suffered because of me." His words, out loud, hurt.

The Porsche breezed through the country with miles going by in silence between the two men.

"I didn't mean for all my personal stuff to come out like that, Butch." He gave him a glance.

"That's okay Doc. I feel like me and you got something in common now because you shared that with me. I can trust you more."

"Thanks, Butch." Alex pushed the Porsche to eighty five and relaxed into the seat.

Alex and Butch looked like the Odd Couple, but it felt comfortable. The kind of comfort that two friends have who can just sit and drive, look out the window without saying a word and it's okay.

"You have a special relationship with Charles," said Alex. "You probably don't know, but I see so many families that are so..."

"Fucked up?" Butch finished it for him.

Alex chuckled and nodded, "Yeah. It's refreshing to see a father and son who really like each other."

"He's my best friend." Butch stared out the window as he spoke.

"Maybe someday I'll have a son." The words sounded strange as soon as they left his mouth.

"You have to work at it Doc, it don't come easy. But I like Charles. I like who he is. So it's easy for me to like being around him. I'd rather hang out with Charles than anyone else."

"You'd do anything for him?"

"Yep, you bet."

"Would you lie for him?" Alex heart pumped.

"What's that supposed to mean?"

Alex could see Butch's eyes in his peripheral vision. "I'm just asking Butch. Not accusing, just asking."

"You think I'm covering up something? I was found not guilty. I ain't covering up nothing."

Alex took a left onto tenth street. "Butch, I know you were found not guilty. But the killing of Len Lamont is weighing on you. I was wondering if anything else was weighing on you?"

"Like what?"

"I don't know that's why I'm asking." The Porsche restrained itself as it crawled down tenth street and stopped at the light. "There was so much interest in that bat. I was just wondering if there was some justification for it."

"Dr. Dalton, there was no bat. I hit him with a rock and they made up that bat story. How many times do I have to keep saying that?"

"Did Cindy make up seeing a bat."

"I don't know what she saw, but it wasn't no bat."

"Did you ever talk to her about that? I mean that really made the DA think you were hiding something."

"I don't want to talk about their lies."

The comfort level vanished. "Where you taking me? Maybe you should just take me back to the hospital." Butch sifted in the seat to face Alex, "The whole prosecution team said I used a bat and hid it. But I told everyone the same thing and the jury too. I was on the ground and Lamont was on top of me hitting me and I reached out and grabbed that rock and whacked him with it. That's it."

"Okay, then Butch, it's very important that in your mind you must start accepting that. If there's no other burden inside you, then forgiveness and acceptance is the answer to your sanity. You must believe it in your heart." Alex slowed the porche. "I don't think you want to hear this, but those tattoos represent your anger. At society,

259

authority...whatever. And it keeps people away from you. But underneath all that exterior," Alex eyes moved about Butch's body, "you're a decent, genuinely nice guy." Alex shifted his eyes ahead. "Your full of guilt and loneliness. Medication can help, but it's what's inside you that will ultimately cure you."

Alex pulled into *Hog Heaven*. "We'll keep working on it together."

The tension eased up a bit and Butch said, "So what you is saying is that I got to cure myself?"

Alex nodded.

"And you're going to help me do it?"

"I will." Alex turned and smiled at Butch. "And we're going to start right now."

Butch looked through the windshield at the motorcycles all lined up in a row. "Why you taking me here?"

"Have you been here before?"

"Yeah, I've been here." He fidgeted in the leather seat. "Not since everything happened."

Alex smiled as he pulled into an empty space. "Well Butch, I thought it would be fun for you to teach me to ride."

Butch's burst around in the seat toward Alex, his eyes sparkling. "You serious?"

"You think I'd take my Friday to just ride around and do therapy with you?"

"Will they let us take one out?"

"I've already arranged it." Alex grinned. "I told the owner we needed a Harley. Nothin' else would do."

"That's all they got here is Harley's."

"Oh."

Butch looked uneasy.

"What's the matter?"

"The owner still Ruddy?"

"I guess so. I spoke with a Ruddy Moody."

Butch nodded, his eyes moved around. "That's him. Silly name and all."

"Come on, let's have some fun." Alex winked and opened the car door. Butch got out and they walked along a procession of new Harleys guarding the double glass doors. Alex felt giddy, his eyes coveting each one, gazing over thick tires with chrome wheels, gas tanks emblazoned with colors and designs that screamed for attention. And the handlebars. Those handlebars made the Harley.

Alex pulled open the showroom door and they walked in. A high pitched, southern voice boomed across the room. "Hoooolllly shiiiiit. Is that you? Butch Allee?"

Wearing a black leather vest that strained against belly fat, tattoos covering both arms -- from fingers to uncovered shoulders-- and gray hair pulled tight into a ponytail, Ruddy lumbered toward Butch. No open hand, Ruddy threw his arms around Butch's body and hugged him. Butch went up on his toes and slapped Ruddy's back.

"Hoolllly shiiiiit it's good to see you ,Allee." Ruddy took a step back and grinned though his long Fu-Manchu mustache. "I heard all about that Lamont thing. You doing alright?"

"Yeah, I'm okay."

"I heard bad things about that boy," said Ruddy. He shook his head like he didn't want to hear anymore, then he grinned again. "Come to get a new bike?" His eye's shifted between Butch and Alex. "Look, you buy a bike," he threw his arm around Butch's shoulder, "and I'll take off my profit for you. My cost." He stepped back and circled Butch like a woman walking around a mannequin admiring the dress. "Goddamn, you lookin' good Allee. Ya cut your hair."

Butch seemed in his element and a smile broke through his beard. "Yeah, I miss my hair. But I like it shorter, it's easier to wash."

"Wash mine once, maybe twice a month." Ruddy laughed. "Any new ink?"

Butch stretched out his arms, fingers spread, "No new ones. Got to save a little money before I get another one."

"Who's this with you?" Ruddy through a nod toward Alex like he wasn't there.

Before Butch could answer or feel uncomfortable Alex stepped forward, "I'm Alex Dalton. Butch is going to show me how to drive one of these."

"Ohhh right, you're the one who called. Sure, sure, got our best bike picked out for you, come on over here. Jeeeessuuusss Christ. Can't believe you're back in town. Follow me." Ruddy wobble-walked with Butch toward the side door with Alex lagging behind.

Ruddy was huge and wide, but at the same time seemed to sashay next to Butch. It didn't fit. Alex checked out Ruddy's boots. Old boots, the heels heavily worn toward one side. It gave Ruddy a wobbly sway, like a drag queen in worn out stilettos.

They walked outside toward a low slung, fire-red Hog with sweeping handle bars and a rolling seat.

Butch was in awe of the machinery before him. Alex thought maybe he made a mistake.

"Look at this baby!" Ruddy's fat hand patted the leather seat. "Fifteenth Anniversary edition of The Fat Boy. Everything on this: Shotgun exhaust pipes, twin cam 88B power train, surfboard foot pads. I customized it too. Put on the old suspension for a smoother ride, classic Harley bars. What a beauty." Ruddy was lost in his own dreamy words. He turned to Alex and winked. "You know how they got the name for the bike? Fat Boy?"

Alex shook his head.

"It's ole' Harley folk lore," Ruddy leaned toward them like he was fearful someone from Harley had a listening device on the bike, "the story goes that Harley wanted to squash those Jap bikes invading the Yoonited States. So they named it *Fat Boy* after those Peace Missions at Hiroshima and Nagasaki." Ruddy's lips curled back revealing chipped yellowing teeth, nodding his head he seemed be right back there dropping The Bomb. "We did 'em good we did."

"There were two atomic bombs," said Alex, his eyes searching the air. "They named them like their planes...Fat Man and--"

"--Little Boy," finished Ruddy. "Yup, The Bomb. *Bombs* to be exact. Took two of 'em to get 'em to their knees. So Harley combined 'em into Fat Boy and named the bike after it." Ruddy straighten, "Harley'll never admit to it, but I think it's true." He twitched his eyebrows. "Fun story anyway. Hey you want helmets? Got to offer helmets it's the law." He seemed embarrassed asking. "But you know Wyoming, our senator keepin' us helmet free."

"Wind in our hair," added Butch.

"You want a helmet, Dr. Dalton?" Butch asked.

"Are you wearing one, Butch?"

With a look of surprise and repugnance, like a boy being questioned if he ever wore dresses, Butch snickered, "No helmet has ever touched my hair."

"No shampoo or scissors either, " Ruddy added. They busted out laughing.

Seeing Butch laugh made Alex feel proud. But he felt like the odd man out. Such close camaraderie in the face of future head injuries. It made him uneasy, but then he said, "Okay, no helmet. I'm trusting you Butch."

"Live free," said Ruddy. "You two take her out let me know what you think? I got some repair work in back. No rush now take your time." Ruddy's demeanor changed and with a stare he asked, "You doin' alright, Allee? You know, with that trial and everything."

"I'm getting some good help. Thanks."

Ruddy gave Butch a wink, then chopped the air with his hand. "Peace brother." Butch returned the gesture, then in ritual form, chin-nodded each other. With that Ruddy turned and wobbled to the repair shed out back.

"He's supportive of you," said Alex.

Butch wasn't listening, his attention was glued to the sleek, shiny bike leaning on the kick stand before him. They stood there a few moments, "You ready?" asked Alex.

"I ain't never rode a new one before."

A tinge of sour crawled into Alex's throat. "You know Butch, I think I'll get that helmet."

Butch swung his leg over the bike and settled into the soft, form fitting seat. He sat there for a moment or two, his back straight, his hair hanging down to his collar.

The image looked strange to Alex: A cutting edge driving machine with Butch on top of it.

"Feels funny with no duct tape on the seat," he said to Alex. Butch's hands gently reached out, like they were to touch something sacred, his fingers wrapped around the black handles as the words *fuck* and *love* disappeared from view. He pushed the bike forward and the kick stand flipped away. He looked back and down to the side. Then smiled and looked at Alex. "I miss the kick start." He jerked his head, "Go ahead and git on, Dr. Dalton."

Alex took a step toward the thirty thousand dollar bike. It's loud guttural howl was muffled by the helmet as Butch ignited the hog with a push of a button. The space for Alex to sit was tight. Too close to a patient? Too close to Butch? Maybe this was a mistake. "I've never rode on one before," he said. Alex's own words echoed from their first session: *Knew it, biker*. He froze. What am I doing? I could get killed today. Lisa's face flashed in his mind, then the detective photo's, then Albert Socorro....

"Just swing your leg over, Dr. Dalton."

Alex's heart was racing, he suddenly felt confined and claustrophobic, he yanked off the helmet, his hair already matted from sweat. He gulped a deep breath. "The...the helmet," he sputtered.

Butch was watching. "I hate 'em too. I like the wind hitting me in the face."

Alex was pale, faint, "Just give me a minute here, Butch." It was the same feeling he had had back at the office a few days ago. Alex slowly walked in a circle. Here he was with his patient, a new Harley, and Albert Socorro was haunting him. Get a grip. Alex slowed his steps and consciously breathed. He was embarrassed pacing in circles, but he felt better and the panic slipped away.

The joints in his fingers were screaming as he realized he was gripping the helmet so hard. He relaxed his hold and took in a long, deep breath, then slowly letting it out. He raised the helmet to slip it on and the panic surged, his breathing trembled. His chest tightened and Alex sunk into a squat using the helmet as a stool in front of him, between his feet, resting his weight on it. The vulnerability was strangling his confidence, just like it did after he knew Albert had been in his home that day, killed his wife and raped her.

A firm arm wrapped around his shoulders and he listened to a calming voice, "Dr. Dalton, we don't have to go for a ride."

Just like that, in an instant…it was gone. His chest relaxed, vibrant air filled his lungs and saliva drenched his parched mouth. He turned his head looking Butch directly in the eyes. Green eyes. For the first time Alex noticed his cat-green eyes. There was worry in them with lines of concern running from each corner. He was so close he could see the fine outline of the flames where the artist cut his skin allowing the ink to permeate permanently into his flesh; each pore and wrinkle filled with red and blue. For an incredible instant, Alex felt supported and calmed by Butch Allee.

"I'm okay, it's just a bit hot in that helmet," he lied. Butch slid his arm under Alex's armpit, cradled his back and helped him to his feet. The helmet sat on the asphalt.

"You sure you're okay, Dr. Dalton?"

"Yeah, just give me a minute here." Breathing helped. Relaxing helped. Butch's support helped. I can't keep hiding this shit, he thought. "Let's go have some fun!"

Butch slid back on the Harley and waited.

Alex lifted his right leg, unbalanced and feeling awkward, he held onto Butch's shoulder, raised his knee further and pushed his foot over the seat toward the other side. He kind of hoped-skipped a step closer and plopped onto the seat. So much for being graceful.

The bike strained for freedom as Butch played with the throttle, and without warning he released it.

Alex jerked backward, his spine smashing against the sissy bar, he grabbed Butch around the waist like a girl and instantly felt silly and very un-masculine. His hand frantically searched for the seat strap and he grabbed it. He couldn't see anything through the flying gray hair as Butch throttled the bike and roared down the street.

Butch banked a curve and Alex resisted the primal urge to grab hold of a body. The power in the bike reminded him of his Porsche...without doors. The wind bit at his face and it felt good.

Butch headed toward the outskirts of town past farms, rows of cut corn and cows. His body, taking the brunt of the wind and cold, protected his Doctor. It was an amazing bike; fine tuned, smooth ride, the sweep of the handlebars was perfect, his grip firm but loose and his arms, extended outward and upward hung with ease and comfort. Butch felt himself melt into the bike as he pushed it to seventy miles an hour, his shoulders loosening. With a subtle shifting of his weight the bike responded by veering left or right. It wasn't like Butch was riding the bike, he was part of it.

The vibration of the seat between Alex' thighs and the steady drone of the engine helped Alex unwind. It would be perfect if he could just keep that hair out of his face. Alex turned his head and through the slit in his helmet watched farm life speed by, he broke out in a grin. This is more fun than a Porsche any day. He was hard pressed to remember the last time he felt exhilaration. But it was there now, pure excitement, a release of emotions, his mind clearing with the bikes speed and his increased comfort of Butch being in control. He was living the present and Alex liked it.

Then a few exhilarating moments from his past suddenly sped into his head: The time he and Lisa came eye to eye with a Tanzanian Cape Buffalo. The huge black brute charging with sweeping horns thrust toward Alex's belly, the shot, the buff skidding only three feet from his Russell boots and Lisa standing just off to his side, her .375 H&H rifle at her shoulder with wisps of smoke curling from the barrel, his own rifle only half way up. Then, the first time he had sex with Lisa, at her parents house, in the very bed she grew up in while her Mom prepared coffee and desert only a few feet away in the kitchen with her Dad watching TV in the living room. Then his wedding day, ebullient emotions, family, friends, jetting off to Rio.

Just as fast as it came, it was gone. He felt suddenly empty. All these fun moments were long ago...before Lisa died...before *he* died, emotionally.

Butch slowed the bike, turned around in the center of the two lane road and headed back toward Greeley.

He leisurely drove into the parking lot, came to a stop and put his feet down to steady the bike.

Alex was sorry it was over. His feet were glued to the surfboards when he realized Butch was holding up the entire weight of the bike and him. He put his feet down and then slid off.

Butch lowered the kick stand and turned off the bike.

Alex quickly regrouped and allowed himself to go back to the excitement, the fun...the present. He slipped off his helmet, beaming. "That was great! That was fun, Buch!" Alex was like a kid. "More fun than I thought." He watched Butch dismount, and he looked content. Peaceful. "You really can drive that thing." Alex strutted around the bike like it was the damn coolest thing he had seen in years. "That was amazing!"

Butch chuckled, "Didn't get sick, huh Doc?"

Alex laughed, "No." He paused. "It helped. It was great! Really great."

"It sure is a nice bike," said Butch standing back and staring at it.

Ruddy walked up, "So goin' to get one for yourself buddy?"

"Hey Ruddy, I'd love to but can't right now," he stroked his beard, "sure is sweet."

"How 'bout you? Trade for that Porsche of yours."

Alex gave him a wink, "I'm tempted, but I think I'll wait. Thanks for letting us take it out, I really do appreciate it."

"Any time."

A few moments of silence slipped by as all three gawked at the Fat Boy. Then Ruddy said, "Butch. When you get some free time give me a call we'll go out have a beer and chew old times."

"I'd like that."

Ruddy nodded, "Remember Butch, my cost." He and Butch exchanged 'chops' and Butch said thanks.

Alex and Butch walked toward the car.

"I needed that, Dr. Dalton."

"Me too, Butch."

Fifty

Sandra just about strangled him. "Are you crazy!?"

Alex rolled his eyes, "Yeah I probably shouldn't have, but I had fun." He let her have a big grin.

"Fun? That's what you had?" Sandra was aghast at Alex's judgment. "What if he wrecked the motorcycle? What would the papers say about that? 'Patient on a day pass kills his doctor.' That would help him. Big time. He'd really kill himself then. How'd you feel about that?"

"I'd be dead remember, it wouldn't affect me much."

"Stop being sarcastic. If the licensing board found out you could be suspended."

Alex looked at her without blinking, "The board will never suspend me Sandra I donate too much money to the place, besides I didn't do anything wrong. It was therapeutic. He needed to get back out there and ride. You should have seen his face when he got off that Harley. It was him, Butch Allee, not some psychotic patient. I can clinically justify it."

"You think you can clinically justify anything."

"Oh, come on Sandra. It was therapeutic."

"For who?"

He grew quiet. "For both of us."

"Alex. The doctor is supposed to treat the patient, not the other way around."

"Look, you have no idea what I've been through the past years and this was eye opening for me. It helped Butch too. I know counter-transference and this wasn't it. This ride was

..." Alex grappled for the right word. "...great." He turned away from her.

Sandra softened. "Alex, I'm just thinking of you. I don't want you to get hurt or suspended. I'm glad it was helpful for you too, but you have to be careful." She sat on the chair in his living room and looked out across the city.

"I don't need the money, Sandra., maybe I should quit. Get a hog and ride cross country."

She shook her head, "Oh God...your going through mid-life!"

Alex walked up to her, knelt on the hardwood floor and placed an open hand on each knee. "I'm glad your worried about me. No one's worried about me in years. I"m glad it's *you* who's worried," he said, looking deep into her eyes.

She leaned forward, her lips closing the distance between them and kissed him gently on the mouth.

He slightly pulled back, "I'm getting a tattoo."

"Stop it."

She kissed him harder and he pulled her onto the floor. They laid there holding each other. He stroked her hair. The closeness they shared felt so good. "Let's go to my room."

She kissed him again, then said, "We work together. Are you good at secrets?"

"Too good."

The sheet's were pulled up above her breasts as she sat in his bed. Alex handed her a glass of wine.

"You've got a nice ass for an old man," she said watching him walk around the bed, then setting his wine goblet on the side table. He climbed in.

"It's genetics.")

"Alex. Look, we have to talk about this." She adjusted the pillows with her free hand and then turned in bed to face him.

"Us?"

"No. *Us* is fine. I meant Butch Allee."

He clasped his hands behind his head and stared straight ahead. Breathing through his nose he could smell it. That thick, bitter-sweetness wafting up from beneath the sheets. A combined pungent aroma of sweat and heat that smells good in the bedroom...or in the kitchen or the back seat of a car. That smell that had been absent in this room for years.

"We're both naked drinking wine and you want to talk about Butch."

"Alex. I've never seen you get personally involved with a patient before. What's up?"

Without looking at her he said, "I don't want to talk about it right now."

"Alex! You're an attorney and psychologist, talking is all you ever want to do. Come on, I'm not being judgmental I'm just interested in what's going on for you."

He turned to look at her and watched as the sheet slid down off her breasts and gathered at her waist. Her eyes soft and gentle...interested. "Let me in," she said.

Tears welled in his eyes and he turned away. His hands twisted at the sheet about his waist.

She put her wine glass on the side table and cozied up next to him. "What?"

"You are in."

Fifty One

Four Months of Solitary

Dearest Loved Ones,
7 more days until trial. I'm sorry I was down during our
family meeting. I'm glad you are a forgiving family. I'm
not going to let Satan win. I don't want him in my life with
hate. It's so hard in here. As soon as you's are gone I'm
missing you's. Please be strong. None of us is weaklings!
Let's all be strong. The closer it gets the more paranoid I
get. I'm thinking minimum 18 years. Maybe I should
make a deal. Write to Parker and make a deal. Maybe with
10 I could be out in 7 that wouldn't be so bad. I'm being
real here, maybe I would be 53 when I get out. Here's what
I'm thinking. Up to now Parker and McCallum has had the
train they've built the tracks even to the point of breaking
the law. All my ideas have failed. I don't want to give up
faith. In Mark, the courts, the cops I have no faith in them.
I have to be real. Nothing has gone mine or Charles way.
Think about it. Sometimes I feel the Judge, Mark and
Parker are playing a game with me. Maybe I need to talk to
Parker and make a deal. I know in your four eyes I'm
innocent, but not in others eyes. I don't care about the rest
of the world! I have upstanding citizens of the community
to fight. I really don't believe I can beat them. Their's Ned
Phillip the pastor, McCallum the cop, Parker the Attorney.
The average person believes in the police. I'm an ex-con.

Tatoos and I'm a hard core person. I have to get 12 people to look beyond my record and looks and I have to be compared to a pastor, a cop and an attorney. Think about what the average person thinks comparing me to them. I'm feeling desperate. I heard talking that the Judge and Parker were around having coffee and with Mark. They is just too buddy buddy. I'm scared. Another guy in here says Mark hasn't done anything for him in here. He's doing 23 years if they find him guilty. He's thinking of firing Mark too. It's hard on me. I really feel I need to talk to Parker just to see what's out there. If there's no deal to be had then I know what's waiting for me. What ever decision I make I hope you support me. I don't know what to do. Please God help me.

Love you all deeply

Butch

Dad

The fear was ever present as the the trial grew near. Butch was writing home, obsessing, and battling the voices. He was exhausted and desperate and couldn't stop his mind from racing. Should he make a deal with Parker or trust Mark Moore? He could face decades in prison or twelve people just might set him free. Either way he'd be out of solitary, the crushing loneliness of solitary was the worse part. He'd even go back in the same cell with Palo just to have someone to talk to.

Butch set the letter on his plastic stool, crawled into bed and slept unusually deep.

Butch awoke. He had heard something, but it was dark and sleep tugged at his mind. A guard? He wasn't sure, but what ever it was was not there now. He lay back down, his lids heavy. Then a rumble, his entire cell shook and he bolted upright in bed. He was sure the mortar between the concrete blocks was cracking, shifting and then a crushing thunder erupted around him and he felt the wall was going to collapse on top of him. Butch huddled defenseless on his cot. Then another sound overtook the thunder; a rhythmic clatter. Hoofs. It sounded like horses galloping down a cobble path, closer and louder; and then they seemed to be all around him. He could smell them, hear their snorting, their breath echoing against the cell walls.

The darkness split apart and a brilliant flash of white filled his stark room. Butch squinted, his eyes stinging, he brought his arm up across his face. Like a small earthquake the walls crumbled and three stallions, each ridden by a King, jumped over the rubble and into his cell. Butch trembled and the air grew icy cold.

His cell instantly felt huge, plenty of room for three horses with Kings. The stallions pranced and pawed at the cement floor each a different color and all three wearing golden saddles adorned with jewels and bridles of silk. The three Kings, Black, White and Asian wore no armor, just flowing robs, jeweled necklaces, rings and golden arm bands. Each wore a crown of gold laced with precious stones.

Butch didn't move except to lower his arm. He felt a breeze and looked up, the ceiling was gone and the night shone through with a buttery moon and sparkling stars. It had been months since he had seen the sky. The night air was bitter, and breathy steam shot from the stallions nose. The Black King pointed a jeweled finger at Butch who was cowering on his cot, and he spoke with thunderous authority, "Do not worry. Do not be afraid for you will be saved."

The yellow horse rose up and pawed the air as fire blew from his nostrils. The Asian King grabbed the horses long blonde mane and pulled back. The stallion dropped his front hoofs to the ground, then with the elegance of a ballerina knelt and the King leaned forward.

Butch could see his face, but it really wasn't there, an apparition of a face. There were Asian features, but no features. Butch was sure he was going crazy and terror spread through his body. Even with the cold night air he was sweating.

The King spoke without moving his mouth. There were words, and Butch heard them, but they seemed to be part of the wind. "Your time is near. Make peace with yourself. You will be taken care of." The horse rose up off his knees and seemed to pose, stone still.

Then all three turned and galloped from his cell disappearing into the night. The walls closed in and the ceiling slid down and the room went dark. Then, just as quickly, the room filled with light again and a man stood in the cell doorway.

"Get your fucking ass outta bed, Allee. You're going to see the doctor."

Butch wondered if this man was real or not. "Who are you?"

"Fuck you, Allee. My superiors said you need to be presentable for court. Get up."

Butch was still trying to make sense of what he had seen. He had heard Pastor Phillip preach of visions before but had never seen one himself. The guard yelled at him again, "Get up you lazy fuck!" Butch flinched. The guard was real.

He pulled himself out of bed and stood. He was stiff from sitting in one place. How long had the Kings been here? Were they really here? He couldn't judge reality or the time.

"You need a shirt Allee, I don't want to be lookin' at all that skin shit."

Butch did as he was told and slid on a shirt and turned around waiting for the guard to shackle him.

"This is the part I like best," said the guard. He stood close to Butch breathing into his ear, "What I'd really like to do...is chain you up...and skin you alive." He let the words linger. "Hang you upside down in my garage, just like the Thanksgiving pig I butchered. I'd call my kids out to watch." He smacked his chew. "I'd start at your ankles, cut a nice clean circle. Then take my pliers," he exhaled loudly, "grab a chunk of your flesh...and rip! Right down to your knee." Butch stared straight ahead not moving a muscle. "I'd grab my skinnin' knife--" The guard pressed his finger against Butch's leg and slowly scrapped his gnawed fingernail against the stiff prison fabric – "and I'd slice that ugly tattoo skin right off your thigh. That bright, red muscle'll be all laid open, fly's be all over it layin' eggs in your meat and you'd be twistin' and jerkin' and screamin'." Then I'd start on your other leg."

The night sergeant walked by the open door, "Hey! Dyer! You getting Allee down to medical?"

Butch stiffened. *Dyer?*

"Yeah, I'm just getting him secured. We'll be right there." The guard attached the cuffs and leg irons then walked Butch out the door and down the hall.

"You're name is Dyer?" Butch asked.

"Didn't you know, Allee? My Uncle Coby's told me all about you. Why don't you try runnin' Allee. I really need some taser practice."

Butch shuffled down the hall, the guard intimately close. They entered a bland exam room. No pictures, no medications, no instruments; which meant no weapons. Butch sat on the stool and waited. Officer Dyer stood next to him. The door opened and a boy in a white coat walked in reading a chart. "Mr. Allee?" he said without looking up.

"Yes, sir."

"I'm Dr. Rodriguez. In looking over your chart here, and what the guards have said, looks like you've been hallucinating. Is that right?" He sat on a stool and looked at Butch.

"You the doctor?" asked Butch.

"Yes he's the doctor Allee, now answer his question."

Dr. Rodriguez said, "Officer Dyer, I can handle this."

"You look too young to be a doctor," Butch responded.

Dr. Rodriquez chuckled, "I'm three years out of residency. Night duty. I've been working here for about a year and a half. Mr. Allee is it true that you've been hallucinating?"

"I guess so. I've seen things in my cell."

The doctor glanced at Dyer and frowned. "Mr. Allee you don't look good. Any problems here?"

"I've been in solitary for four months now."

"Four months?" He looked at Dyer. "Why was this man in solitary for four months, and this is the first time I've seen him?"

"I don't know sir, I don't make the medical recommendations."

Dr. Rodriguez stood up. "Look at him officer. This man is underweight, his hair is matted, he needs a bath and he's hallucinating." Dr. Rodriquez' face hardened. "Do you think this is proper treatment of a prisoner, Officer Dyer?"

Dyer fidgeted. Just five minutes ago he was skinning Butch alive, now he was being skinned himself.

"Answer me, Officer."

"No sir. He needs medical attention."

Dr. Rodriguez clenched his teeth and flexed his jaw as he wrote a prescription. "Mr. Allee I'm going to prescribe an anti-psychotic med for you. It should take care of those hallucinations. I'll have it delivered to your cell later tonight." He looked at the chart again now reading it more thoroughly. "This is why they sent you to see me now, our trial is next week." His stared at Dyer. "This is going to be written up Officer. This treatment is inexcusable."

"Yes, Sir."

"Take Mr. Allee back to his cell and see that he gets a shower *tonight*. Mr. Allee, I'll check on you tomorrow."

"Thank you, Doc." Butch smiled weakly at the baby faced doctor.

Officer Dyer and Butch left the medical office and walked down the hall. Butch in front. Butch thought now was a good time to ask. "I want to see my family. Will you get a message to the night operator and have them called?"

"Fuck you, Allee. I'm getting written up because of you. If anything happens to my seniority I'll get you Allee. Remember that."

"I want to see my family." He felt a sharp shove between his shoulder blades.

"You'll see 'em on trial day."

Butch stopped in the middle of the hall, cells flanked him on both sides. "I have a right to see my family."

"You know what, Allee? If you don't start walkin' right now I'll go visit Cindy myself tonight...and it won't be for fuckin'."

The air in the hallway grew cold and stampeding hoofs floated on the wind. Butch's eyes widened as the same white stallion galloped toward him, perched high in the saddle was the White King. The stallion slowed, trotted and abruptly stopped in front of Butch who could clearly see the king's eyes red with anger, his hair wild and un-kept flowed out from under his crown.

The king spoke: "Now is the time." Jerking the horse around the King galloped back down the hall and disappeared.

The air warmed.

"Walk! Asshole!"

Butch stood there. *Now is the time?*

"You better walk Allee or--" He didn't finish his sentence. Butch spun around and body slammed Dyer against the wall between the cells. Dyer screamed for help and reached for his revolver. With the commotion, inmates rushed to their cell doors and the corridor erupted into yelling and hollering.

An alarm sounded.

Butch hopped over his bound hands so they were now in front of him, and circled the chain around Dyers neck. Leaning all his weight into Dyer he pinned him to the wall and forced the chain tighter against Dyers throat. Through clenched teeth Butch said, "I want to see my family."

Dyer's fingers scrambled and searched for his gun, his taser, anything he could grab, but Butch's body blocked his access. With his free hand he struck out wildly hitting Butch in the back and shoulder. His blows ineffective against Butch's rage.

"I want to see my family." Butch's forearms bulged and he twisted the chain tighter against Dyer's neck cutting off his blood flow and air. Dyer gurgled, his knees buckled, his fingers stopped searching for his weapons.

The yelling, the hooting, the alarm -- it drowned out the sound of running boots -- a flash erupted in Butch's head, and then blackness.

Butch awoke on the cement floor with a splitting headache. He glanced about. He was back in his cell. He felt the knot on the back of his skull: Soft, mushy, painful. He grimaced, then forced himself up and to the basin and splashed cold water on his face and head and neck. He ran his fingers through his hair. No shower yet. He laid on his cot and pulled his knees up to his chest.

He didn't know how much time had passed, but he awoke to the familiar and comforting voice.

"Hey, Butch. Butch? You awake?" The voice seeped through the opening in the door.

Butch stirred, then sat up.

"Butch, you gotta get up. I got a mid-night snack for you and some medicine from the Doc."

Butch was groggy. "I'm up. I'm comin'." Butch nearly fell as he lowered himself to the floor and peered through the slot.

"Hey, I heard about you tryin' to take out Dyer. The word here is you had him too. To bad you didn't do him in before they knocked you up." A plastic tray slid through and Butch took it. "Got you some chocolate cake. Them meds, I gotta watch you take 'em so I can log it in."

Butch took the two pills off the tray and popped them into his mouth and dry swallowed them. For the first time he saw eyes staring back at him through the slot: Blue-grey eyes, circled by weary, wrinkled skin and bushy grey eyebrows. Warm, caring eyes.

"Sorry buddy, but I got to see in your mouth. You know guys cheek 'em then overdose on 'em later." Butch opened his mouth wide. "You need 'em though. They's treaten you pretty bad here."

Butch took the cake and plastic spoon and gave the tray back. "I like chocolate cake. Any ice cream?"

A short laugh. "No-go on that one Butch, sorry buddy."

"I was just jokin' with ya."

"Your trial is in a week. They're tryin' to break you before trial. Make you look like a killer. Don't let 'em get you Butch. Be strong. I hate to say it, but what ever they do to you don't hit anyone anymore."

Butch knew he was right. Those words: the trial in a week, looking like a killer. He felt lonely and scared. "I don't really feel like talkin' right now."

"Ok, no problem buddy. See you tomorrow."

"Where's Dyer?"

Butch heard a heartfelt chuckle, "He went on leave for a few days. I wonder why?"

Butch felt some relief with that. "Thanks for the chocolate cake."

The cell went dark as the door slot slid shut.

Fifty Two

His heart beat faster, the excitement was overwhelming him. Butch desperately needed to see Charles. He waited in the cubicle the phone already in his hand. When Charles walked in and sat down Butch felt a mass of emotions. "Hey Charles, man I miss you so much." Tears welled in his eyes.

"Hi Dad. I miss you too."

"Four days to go." Butch tried to be upbeat, but he could read Charles and he saw the fear in his eyes. "We're goin' to win this. Mark Moore is confident I'm goin' to win. And If I win, then you win too. It's plain and simple self defense."

Charles held the phone tight. "I'm scared."

"I know Charles but you'll get through it."

Charles looked like he was going to cry. It was hard enough for Butch to hold it in, but to expect that from a seventeen year old was way too much to ask.

"Dad. They gave me a new attorney. She says maybe I should plea bargain. Get it over with."

Butch felt sick. "No way Charles. You're innocent." Then it hit him, right in the gut. A crushing sense of helplessness. He wasn't able to be a good Dad, being locked up, they took that from him. He couldn't hold it in and the tears flowed, "Charles, I'm so sorry your alone in this. I wish I could, I wish, I..." he sobbed. "Charles I just want to hold you." Charles put his hand on the glass and Butch reached up and touched it with his.

"Dad, I'm really scared. I don't think I can do this. What if they find me guilty and I go to prison. I won't make it."

Butch tried to pull himself together. "Your trial is after mine. If the jury finds me innocent then your trial is basically over. Charles we're both innocent. We have to believe in the jury system." Butch couldn't hardly believe what he was saying.

"But they send innocent people to jail all the time, and it was Len Lamont, Dad."

"It don't matter. After my trial we'll deal with yours. But don't plea bargain. You're innocent Charles."

Charles searched his Dad's eyes hoping he was right. "The beating that happened in there..." his words trailed off. "I'm not tough enough, Dad. I'm not like you."

Butch just wanted to smash the glass, grab Charles and run. Run forever if he had to. Those fucking ass-holes caused this and his family was paying for it.

"I really miss you Dad."

His heart ached. "I know. I miss you so much. When I'm lying there in the dark I think about our talks and going to Jackson lake and camping; all the good times me and you had." He choked up. "Four more days and this'll be over. You'll see." Then he felt some excited anticipation. "When this is done, we'll get your car painted." He broke out in a grin.

"It's done, Dad. I finished it about a month ago."

"Oh...great." Butch kept the smile, but inside he was crushed. "I can't wait to see it."

Then those dreaded words: "Times up" said a guard.

"Got to go. I love you, Charles."

"I love you too, Dad."

Fifty Three

The day of the trial.

"*Mister* Allee you have to hold still or you'll look a mess," said the hair stylist as she blunt-cut Butch's bangs so they hung straight down, covering the flames on his forehead. Butch jerked his head away and looked at Mark Moore who was reviewing notes. "Why do we have to do this?" The stylist rolled her eyes and tapped her foot.

"I don't want the jury to see *any* tattoos on you, and face it Butch that ones hard to cover up. Cutting bangs is the only way to do it. I don't want to prejudice them right off the bat. I want you clean cut, neat and polite." Mark examined the bangs. "You look like an old Dutch boy."

Butch turned back around and the stylist continued cutting and combing, then gave it a light shower of hair spray. Butch pulled his head away again. "I ain't never put that on my hair."

Mark was buried in his notes but glanced up at Butch's protest. "Just let her finish Butch, you don't have to use the hair spray tomorrow. Jesus Christ you're worse than my wife."

The stylist put the finishing touches on his hair and stood back to look at her work.

"Well don't you look handsome," replied Cindy as she stood in the doorway of his holding cell.

"Hey, Cindy," Butch grinned looking like a little boy. "They's puttin' your hair spray on me."

"Oh my God, Butch. Next you'll be wanting a suit and tie."

"He's already got it," said Mark without looking up, pointing to the dark suit on the hanger. "First impressions."

Butch felt sick, his gut knotting. *First impressions.* He hated that. "Mark, there's twelve people waiting for me right?"

"Yes." Mark finally picked up the apprehension in Butch's voice. "The trial should last about four to five days. The jury will be there the entire time. Remember? We discussed this. You'll be sitting next to me at the defendants table, but Cindy can't be there. She's a witness. She can be there when the verdict is in but not before."

Butch felt the blood drain from his face and his heart pounded in his chest.

"Ok, lets get that suit on you and then we'll be ready," said Mark. "Is he done?" he said to the stylist.

"All done."

"Thanks. I'll call you if we need to." The stylist packed up her things and left.

Butch watched Mark slip the suit coat off the hanger. "I think the last time I wore a suit was when my Dad died." His hands trembled.

Mark took the pants and draped them over the metal bar of the cot. There was tension in the air.

Butch felt light headed and started to sweat, Cindy noticed immediately.

"You're going to be fine Butch. Charles told me what you two talked about when he visited. I want *you* to remember what you told him: You're innocent. You're the victim here. Len Lamont came to our home to hurt *your* son and you did what every good Dad would do. You protected your son." She took hold of his face between her hands, and through her fingertips she could feel his fear. "You're a good Dad. And you're innocent."

He needed to hear it, wanted to hear it. His chin trembled and then the tears...and then panic. "I can't do this. I can't go out there." He turned away from Cindy and paced his cell, his fingers nervously digging at his beard, "I can't Cindy. It's been six months, I can't go out there." Desperation covered his face, "Mark can I just stay here?"

Mark shook his head, "I know it's hard, but you have to be out there with me."

Butch flopped down onto the cot and wrapped his arms about his body. He rocked, and gasped through his open mouth. "Everyone out there knows what I did. They know me. They're going to look at me and think I'm a killer. Mark they're goin' to think I look like Charles Manson. They're going to see a killer sittin' there. I can't do it." Then, for a brief moment he calmed. "Mark, I'll plead guilty. I'll just do that, yeah, that's what I'll do. Mark let the judge know. Let him know I changed my mind." He licked his lips, then ground his teeth and squinted. He knew it sounded insane, and then panic shot through his veins. He seemed to be in excruciating pain and put his hands over his face and cried. Cindy sat next to him and rubbed his back as he collapsed into her body. It was rare that Butch cried.

Mark waited. Butch needed to get this out. Get it done and over with now rather than in the courtroom. He waited about four minutes then he glanced at his watch. He gently walked up to them and knelt down. "Butch look at me. You have to trust me. I know we're going to win. This is a self defense case, and Cindy is right, you protected Charles. The newspapers and the news are liars. They're only after headlines. But now it's your turn." Mark cleared his throat, "It's time to tell *your* story.

Fifty Four

Aspen Grove

Alex was on the edge of his seat. When Butch finished recounting how he tried to kill himself and then the trial, Alex leaned back and felt exhausted by the whole thing. "What happened to Charles?"

"Charles was so scared he kinda broke and couldn't do the trial and his attorney got him to plea bargain to a *no contest*. He was sentenced in juvenile court and got two years probation, a restraining order to stay five hundred yards from any Lamont and he had to move out of Kersey county. I'm still really mad at his attorney. Charles never got to hear that he was not guilty. He needed to hear that, I think that would have helped him. All that I went through, how can a seventeen year old go through the same thing. He just needed to get it behind him."

"And he's in jail right now?"

"Yeah, for them drugs. I wasn't there to guide him. I feel like I lost my son because of all this."

"In some ways you did, Butch. But you can get that relationship back. Work on it. Maybe both of you do some therapy together."

Butch mulled the idea over in his head. "What's next? For me?" he asked.

"Well Butch, you're stable right now, the psychotic process is gone. But this is just the beginning. You need to stay in therapy, deal with the guilt you have and work on that depression. Therapy and medication will help you a lot."

"I ain't never been in therapy before. Never really liked to talk about my problems with anyone. Except my family."

"I know, Butch. But therapy will help."

Butch looked at Alex. "I like *you* Doc. Can I come and talk with you? I'll get a ride here. Maybe Charles can come and talk to you after he gets out of jail."

Alex thought a moment. "Normally we refer patients to outside doctors, but let me see what I can do."

Butch smiled. "Thanks Doc, I hope so." Butch got up and walked out.

Alex leaned back in his chair and Sandra walked in.

"Just saw Butch. He's looking well."

"He's slowly getting there, but needs a lot more therapy to get him through this."

"You've done a good job with him so far. He needed you."

Alex looked up at her. "You know, I think I needed him."

Fifty Five

The Porsche sped up the forested mountain. Evergreen
trees always look taller when driving up hill, and they were
different from other trees, never changing color or dropping
leaves. They were the same whether it was summer or
winter: always green, always cone shaped. They seemed
strong and sturdy. Consistent. So different from humans.

Lisa, and Evergreen Cemetery were at the top of the hill.

The usually lonely but routine drive was not what Alex
was feeling today. The past weeks with Butch, and Alex's
awakened awareness of his own internal struggles filled him
with apprehension.

The Porsche sped past the evergreen forests, the
meadows where elk came to graze, past the glacial rocks that
held fossil stories of ancient life.

He slowed the Porsche and pulled up to the gate. It was
easy parking on a Thursday morning. He opened the door
and grabbed his coat from the passenger seat and slid into it.
The woolen coat was dense and warm, comforting. The cold
bit at his nose and cheeks. He felt in the pockets, and pulled
out some gloves and slipped them on, then walked through
the gate toward the east.

His walk was slow. Deliberate and heavy. In the past he
sometimes looked at other grave sites reading the names and
dates but not today.

He and Lisa hadn't picked out any grave sites. Who
would think of doing that in their thirties. Or forties even.
So Alex chose this site. The plots faced east, warmed by the
morning sun and there was a stone bench right next to the

plot for visitors. Alex sat on the cold stone slab. He leaned forward, his forearms resting on his knees, his hands clasped. He always sat silently for a few minutes, as if waiting for Lisa to become aware that he was there.

"I've been lonely."

He didn't say anymore. A jay screeched at a squirrel in the pine tree. Then it was quiet again.

Minutes passed.

"I'm not letting anyone in, Lisa. And I need to. I'm not blaming you. It's me. I tell my patients to understand and listen to themselves. But I haven't done it for years." He rubbed his hands together, clasping and unclasping his fingers as the cold crept through the wool. "I've been holding onto you,...I'm afraid that, that if I let someone get close...I'll lose you forever." He swallowed, then gazed down at the grass, moist with frost.

"I met someone. Someone who's changed me. A patient of mine actually." He took a long slow cold breath. "Lisa, I need to let go. I guess I wasn't aware of it, or maybe I didn't want to be, but all these years...I've been full of...hate. It became my reason for living. And working. I think...all these years I've been trying to avenge your death through my work, and I know you wouldn't want that. And...I can't do it anymore." He lifted his head and stared at her headstone.

A few more minutes passed and the sun warmed the air melting the frost.

"You know I haven't dated since I lost you. But I'm seeing someone now. Not serious."

Alex shivered.

"You won't believe this, but I want...to be a Dad." His emotions overwhelmed him and he sat upright taking in a breath, blinking the tears away. He looked upward at the blue sky. "You know, we talked about kids...I guess I didn't want to sacrifice my time for kids. I've have this patient who doesn't have much. But he has a great relationship with his son." His emotions swelled and it took him off guard, and he choked on a sob. "Uhm, I think I'm ready for that...having a child."

He cried now, letting it out. "I'm sorry, I wish I could have had a baby with you." Alex wiped his eyes with his gloved fingers and sat awhile softly crying. "I miss you so much, Lisa."

Alex calmed and watched a squirrel run back and forth on a tree limb. "Lisa, I need to be who I was before you were killed. Not the attorney, but the person you feel in love with. I haven't liked myself for awhile. And I need to."

He stood. Then gently touched the top of her headstone.

"There's one more thing I need to do."

Fifty Six

"This way Dr. Dalton." The guard was formal and walked in front of Alex off to his right side. "Are you sure you want to do this?"

"Let's go." Alex was impatient.

The alarm sounded and the steel door laboriously unbolted then painfully, slowly slid open. "Two guards are already in the room Doctor, they have to stay with you. They'll notify me when you're done." The guard looked at him like this was a very big mistake. "He's all yours." The guard walked back down the hall toward the security door they had just came through and signaled to the camera.

Alex hadn't move. The steel door to the room was open and he peered in from where he stood. He could see one guard standing tall and stiff, his belt heavy with tactical gear. The steel door hid who ever else was in that room.

He was sweating. Do it, he commanded.

Alex walked in.

And there he was.

It startled Alex at first, unnerving to see him sitting there, ankles and wrists leather bound to the metal arms of the security chair, a wide chest belt pulled tight and secured so he could not move. Those tattoos; from his finger tips up his arms all the way to his biceps till they were covered by his short sleeve prison coveralls. Tattoo blue, along with reds and greens and yellows all covering his hands, arms, even on his neck. He was older, grayer and looked worn and tired. It's what solitary does to a man. Alex knew. Alex sat in the only chair, positioned in front of the man about eight feet away. A safe distance.

The man's expression was blank. Not flat, not depressed, not angry...just blank. But those eyes. Alex never forgot those eyes. The puppy dog expression in those eyes, disarmingly friendly, but underneath was sickness. Pure evil.

"I'm Doctor Dalton. Do you remember me?" Alex searched for a hint of expression in the mans face. "I was your attorney...then you killed my wife."

"Lisa." A grin snaked along his lips. His words were slow, deliberate, no need to talk fast. "You introduced yourself as Doctor."

"I quit law and became a psychologist." Alex wasn't here to inform Albert Soccoro about his career change and small talk was not in the cards. "I don't need much time. But I wanted to talk to you." Albert looked stiff and uncomfortable in the restraints, but there was this calm, like he'd been through the routine before.

"I want to be very clear with you." Alex gaze bore into Albert's puppy eyes. "You're a horrible, sick, demented human being. You belong right here and nowhere else. But I made a mistake. When I was your attorney I let you walk free without any treatment or follow up. What I know now, is that you needed help and I let you walk. I let you down. I did my job representing you, but I didn't do enough...and because of that...I suffered for it."

"You came here to cleanse your soul, Alex?" Like a slight tremor Albert shook his head, "Its too late." Albert's chest expanded, fighting against the belt. "I'm here to die Alex, so why don't you just go back to your rich-ass home and fuck some whore for me."

His stare penetrated.

"As I remember it, Alex...Lisa was a challenging lay." Cracked teeth grew from his sick smile. "A bit cold towards the end."

Alex felt like he was going to puke. "You belong here you sick fuck and you are responsible for killing my wife." How could he have let this guy just walk out of that courtroom? "Maybe I could have prevented you from killing her...I could have asked the Judge for court ordered treatment. But that's where I failed, and I have to live with that."

Albert was stoic.

"When I represented you I didn't care who you were or what kind of fucked up life you had. You were a client, I didn't like you or dislike you. I did my job. I did a good job. After you killed Lisa and I testified against you...I hated you. You took her life and entered mine forever. But, I'm not going to allow that to continue. In my mind, from now on, you stay here."

Alex stood up and Albert followed with his gaze.

Albert stretched out his tattooed neck so his face grew red, "You're tormented, Alex. The truth is *you* killed Lisa. I was just your pawn. *You* killed her. And both of us are suffering for it. You're a sinner Alex." Albert let his tongue slid along his lips. "A sinner. Let him who is unclean stay unclean. *Revelations*, Alex. You can't escape it."

"You're wrong. You have no life Albert, but I'm taking mine back."

Alex looked at the guard. "I'm done."

Fifty Seven

Aspen Grove

Alex shuffled through the papers on his desk, looked under some charts, then pulled open the right desk drawer. He grabbed the worn paperback and read the title: "*Gitanjali. Rabindranath Tagore.*" He thumbed through and stopped at the marked page. He read:

> *Thou hast made me known to friends whom*
> *I knew not.*
> *Thou hast given me seats in homes not my own.*
> *Thou hast brought the distant near and made a*
> *brother of the stranger.*
> *I am uneasy at heart when I have to leave my*
> *accustomed shelter; I forget that there abides the*
> *old in the new, and that there also thou abidest.*
> *Through birth and death, in this world or in*
> *others, wherever thou leadest me it is thou, the*
> *same, the one companion of my endless life who*
> *ever linkest my heart with bonds of joy to the*
> *unfamiliar.*
> *When one knows thee, then alien there is none,*
> *then no door is shut.*
> *Oh, grant me my prayer that I may never lose the*
> *bliss of the touch of the one in the play of the many.*

He closed the book and held it in his lap. No door has been shut, except my own, he thought.

"Hey Doc? You ready?" Butch stood at the entrance to his office. Alex looked up and a verse floated into his head: *A brother of the stranger.* Alex felt sad. "You're leaving today."

"Yeah." Butch sat down.

There was an unspoken connection as they looked at each other. "You've helped me a lot Doc. You had the answers I needed."

Alex felt uncomfortable. "To be honest Butch, I really *didn't* have the answers." Alex then said, "Sometimes when people help each other, neither one has the answers...you just get in there, wallow around and find 'em together."

"It's trustin' each other." Butch said.

Alex nodded, "It is, Butch. By the way I checked with the staff and it's okay with them if you want to come up here and talk with me."

Butch smiled, "Good. Thanks Doc."

"On your way out, check in with the nurse at the desk and she'll schedule our next session."

They were silent a few moments.

"You know Butch, everyone involved in this incident lost something. Len Lamont lost his life. You lost your life, at least for a while. Charles lost a dad. McCallum, Parker, they lost too. Most people would think a not guilty plea was good. It means you won, you get to walk right out of court and get on with your life." Alex took a breath. "But you and I know differently."

Butch nodded.

"Medication doesn't solve any problems, and there's a lot more to work on, Butch. And we'll get there together." Alex stood. "So, I guess I'll be seeing you next week."

"You will. Thanks Doc."

"No, Butch. Thank you."

Butch walked up to Alex and threw his arms around him. "You're okay, Doc." Butch stepped back, chopped the air with his hand and walked out of Alex's office.

Alex stood there and let the good feeling linger. He sat back in his chair and reached for Butch's chart. On the discharge page he wrote:

> *Major Depression with psychotic features.*
> *Improving with therapy and medication.*
> *Post Traumatic Stress Disorder, severe.*
> *No evidence of anti-social personality*
>   *disorder.*
> *Continue with outpatient therapy.*
> *Appointment made for next week.*

He signed his name and closed the chart. Alex walked out the front door of Aspen Grove and stood there.

He felt good.

A slight breeze brushed his face as he glanced over and saw Sandra waiting for him at his parking spot. She gave him a little wave and he grinned. Alex walked toward her and gave her a hug and a quick kiss on the lips, then slid on his helmet and handed one to her. For some reason Alex turned around. Butch was watching them through the window.

Right then Alex wasn't seeing the tattoos, the long graying hair or the beard...he saw a man trying to put his life back together; ending his solitary confinement. Their eyes connected and Alex chopped the air with his hand.

Butch grinned and saluted back.

Alex turned and slid his leg over the brand new fire-red *Fat Boy* steadying the bike as Sandra climbed on. Alex hit the ignition and the engine roared to life.

Butch watched them ride off, then turned around and packed his bag to go home.

Fifty Eight

On his way out, Butch stopped by the discharge desk, signed some forms, and felt a tinge of uneasiness about leaving. The nurse gave him copies of his discharge orders and then said, "Is someone picking you up Mr. Allee?"

"Yeah, my wife Cindy, she should be here. I'll just wait outside." The nurse smiled, and Butch shoved his papers into the side pocket of his suite case.

Butch waited on the curb outside the Aspen Grove front door. The day was bright and clear. What was he going to do now? What would tomorrow bring? How was he going to put his life back together?

His thoughts were abruptly interrupted by the backfire of a tuck and the screeching of brakes as a Ford pickup broke into view. The beat-up pickup rumbled toward him, swung up to the curb and stopped. The door burst open and Ruddy jumped out.

"What the hell! *You* pickin' me up, Ruddy? Where's Cindy?"

"I ain't pickin you up, brother...I'm delivering." Ruddy jumped up on the back of the pickup, threw off a tarp and beamed. "This is your's Allee!"

Butch stared.

Ruddy unlatched the trucks tailgate, kicked down the back ramp and then unstrapped the brand new Harley *Fat Boy*. He rolled the bike onto the pavement before Butch. "Here's a note for ya."

Butch took the envelope and opened it.

297

It read: *No more solitary, Butch.* It was signed, *Dr. Dalton.*

Butch choked up. He stuffed the note in his back pocket.

Ruddy handed him the keys and Butch swept his leg up and over, and straddled the Harley. The seat, the weight of the bike, the sweep of the handlebars, it felt like... freedom.

He brought the bike to life, and chopped the air at Ruddy.

With a rumbling roar, Butch flew out the parking lot toward home.

The End

Other books by Brett Valette

Come Together.

The psychological thriller where deadly delusions become reality, and taking a life means giving life; even to the dead.

Does the Beatles final album, "Abbey Road" hold hidden messages? Did John and Paul pen secret instructions to follow, in case one of them died? Simon Picasso thinks so. And he's going to follow them and reunite the Beatles for a final world concert.

But first, he must become 'Old Flat Top' from the song 'Come Together.' His gruesome performance opens with the murder of a Jewish couple; the man's eyes are scooped out, a section of the woman's spine removed. It's written into the song.

Detective Frank Muldower thought he'd seen it all—until Simon Picasso entered his life.
Being gay and middle-aged, Frank has his own problems—ex-wife, estranged son—but his life takes a back seat when Simon's bizarre ritualistic crimes make the headlines.

To catch this killer, Frank and guilt-ridden new partner Karen Collins must figure out the clues and predict his next move. That means learning how Simon thinks. And the only way to do that is to travel the very darkest, twisted alleys of the human psyche.

Frank calls on his buddy Avi Salono. Born without arms or legs, Avi's a hyper-sexual, manic genius who's helped Frank unravel the twisted minds of killers before— but no one like Simon. And never involving secret song messages. Even Avi can miss a clue, but missing a clue with Simon…means you die.

Available at Amazon.com

www.ingramcontent.com/pod-product-compliance
Lightning Source LLC
Chambersburg PA
CBHW071949040426
42447CB00009B/1294